THE ULTIMATE S(

PRACTICE GUIDE:

A Revolutionary Approach to Organizing & Planning Your Practices

by

CINDY BRISTOW

Softball Excellence
Tampa, FL
www.softballexcellence.com

THE ULTIMATE SOFTBALL PRACTICE GUIDE:
A Revolutionary Approach to Organizing & Planning Your Practices

Published by Softball Excellence -Tampa, FL.
Phone: 813-368-2048
Fax: 813-315-6216
Email: cindy@softballexcellence.com
Website: www.softballexcellence.com
Printed in the USA

ISBN 978-0-9701138-5-6
Library of Congress Control Number: 2006905849

To give me additional input or feedback on any portion of this book, to ask me any questions, to ask for permission to reproduce any portion of this book please email me:
cindy@softballexcellence.com

To order any coaching materials, to sign up for the Softball Excellence Coaching newsletter, or to find any of the drills listed in this book please visit my website:
www.softballexcellence.com

DEDICATION

To Dan Ems Jr. - my brother-in-law

While working two jobs you still find time to coach your son's baseball team (my nephew Danny) and give time to your family. Your willingness to sacrifice your time (and sleep) and constantly find ways to improve yourself for the sake of your players is truly remarkable. I admire you, and all the coaches out there just like you!

My hope is that this book can help you in some small way...

Table of Contents

Introduction 7

THE MUST-HAVES 9

Must-Haves for YOU 11

PREPARATION YOUR WAY 11

Type It, Write It, Think It 11

SOLID PLANNING 13

Total Time for the Season/Year 13

Season Needs 18

1st Game Needs 22

Position Needs 24

Individual Needs 25

MAKE GOOD CHOICES 28

List All Your Info 28

Combine When Possible 30

Turn Your Planning into Practice 31

Drill It & Fill It 33

Don't Forget the Game Part of Softball 36

Prioritize 38

BE A CONSISTENT YOU 41

Whoever You Are in Games - Be in Practice 41

CHAPTER SUMMARY - MUST-HAVES FOR YOU 42

MUST-HAVES for PRACTICE 43

SKILL BUILDING 44

Kids Learn by Doing 44

Young Kids vs. Older Kids 46

Everydays 51

COMPETITION 58

Against the Clock 58

Against Yourself 63

Against Your Teammates 65

Competitive Challenges 69

ACCOUNTABILITY & CONSEQUENCE 73

Posting Results 74

Table of Contents

Winners and Losers . . . 76

"Just One More" & "End on a Good One" . . . 78

PACE . . . 80

Game Pace vs. Practice Pace . . . 80

CHAPTER SUMMARY - MUST-HAVES FOR PRACTICE . . . 83

BE CREATIVE 85

EQUIPMENT CREATIVITY - WHAT GADGETS MATTER? . . . 86

INDOOR PRACTICES . . . 89

SAMPLE PRACTICES 91

PRACTICE INTRODUCTION . . . 92

BEGINNING PRACTICES . . . 93

ADVANCED PRACTICES . . . 110

Practicing with Small Groups . . . 112

Whole Team Practice Situations . . . 120

Defensive Only Practices . . . 128

Offensive Only Practices . . . 134

Combined Practices . . . 142

CHANGES FOR PRE, IN, & OFF-SEASON 153

PRE-SEASON . . . 153

Skills & Conditioning . . . 153

IN-SEASON. . . . 154

Repair & Prepare . . . 154

OFF-SEASON . . . 155

Learn, Experiment, Improve . . . 156

Introduction

Let me ask you a question, when was the last time any of these questions popped into your head?

"What are we supposed to do at practice today?"

"How can I make my practices better?"

"How can my practice not be so boring?"

" How come my team can do it in practice and not in a game?"

If you've ever asked yourself any of these questions you're not alone. Almost every softball coach on the planet has wondered these same things and yet most of us continue to struggle through practice without having any real clue how to change or fix things.

It that sounds like you then you've come to the right place! This book will help you answer all of these questions and more!

My last book on practice organization – Keys to Holding Great Practices, 2000 – was my best attempt at the time to share with you my methods for creating practices that would lead to success on the ballfield. It's not that anything in that book wouldn't lead you to success, they would and in fact they lead my professional team, the Florida Wahoos, to the Women's Professional Softball League championship that year. The problem was that everything in that book was written for and targeted toward athletes of an elite caliber, which really aren't the players that most of us are dealing with. So, it's time to write a newer and better book on a subject that is still my favorite area associated with softball – and that's practice!

This book will teach you all the things you need to know to hold great practices that are well organized, that are fun for you and your players to attend, that allow your players to improve their skills and most importantly, practices that will lead to your team playing better in their games.

I absolutely LOVE practice and my goal is to help you feel the same way by the time you've finished reading this book. Practice is what makes or breaks your team for games. It's where you help your players improve on those skills they just can't seem to grasp or the ones they just can't seem to do well under the pressure of a game. Practice is where you can get creative and figure out ways to solve problems that are frustrating either you or your players or both. To me, practice has always been like a blank canvas that I could always draw on and create any kind of player or team that I wanted (within the skill range of what I had). Games, on the other hand were something I didn't have as much control over.

I think that too many coaches overlook the importance of practice and simply focus on their games. Most teams practice a minimum of 2-3 times more than they play so overlooking something that happens that much can be a very costly mistake. I'm convinced that coaches would focus more on practice if they felt more comfortable on what to do with their practice time, where everyone should go, how to handle their lack of equipment and basically how to get everyone doing things that will help them improve their skills and therefore help the team win more games.

After reading this book you're going to know how to do just that, so hang in there and let's get started!

The Must-Haves

Creating great practices involves understanding two different sets of what I call the "Must-Haves". These are just what they say – things that you MUST HAVE either in your practices or in your mind in order to create practices that will improve your player's skill and knowledge of the game, improve their ability to succeed under pressure, and ultimately help your team win games.

Before you panic thinking that having a long list of "Must-Haves" only adds to your coaching pressure, I'm going to walk you through each of these things and give you lots of examples on how to include each element into your thinking and then into your practices. These "Must-Haves" fall into two categories; Must-Haves for YOU and Must-Haves for your PRACTICES and each one contain things that will help make it possible for you to always create great practices. Let's take a look at elements within the Must-Haves for YOU as the person that is planning, creating and designing your practices:

***MUST-HAVES* for YOU:**

1) PREPARATION YOUR WAY

a. Type it, Write, it, Think it
b. Make it Work for You

2) SOLID PLANNING

a. Total Time for the Season/Year
b. Season Needs
c. 1st Game Needs
d. Position Needs
e. Individual Needs

3) MAKE YOUR CHOICES

a. List All Your Info.
b. Combine When Possible
c. Turn Your Planning Into Practice
d. Drill It & Fill It Out
e. Don't Forget the *Game* Part of Softball
f. Prioritize

4) A CONSISTENT YOU

a. Whoever You Are in Games - Be in Practice

We'll look at each of these elements in detail in the following chapters so for now, just glance through the list and see how many of these things you might already be doing.

We should also look at the Must-Haves that your PRACTICES need to include. These are elements that should be present in some form for all of your practices, and again, we'll look at each of these in much greater detail in the chapters to come. So for now, just glance through this list:

***MUST-HAVES* for PRACTICE :**

1) SKILL BUILDING

- a. Kids Learn by Doing
- b. Young Kids vs. Older Kids
- c. "Everydays"
- d. Putting the "Everydays" Into Practice

2) COMPETITION

- a. Against Yourself
- b. Against Time
- c. Against Your Teammates
- d. Competitive Challenges

3) ACCOUNTABILITY & CONSEQUENCE

- a. Posting Results
- b. Winners and Losers
- c. "Just One More" & "End on a Good One"

4) PACE

Must-Haves for YOU

Again, these are the elements that YOU as a coach need to have and know when you sit down to figure out what you're going to do today and each day at practice.

PREPARATION YOUR WAY

Before you plan anything for practice you've first got to do so in a way that's comfortable for you. You're either going to type things out, write things down or think it all through and keep it all organized in your head. Whatever method you use needs to be easy and comfortable for you. Don't make the mistake I did when I first got into coaching when I used the same forms that other more successful coaches used for their practices and simply changed the information to be mine. That method was horrible for me since I could never make all of my information fit into their forms so I ended up leaving things out of my plans and ultimately, and more importantly, I was leaving those things out of my team's preparations.

Type It, Write It, Think It

Taking a look at one of my old practices you can see that I like to write my practices out by hand. I type OK, and I'm pretty good with the computer but I think much faster than I type, plus I like to draw out where everybody and everything goes during practice (as you can see from the practice to the right) and doing all that on the computer just doesn't work for me. I'm a visual person and like seeing diagrams much more than I like reading words.

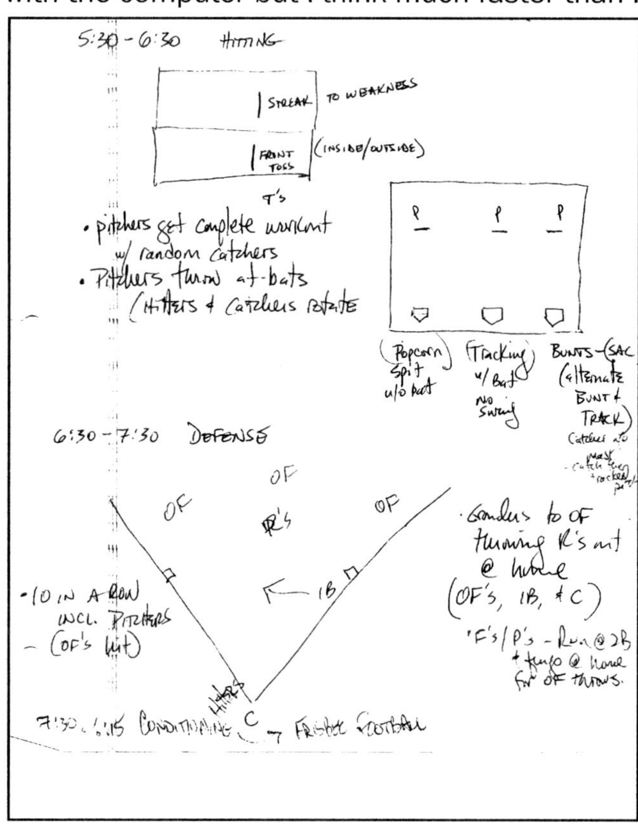

So, I write it down. Now that means nobody else can even begin to read what I write or figure out what I'm talking about but for me it works. If you're someone who writes out all your practices but another coach might need to read it (or your players if you post your practices, or an equipment manager) then just make sure you write so people can read it. I never had to really worry about anyone reading my practices until I started writing books on practice and started included my handwritten practice plans, so writing my plans out by hand worked fine for me.

This is a sample of a typed practice plan that shows you a different look and method for listing everything to happen during practice.

SESSION #1 WARM UP & SPRINT TRAINING
2:00 2 laps, Team stretch, 1 min. Push ups, gradual spring training (10)
2:20 Spring Training - do with perfection (boxes)

SESSION #2 OUR MISSION!!!
- Use your mental training during practice
- Goal Books

SESSION #3 BASERUNNING!!!
2:30 Independent fly ball

SESSION #4 TEAM THROW - "Set a Goal"
2:40 Team throw - get better today and every day!!

SESSION #5 TEAM DEFENSE & SITUATIONS
3:00 - team kareokee drill
3:10 - runners at home, 1b & 2b - outfield work (hit off a toss from side) (need P's & C's to run with helmets)
3:20 - team relays & cuts
3:30 - infield work or run
3:40 - 1st & 3rds (Stacy catch)

SESSION #7 HITTING
4:00 Hit Line Drives!!!!!!!!!
- 10 minutes each stations

Station 1	St. 2	St. 3	St. 4	St. 5	St. 6
Bunts & Slaps	Step Behind	Tee opp.	long dis. field	off set mach. drill	shag off coach
Amy	Jan	Lana	Steph	Stacy	Crissy
Juel	Court	AJ	Dedra	Dina	Lisa

SESSION #8 VIDEO TRAINING!!!
4:50 go to office and view FAU & Championship game

SESSION #9 OUR MISSION
5:30 Rate yourself on a scale of A-F on each of your 3 indiv. goals

To me, this is a very sterile type of plan but that doesn't mean it's not a good one - it just isn't a good one for me.

What's important is to use a system of keeping track of what you're going to do each day at practice that will work for you. Pick out a way of listing your practice schedule that works best for YOU!

The one system that I'd recommend staying away from, unless you have a photographic memory, is keeping track of your entire practice plan in your head. Most of us aren't too good at this and the more things we have to remember the less reliable the whole thing becomes. I'd recommend you either hand write or type out what you plan to do each day at practice so you can follow it and remember it once practice starts and things heat up.

Once you figure out what method works best for you in regards to writing down your actual practice you need to figure out what it is you're going to write down. That's where our planning comes in.

SOLID PLANNING

We don't plan to fail, we fail to plan!

Planning is critical to making your practices any good at all. Great practices don't happen by luck, they are a result of thoughtful, careful planning. If you don't see yourself as a great planner and you're more the type of person that is pretty quick on on your feet and tend to just makes things up as you go well take heart, I'm like that too. But I also realize that there are times when that type of fast-thinking is very helpful, but practice planning isn't one of those times. If you're the kind of person who can't wait until you get out on the practice field to start thinking about what you're going to do that day well you're going to have horrible practices as a result. So, if you're sick of bad practices and you're wanting to figure out how to make good ones all the time then "figuring" is one of the skills you're going to have to use. We'll call it planning for the rest of this chapter since planning is nothing more than figuring out what you're going to do but doing it ahead of time instead of on the spot.

In order to help make our "planning" easier to talk about and understand I've broken the planning process down into five different parts:

a. Total Time for the Season/Year
b. Season Needs
c. 1st Game Needs
d. Position Needs
e. Individual Needs

Each part is slightly different and yet crucial in the overall planning picture. Let's take a closer look at what each of these five different planning concepts are and how they can help us make better practices.

Total Time for the Season/Year

To me, this is THE MOST critical part of the entire planning process. Now keep in mind that by nature, I'm not a planner, but I do recognize the value that knowing how much time you have to do something and knowing what all those somethings-to-do are can really help you get them all done. And that's the gist of this chapter - knowing how much total practice time you have for your season or year. So let's look at how to do that.

BRIGHT IDEA

Add up the total number of hours your team will practice all season so you can figure how to best spend your practice time!

The easiest way to figure out just how much practice time you have for your whole season is to fill-in some blanks. But in order to do so you'll need to know the following:

1. How long does your average practice last?
2. How many total practices do you have all season?
3. How much total practice time do you have all season?

Once you know your answers to these questions you can put them into the following grid and come up with your own Total Practice Time for the Year. I'm going to do one for two different types of teams and seasons; one is for a Summerball-JO Team and the other for a High School team. You'll see how the basic idea is the same for each one just some of the numbers and circumstances will change slightly.

School Team Example

What follows is a great list of questions to help you begin to figure out how much Total Practice Time you're going to have for the entire season or year. I'll answer these questions using a make-believe High School Team that we'll call the Excellence HS Eagles, and we'll use the following information about their season:

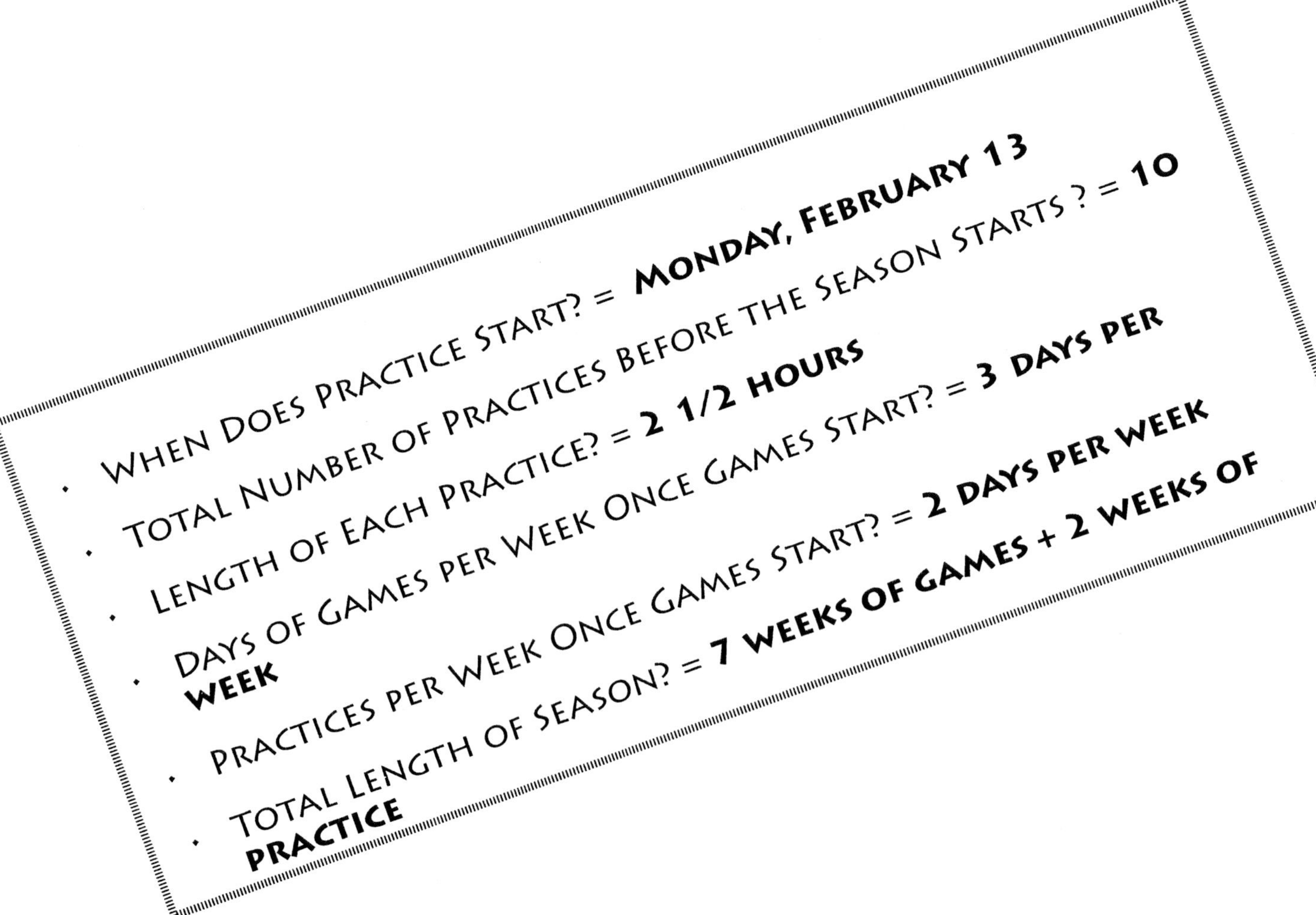

- WHEN DOES PRACTICE START? = **MONDAY, FEBRUARY 13**
- TOTAL NUMBER OF PRACTICES BEFORE THE SEASON STARTS ? = **10**
- LENGTH OF EACH PRACTICE? = **2 1/2 HOURS**
- DAYS OF GAMES PER WEEK ONCE GAMES START? = **3 DAYS PER WEEK**
- PRACTICES PER WEEK ONCE GAMES START? = **2 DAYS PER WEEK**
- TOTAL LENGTH OF SEASON? = **7 WEEKS OF GAMES + 2 WEEKS OF PRACTICE**

What does all this mean and how does it help us? Well, lets look through this list and see just what information we have that we can use to figure out what our Total Practice Time for the Year/Season is going to be.

Let's start by figuring out exactly how many total practices we could possibly have all year:

- Total number of practices before the season starts ? = **10**
- Practices per week once games start? = **2 days per week**
- Total Length of Season? = **7 wks of games (14 practices) x 2 wks of practice (10 practices)**

- **Total Number of Practices: 10 + 14 = 24 Total Practices**

Now we know we have 24 Total Practices for the whole season so let's figure out just how much Total Practice Time that really gives us:

High School Team Season:

HOW LONG DOES YOUR AVE. PRACTICE LAST?	2 1/2 HOURS
HOW MANY TOTAL PRACTICES DO YOU HAVE?	24 PRACTICES
HOW MUCH TOTAL PRACTICE TIME DO YOU HAVE? (24 X 2.5 HRS = 60 HRS)	60 HOURS

So if you're coaching this Excellence HS Eagles Softball Team then you know you have 60 Total Practice Hours all year in 24 different practices. What you choose to do with this time is what will make or break your season, but it's also what we'll cover in great detail shortly.

Summerball-JO Team Example

Now let's look at this same formula but this time for a Summerball-JO Team. Let's assume that the Summerball Team can only practice on the weekends during the school year and they do that for 8 weekends. They practice two times each weekend for 2 hours each time. But, once games start the team will practice two days per week for 2 1/2 hours per practice and this will last for 12 weeks.

So instead of feeling like we're all back in grade school doing those horrible word problems in math class, let's just pull out all the important information we'll need by answering our basic questions below:

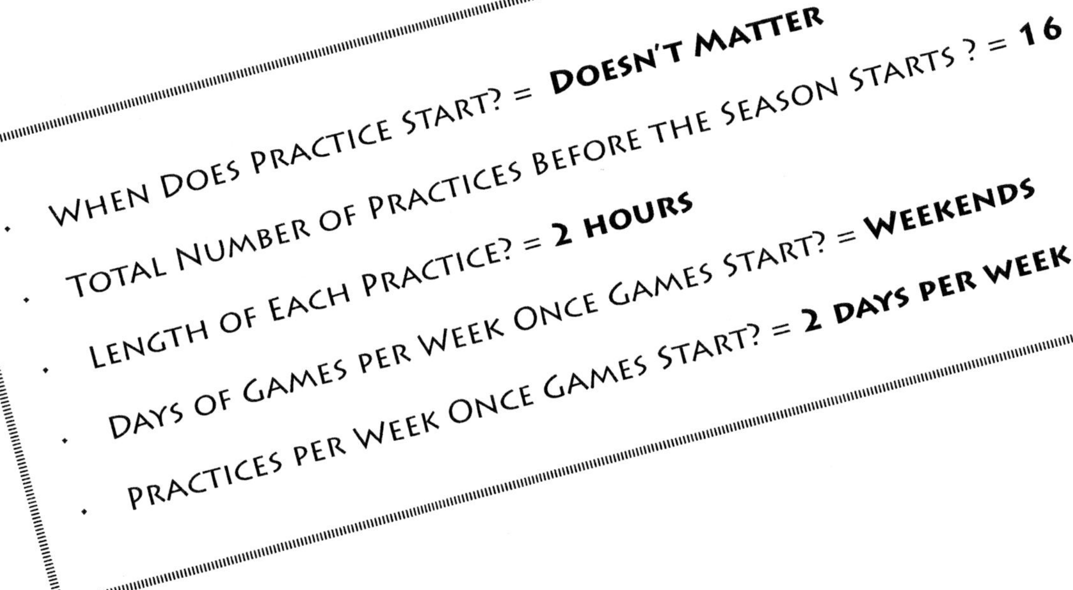

» Total number of practices before the season starts ? = 16

» Practices per week once games start? = 2 **days per week**

» Total Length of Season? = 12 **wks of games (24 practices)+ 8 wks of practice (16 practices)**

» **Total Number of Practices: 24 + 16 = 40 Total Practices**

In this example the team practices for 2 hours during their 8 weeks of weekend-only practices, and then once the season starts they practice for 2 1/2 hours during their twice weekly 12 week season.

Because of this we need to change our Total Practice Time Box slightly to allow for different practice lengths in different parts of a season.

This is pretty simple to do, we just add a few lines to allow for two different practice lengths for two different parts of the season. Here's what that box now looks like:

Summer - JO Team Season:

How Long Does Your Pre-Season Practice Last? ______

How Many Times Do You Practice This Long? ______

How Long Does Your In-Season Practice Last? ______

How Many Times Do You Practice This Long? ______

So, if we take out figures from the previous page and fill in this box, we'll easily be able to find out just how many Total Practice Hours we're dealing with for this team for their entire season.

SUMMER - JO TEAM SEASON:

How Long Does Your Pre-Season Practice Last? **2 hours**

How Many Times Do You Practice This Long? **16 practices**

How Long Does Your In-Season Practice Last? **2 1/2 Hours**

How Many Times Do You Practice This Long? **24 practices**

How Much Total Practice Time Do You Have? 92 hours

Preseason: 16 x 2 hrs = 32 hrs
Inseason: 24 x 2.5hrs = 60 hrs
92 Total Hrs

Season Needs

Once you've figured out how many total hours you have all season to practice, then you've got to figure out what things you're going to spend your time practicing - these are your Season Needs. These are all the skills, plays and things your team will need to know how to do to be successful. Keep in mind these aren't a list of what your fantasy team should be able to do in a season, and it's not a list of all the things **you** know about the game of softball! Instead, it's a realistic list of what your team, the one you have this year, should realistically (for it's skill and experience level and based upon your known competition) be able to know, learn and perform for the season.

So where do we start? First of all you need to sit down and make a list of all the skills you think your team needs to be able to do over the course of this season. If you're a veteran coach and have made a list like this before be careful to make this list for THIS team and not for last years team, or just repeat the same list that you always use. Each team you coach is completely different from the previous one so the more accurate this list can be to the players skill level, experience and talent that you have on this year's team the greater chance your team will actually master all the items on your list.

Bright Idea:

Your season needs are NOT what you want your fantasy team to be able to do, but rather what the team you have this year is realistically ale to do for this season. The closer this list is to reality the closer you'll come to achieving it!

Here's a typed copy of an actual list I used for one of the seasons I coached in the Women's Professional Softball League. As you look through the list you'll notice there aren't any fancy plays listed and that most the things on this list are pretty basic. Keep in mind that although I was coaching professional athletes who had already completed college and played major Division I level softball, we still had to execute the basic fundamentals in order to be successful. That's what the following list represents:

I've circled all the main positions and skills that you needed to focus on during practice. You'll notice that my list for PITCHERS is smaller and less detailed than the other position lists- that's because I was the pitching coach & had a different list for the PITCHERS to follow. Here I simply listed what we needed to make special practice time for.

CATCHERS:

Popups – foul to dugouts
- four to screen

Signals
Pickoff Signals
Bunt Defense
Wild Pitches off Backstop
- high - low

Catcher strengthening and agility series
Blocking balls
Pickoffs at
- 1st base
- 3rd base (off all pitchers)

Know from each pitcher:
- is the glove where the ball ends?
- where the balls starts to break?

(Tell UP if it's where it starts)
EARN IT!
Film them giving signals
Make all signals the same for all pitchers.

INFIELDERS:

TRIANGLES
LF CF RF
3B SS 2B 1B

•Wild pitches off the backstop – high – low and with runners on 2B and on Walks.
•Practicing on a grass outfield to get used to grass infields.

1B / 3B
- Foulballs to dugout
- foulballs to outfield

Balls to backhand
Throws on the Run
Grounders on the grass
Relays
Rundowns
1st and 3rd's
Pickoffs
Steals of 2B and 3B
Bunt Defense
Double Plays
Balls in the:
- 5/6 hole (3B and SS)
- 4/3 hole (2B and 1B)

Balls between the outfielders.

OUTFIELDERS:

▪Balls against the fence
▪Cut offs
▪Gappers:
- between outfielders
- between outfield and infield

•Grounders:
- with runner on 2B
- with the game on the line
- to rightfield with throws to 1B

▪Slapper defense
▪Rundowns
▪Baserunnning:
- leadoffs
- flyballs
- foulballs
- groundballs

PITCHERS:

▪Film them from the front and the side
▪Make sure their timing is the same on all of the their pitches.

HITTING:

▪Hitting a series of the same pitch (Rises, drops, curves) in pairs.
▪Opposite field hitting
▪Positive counts (look for the pitch in the middle of the zone)
▪Negative counts
▪Hit and Runs
▪Steals
▪Slug Bunts

BUNTS:

•Sacrifice:
- left
- middle
- right

•Keep hands at the top of the strike sone
•Bunt and Runs
•Push Bunts
•Fake Bunts

These circles are all the things that my team CATCHERS , INFIELDERS, OUTFIELDERS, PITCHERS, HITTERS and BUNTERS needed to practice throughout the year so I had to make sure to schedule them into our practices.

Here's another example of a team's Season Needs, this time by a great summerball coach (Pete Gonzalez) for his team, the St. Louis Fever. Pete had written and asked me to help him figure out how to know what things his team should be practicing in the time they had to practice. I talked Pete through the same process that we're going through in this book -

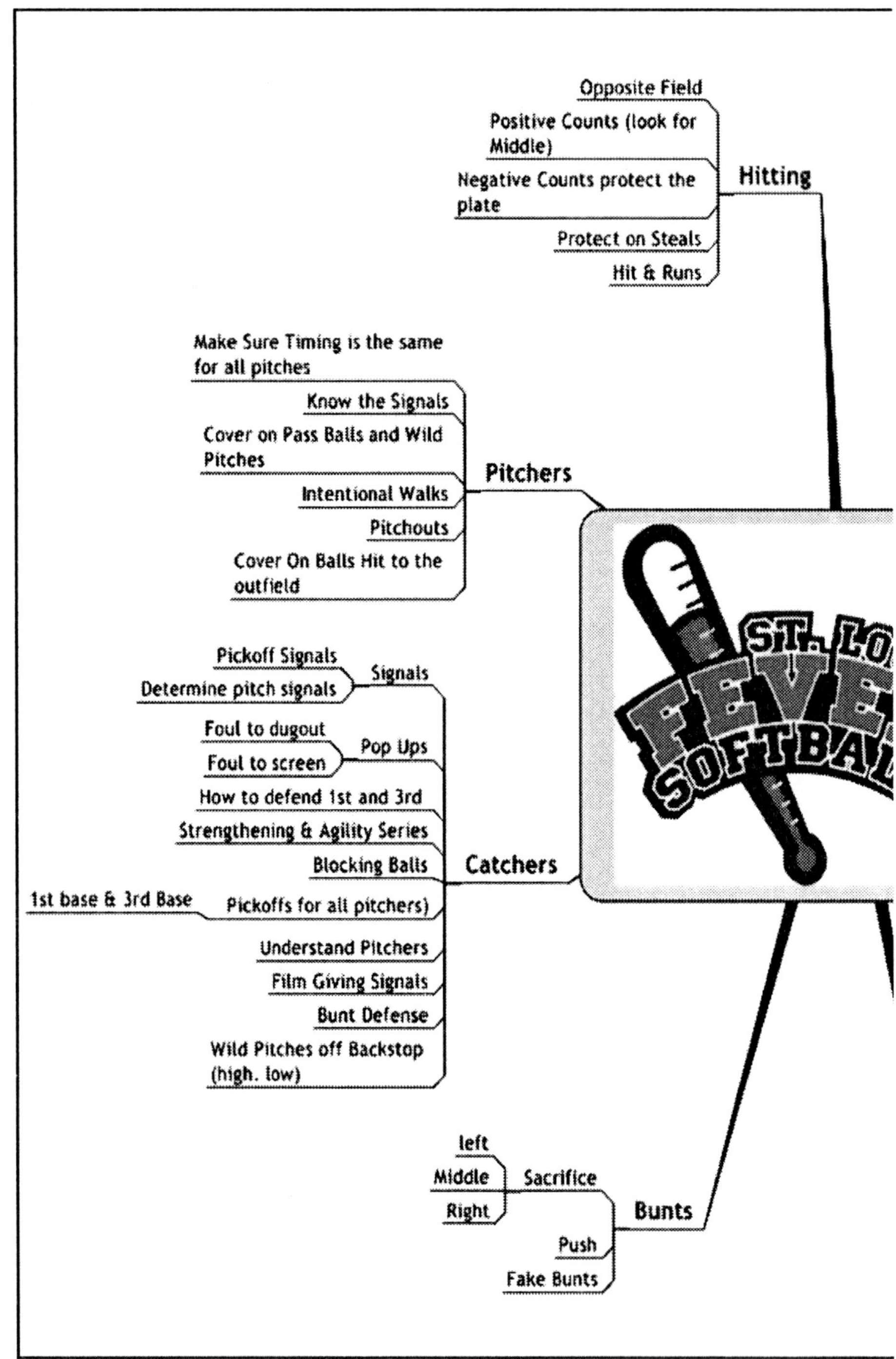

first, figuring out how much total time he had all season to practice and then listing all the things he thought his team needed to practice during that time.

This is what Pete came up with for the St. Louis Fever - and it's quite a complete list. As you can see, Pete's a whole lot more organized in his list presentation than I was on the list I put on the previous page, especially when you consider that my original list was hand written, not even typed.

As we've discussed, it doesn't matter how you organize yourself it just has to be a method that works for you. This method works for Pete, plus, it looks great! Thanks Pete for such a great job!

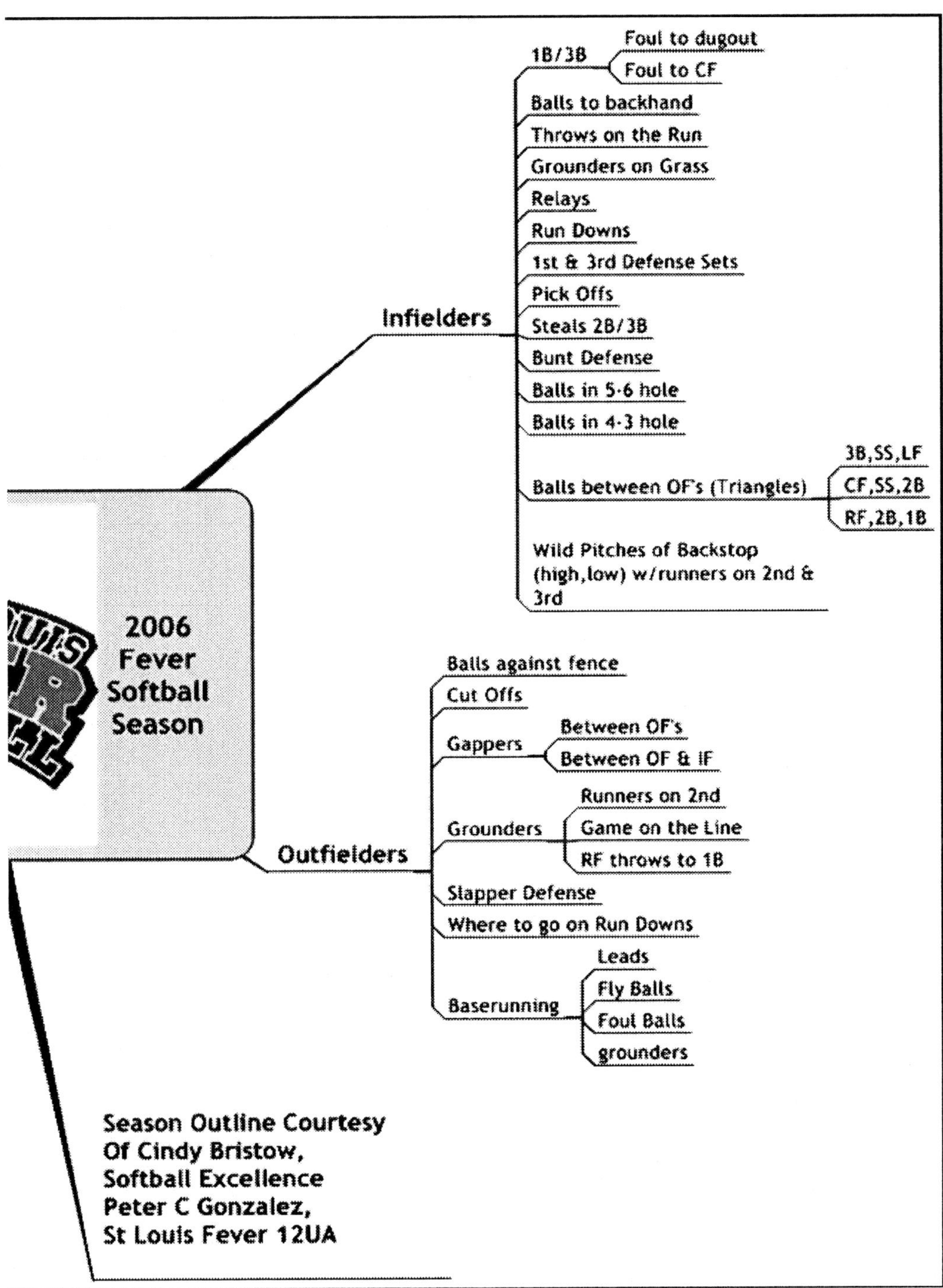

As you look through Pete's list notice how specific he gets with certain positions in certain situations or skills. Be sure to remember that this is Pete's list for Pete's team. While looking at it can help give you a better idea of the things you might need to list for your team to practice during the season, it sure won't help you to simply copy everything on Pete's list and make it yours. Just use this as a guide to help you come up with your list for your team.

1st Game Needs

Now let's all be real about this. There's the list of things that you want your team to practice over the course of an entire season (that's the stuff we just went over). And then there's the fact that once you start practice you probably have less than two weeks until you have to play your first game. Does that sound about right? Some of you will have longer and some of you will unfortunately have less. I know when I coached in the pro league one year we had five days and the rest of the time we had seven. No matter how much time you have before your first game it's never really enough.

That's why we need to create a shorter list of things to practice that we're going to call our 1st Game Needs. This list is just what it says, things we need to practice before our first game.

Pitcher's & Catcher's needs:	Infielders needs:	Outfielder's needs:	Offensive needs:
DEFENSIVE NEEDS			OFFENSIVE NEEDS
P/C	INF	OF	
• SIGNALS	• BUNT DEF	• SLAP DEF.	• SIGNALS
• PITCHOUTS	• SLAP DEF	• CUT OFFS	• BUNTS/SAC/B & R
• INT WALKS	• 1st & 3rd	• RELAYS	• H & R
• BUNT DEF	• PICKOFFS	• GROUNDERS	• SWINGS
	• STEALS	• TWEENERS	• 1st & 3rd
C	• CUTOFFS	- w/ each of	• BASERUNNING
	• RELAYS	- w/ IF	- Leads
• THROWS to 2B			- Fly balls
			- Foul balls
• PICKOFFS			- Ground balls
- 1B			
- 3B			

Here's what my list looked like for my pro team that had 5 days before it's first game: It's certainly not a very big list compared to my Seasons Needs List on page 19, but keep in mind that I couldn't realistically expect my team to have practiced all of the things on that list in five days - even if they were all professional athletes!

When making out your 1st Game Needs list for your infielders you might simply list Bunt Defense instead of listing things like Rundowns, 1st and 3rds, Double Plays, Pick-offs, and Slap Defense since those things take time and practice to do successfully. The only time I'd suggest you list one of these more detailed-type of defensive plays is if you know for sure that your first game opponent does a lot of slaps, for instance, then you'll need to have your team somewhat prepared to face that. Otherwise, cover the basics and build from there.

Look at my two lists different lists - while they're both dealing with things that your infield will need to cover, the list on the left is an entire season list and the short one below is a list for the 1st Game. The entire season list is much longer since you have more time throughout the season to cover things that you don't have time to cover before your first game

Entire Season Infield List:

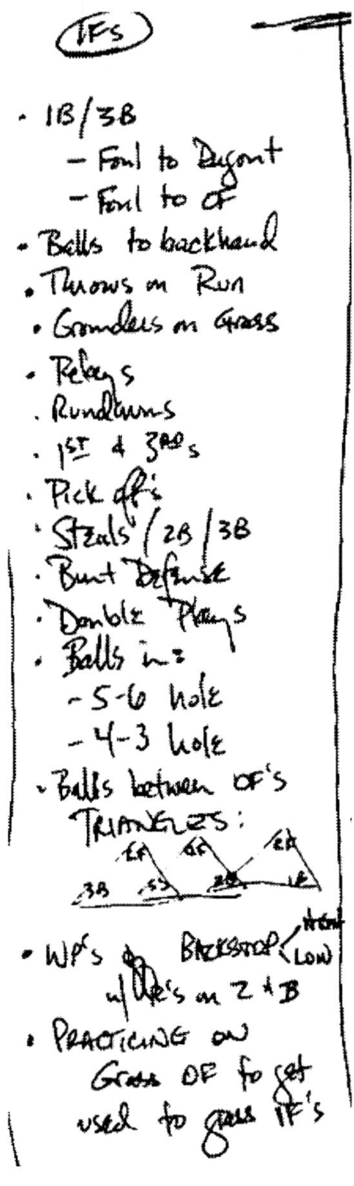

1st Game List for Infielders:

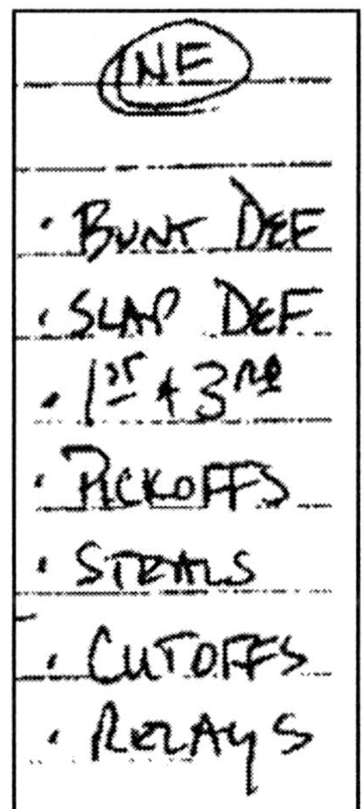

BRIGHT IDEA:

For your first game of the season, shorten your season needs down to give your team the chance to practice the basics they'll need for first game success!

Position Needs

No matter what skill level of athlete you're coaching you're going to have to allow some practice time over the course of your season for the various positions. If you're coaching a first-year T-ball team made up of five and six year olds you'll no doubt spend most of your time practicing throwing and catching, but you're still going to have to teach them something about positions. The older and more skilled your players the more time within your practices you'll have to allow for position needs.

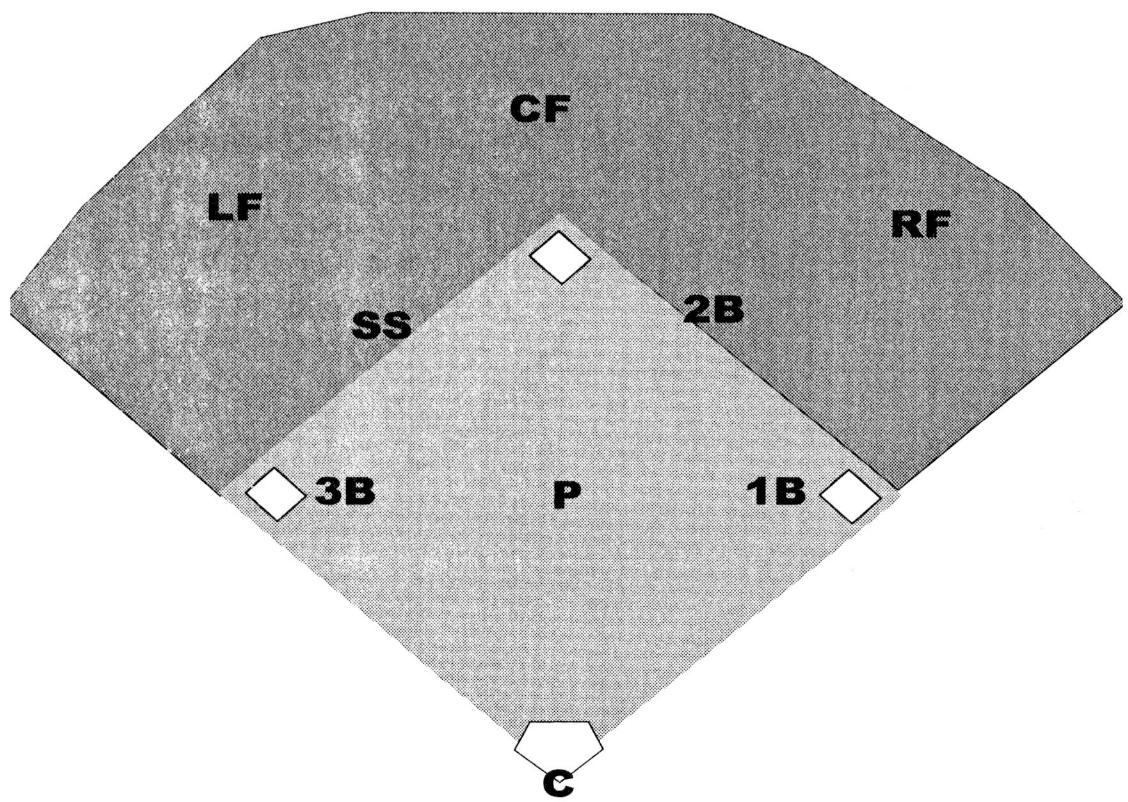

No matter what age and skill level your players are you've got to plan time for your team to practice their position needs, and if you're really smart, allow time for them to practice at least one additional position as well just in case someone gets injured and people have to start filling in.

When you're sitting down to plan out your various position needs for practice don't forget to include the backups, relievers and reserves. Your job as a coach is to prepare your team to succeed and one way to do this is to make sure your players are ready for the "what if's" - those things like injuries and missed games (for things like grades, vacation or disciplinary actions) that happen throughout the course of a year and that really have a major impact on the outcome if your team isn't ready to handle them.

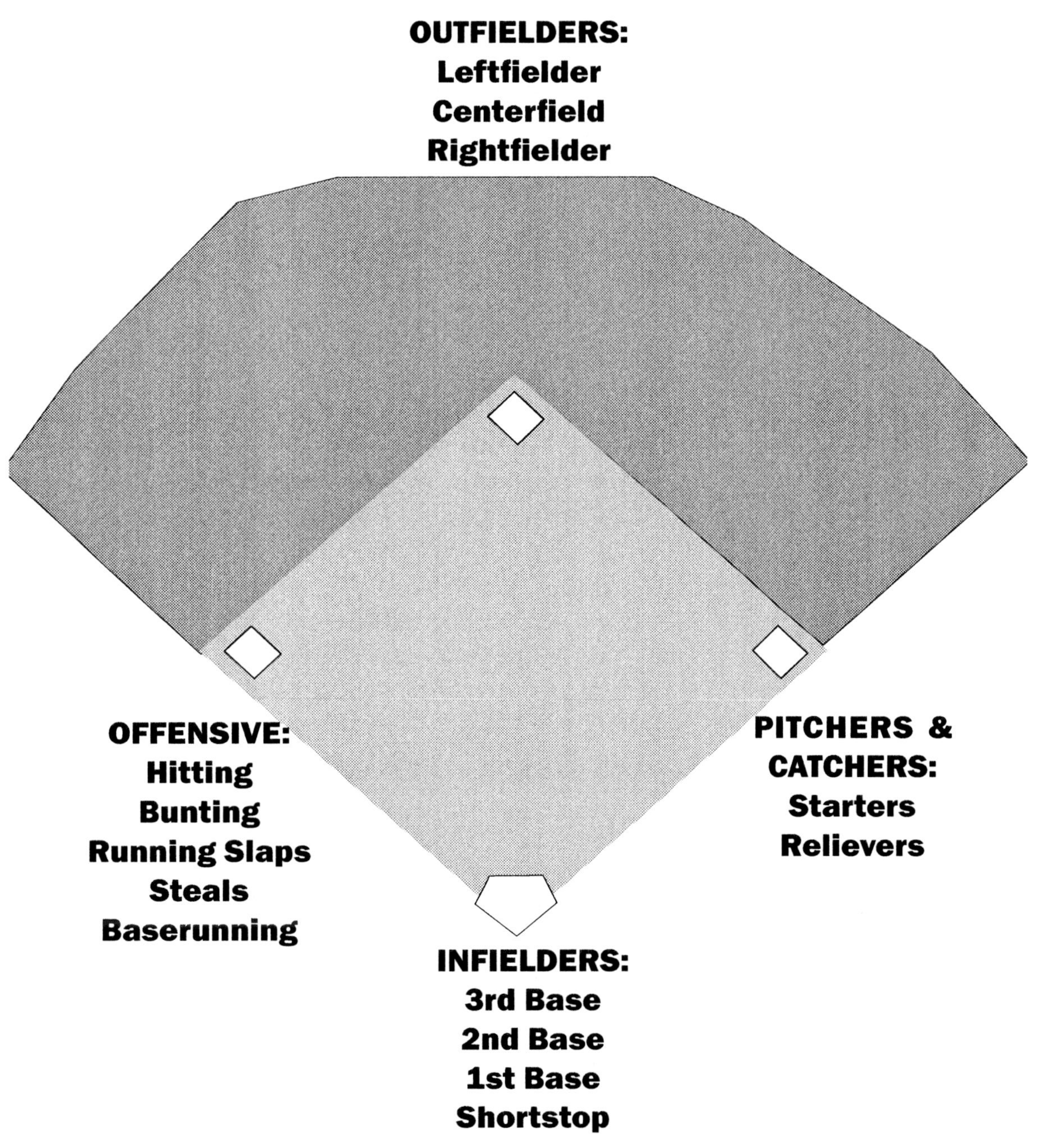

We'll explore ways to work position needs into practice later on in this book, for now, I'm just mentioning it as something that you have to consider in your planning phase.

Individual Needs

Without getting too far into the mental side of coaching, let's just say that as coaches we need to make sure we carve out some practice time for the individual needs of our players. Not all players learn at the same rate and once games start then all kinds of different issues crop up that we've got to try and deal with during our practices.

Later on we'll look at some more in-depth examples of how to work INDIVIDUAL NEEDS into your practices so for now I'm just going to skim over the basics. When you're sitting down to plan your practice for either that day or for that particular week there will be times when you're going to have to make time for certain individual players to get in some extra work.

One of the simplest things you can do during each practice to make sure that each one of your players is getting some of your attention, is to make a list of their names and be make sure you talk to every single player each practice.

I know this sounds like a crazy idea and one that you're thinking doesn't even require a list, but for those of you who have coached before, think back to sometime during last season when things weren't going so well - did you talk to all of your players every practice? Or did you avoid those players that weren't doing so well in order to spend most of your time with those that were?

Ashley
Blair
Kasey
Melissa
Megan
Ryleigh
Steph
Brittany
Asia
Robin
Mallory
Alex
Hailey
Savanna
Morgan

It's hard coaching those struggling players, we aren't always sure what to say to them and we sometimes aren't sure just how to help them. But, the very best thing we can do is to let them know we care about them and that we're working hard to help them.

I know two outstanding coaches who did this exact thing during their coaching careers; one was Jimmy Johnson former coach of the World Champion Dallas Cowboys and the other was Linda Wells former coach of Arizona State University and the 2004 Greek Olympic Softball Team.

Even though both coaches were dealing with world class athletes whom most people would think were mature enough and self-secure enough to not need this type of daily communication - both coaches did so in slightly different ways. Jimmy Johnson would carry around a list of all of his players (just like the list above) in his back pocket and after he spoke to each player throughout the course of each practice, he'd check off that player. He wouldn't leave practice that day until every player's name had been checked off. And he was coaching the then World Champion Dallas Cowboys with Troy Aikman, Emmett Smith and company.

Linda Wells, former hall of fame coach from Arizona State University, on the other hand used a slightly different method but one that worked very well for her. She had her player list on her bedside table and before going to sleep each night she'd go down the entire list and ask herself if she spent time with that player that day in practice.

Whether you use one of these two methods or come up with one of your own, just keep in mind that you need to make the effort to talk to and spend time with each of your players every day in practice. It doesn't need to be more than a simple "how's your day been going?", or "how was school today?", but it will make all the difference in the world to your players which just might make the difference in your team!

Bright Idea:

Make the effort to spend time with each of your players every practice. It's too easy to work with the good ones and spend less time with those that are struggling, but all of your players need to know that you're their coach and that you're there to help them. They don't care how much you know until they know how much you care!

MAKE GOOD CHOICES

This is where the rubber meets the road. Or, if you're not into goofy sayings, it's where everything you've done so far finally turns into an actual practice. Up to this point we've been planning and creating and now you're finally going to turn it all into a practice.

Once you understand the concept involved with creating a single practice then it's much easier for you to plan out a week or months worth. If you're one of those ultra-planner-type people that prefer to have their life planned out as far in advance as possible then you'll be much, much more comfortable planning out an entire season's worth of practices. I'd suggest you hold off on doing that. While that might give you a higher level of comfort too many unexpected things are going to pop up throughout the course of your season that you're going to have to make time for your team to practice and work on so you're better off not planning any more than a weeks worth of practices at a time, especially once games start.

The exception to this is your preseason practice - all those practices before your first game. You can plan all of these out in advance if you feel better doing so because you aren't going to have any games that suddenly show you major things your teams needs to work on, things you might not have planned for when you made out the practice.

List All Your Info

The way we start actually creating a practice is to first list all the information that we've covered so far. Those things like the *Total Practice Time for Your Season* and *Your List of Season Needs* that I covered previously well now's the time we put all that information to use, and here's how we do that.

Make a list of the things you know so far about your season:

Practice Time -

» 60 HRS FOR THE SEASON, 24 PRACTICES LASTING 2 1/2 HRS EACH

If you remember from the box below, we figured out that our imaginary high school team had 60 total practice hours for the entire season.

HIGH SCHOOL TEAM SEASON:

How Long Does Your Ave. Practice Last?	**2 1/2 hours**
How Many Total Practices Do You Have?	**24 practices**
How Much Total Practice Time Do You Have?	**60 hours**

(24 x 2.5 hrs = 60 hrs)

List of Season Needs

We then listed all the things our team would need to work on for the entire season which looked like this:

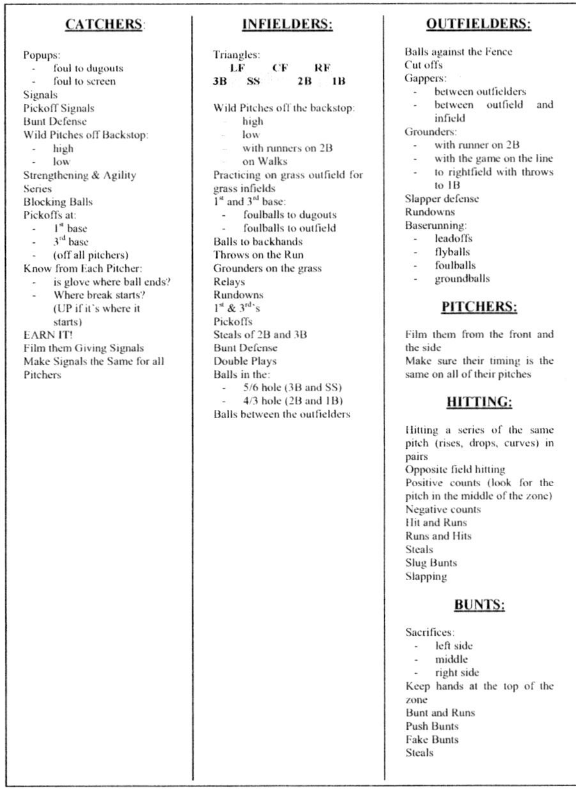

CATCHERS:

Popups:
- foul to dugouts
- foul to screen

Signals
Pickoff Signals
Bunt Defense
Wild Pitches off Backstop:
- high
- low

Strengthening & Agility Series
Blocking Balls
Pickoffs at:
- 1st base
- 3rd base
- (off all pitchers)

Know from Each Pitcher:
- is glove where ball ends?
- Where break starts? (UP if it's where it starts)

EARN IT!
Film them Giving Signals
Make Signals the Same for all Pitchers

INFIELDERS:

Triangles:
LF CF RF
3B SS 2B 1B

Wild Pitches off the backstop:
- high
- low
- with runners on 2B
- on Walks

Practicing on grass outfield for grass infields
1st and 3rd base:
- foulballs to dugouts
- foulballs to outfield

Balls to backhands
Throws on the Run
Grounders on the grass
Relays
Rundowns
1st & 3rd's
Pickoffs
Steals of 2B and 3B
Bunt Defense
Double Plays
Balls in the:
- 5/6 hole (3B and SS)
- 4/3 hole (2B and 1B)

Balls between the outfielders

OUTFIELDERS:

Balls against the Fence
Cut offs
Gappers:
- between outfielders
- between outfield and infield

Grounders:
- with runner on 2B
- with the game on the line
- to rightfield with throws to 1B

Slapper defense
Rundowns
Baserunning:
- leadoffs
- flyballs
- foulballs
- groundballs

PITCHERS:

Film them from the front and the side
Make sure their timing is the same on all of their pitches

HITTING:

Hitting a series of the same pitch (rises, drops, curves) in pairs
Opposite field hitting
Positive counts (look for the pitch in the middle of the zone)
Negative counts
Hit and Runs
Runs and Hits
Steals
Slug Bunts
Slapping

BUNTS:

Sacrifices:
- left side
- middle
- right side

Keep hands at the top of the zone
Bunt and Runs
Push Bunts
Fake Bunts
Steals

Generalize Your Choices

Keep in mind that while there might be a lot of details listed in regards to specific position work, hitting skills or team defense that all of these skills basically fall into some pretty simple categories: throwing, hitting, (bunting, running slap, fielding, baserunning, catching, pitching, team defense, team offense and game situations.

These more general categories are what we'll list in order to help us finalize our practice creation process.

The big question you need to ask yourself is - How much time are you going to allow for each of these general skill areas in each of your practices?

THROWING	TEAM DEFENSE
HITTING	TEAM OFFENSE
FIELDING	CONDITIONING
BASERUNNING	PITCHING
CATCHING	GAME SITUATIONS
BUNTING	RUNNING SLAP

After listing all of our information - here's what we have:

TIME?

» 60 TOTAL HOURS OF PRACTICE IN 24 21/2 HOUR PRACTICES

SKILLS?

» 12 SKILLS TO PRACTICE

THROWING	TEAM DEFENSE
HITTING	TEAM OFFENSE
FIELDING	CONDITIONING
BASERUNNING	PITCHING
CATCHING	GAME SITUATIONS

RESULT?

» 12 SKILLS TO FIT INTO A 21/2 HR. PRACTICE (150 MINUTES)

» 121/2 MINUTES PER SKILL AREA PER PRACTICE

» 121/2 MINUTES X 24 PRACTICES = 5 HRS PER SKILL PER SEASON

That means we have don't have very much time to practice some pretty important things. Now, we could certainly go longer than 12 1/2 minutes in some skill areas but that would mean we'd have less than that for others - and all the skill areas are important since we listed them as critical for our Season Needs.

Combine When Possible

So, what do we do? How can we realistically fit all of our critical season needs into the limited time we have in practice? The answer lies in combining as many skill groups as we can that realistically go together in order to maximize our time.

For instance, in looking at our list of 12 skill groups in the box above, certain ones can naturally be combined in order to shrink down our list considerably:

THROWING - FIELDING
HITTING - SLAPPING - BUNTING
CONDITIONING - BASERUNNING
PITCHING - CATCHING
GAME SITUATIONS - TEAM DEFENSE - TEAM OFFENSE

When we look at this list it shrinks our skill groups down to 5 which drastically changes our amount of time per practice for each skill area as well as over the course of our entire season.

- » 5 SKILLS TO FIT INTO A 21/2 HR. PRACTICE (150 MINUTES)
- » 30 MINUTES PER SKILL AREA PER PRACTICE
- » 30 MINUTES X 24 PRACTICES = 12 HRS PER SKILL PER SEASON

12 HOURS per skill group per year! That's HUGE! By combining skills that naturally go together - like pitching and catching, baserunning and conditioning, throwing and fielding - you can get so much more accomplished in the same amount of time.

Just by combining skills we jumped from giving 12 skills 12 1/2 minutes per practice and 5 hours total per season, to 30 minutes per practice and 12 hours per season! That's huge!

Turn Your Planning into Practice

Now let's get down to business! We know what things we need to practice, how much time we have to practice and - how much time we have per practice per skill group. So we're back to the reason we bought this book - How Do We Organize Our Practices?

Simple. List and organize the things you know, the things we've spent all this time talking about so far and assign a practice time for them. Let's see how this would look in a regular 2 1/2 hour practice with five key skill groups to practice each day. To make it simple let's say that our 2 1/2 hour practice starts at 2:30 and goes until 5:00:

SAMPLE PRACTICE

2:30 - 3:00	Baserunning - Conditioning
3:00 - 3:30	Throwing - Fielding
3:30 - 4:00	Hitting - Slapping - Bunting
4:00 - 4:30	Pitching - Catching
4:30 - 5:00	Game Situations - Team Def. - Team Off.

SAMPLE PRACTICE - 1

2:30 - 3:00	Baserunning - Conditioning
3:00 - 3:30	Throwing - Fielding
3:30 - 4:00	Hitting - Slapping - Bunting
4:00 - 4:30	Pitching - Catching
4:30 - 5:00	Game Situations - Team Def. - Team Off.

Let's say that once you list out all your times and skills like this that you want to make your practice a little more realistic by allowing at least 5 minutes in between skill groups for players to get some water, rotate and the new session to get set up. That's no problem, just adjust your numbers accordingly.

SAMPLE PRACTICE - 2

2:30 - 2:55	Baserunning - Conditioning
3:00 - 3:25	Throwing - Fielding
3:30 - 3:55	Hitting - Slapping - Bunting
4:00 - 4:25	Pitching - Catching
4:30 - 4:55	Game Situations - Team Def. - Team Off.
4:55 - 5:00	Wrap Up

You can always alter your practices anyway that you to need or want to, I'd just recommend that you keep a close eye on the amount of time you're allowing for each skill group for each practice and over the course of the entire season. This slight adjustment of five minutes changes our totals as follows:

» 5 SKILLS TO FIT INTO A 21/2 HR. PRACTICE (150 MINUTES) - SAME

» 25 MINUTES PER SKILL AREA PER PRACTICE - INSTEAD OF 30

» 10 HOURS PER SKILL PER SEASON - INSTEAD OF 12

You can always adjust how you organize your various skill groups, or in what order you practice them. Let's say it's better for you to have your Pitchers & Catchers practicing at the same time that the rest of your players are working on their Throwing & Fielding. Great, that's totally up to you! You'd simply make that change in your basic schedule which would then free up 25 minutes for your to use someplace else - either by adding 12 minutes to the two remaining areas (like Hitting and Game Situations), or else adding the entire 25 minutes to one skill group - your choice.

For this example I'll add 12 minutes to both the Hitting and the Game Situations sections which will now make our practice look like this:

SAMPLE PRACTICE - 3

2:30 - 2:55	Baserunning - Conditioning
3:00 - 3:25	Throwing - Fielding & Pitching - Catching
3:30 - 4:07	Hitting - Slapping - Bunting
4:12- 4:48	Game Situations - Team Def. - Team Off.
4:48 - 5:00	Wrap Up

Drill It & Fill It

Once you've written out the basic shell of your practice, that is you've created your basic skill groups and assigned times within practice for them (like we've just done in the 3 previous examples Practices 1,2 and 3), then what? You're probably wondering what you do with all that time for each skill group?

Well remember all those drills you've been obsessed with learning all these years? This is where they'll come in handy and fit perfectly into your practices.

Depending on the length of the drill and your team's familiarity with it you can do anywhere from one to three different drills in a 25 minute session. The more drills you can learn and plug into these different sessions the fresher your practices will be for both you and your players.

Just try and make sure that the drills you choose for each practice are related to the concept you're presenting that day. Your players won't get better at something just because you talked about it for five minutes, they'll only improve if they get to practice that concept in action.

Let's look at Sample Practice 2 and see how we would fit drills into this type of practice.

SAMPLE PRACTICE - 2

2:30 - 2:55	Baserunning - Conditioning
3:00 - 3:25	Throwing - Fielding
3:30 - 3:55	Hitting - Slapping - Bunting
4:00 - 4:25	Pitching - Catching
4:30 - 4:55	Game Situations - Team Def. - Team Off.
4:55 - 5:00	Wrap Up

We have 25 minutes for each of the five skill areas so let's say we're going to spend the first five minutes of each skill group explaining a concept we want to emphasize that day, and spend the remaining 20 minutes doing 2-3 drills. By adding a concept and a drill or two to each skill group, or 25 minute skill session, Practice 2 now looks like this:

SAMPLE PRACTICE - 2

2:30 - 2:55 Baserunning - Conditioning

- **2:30 - 2:35** Explain today's concept
- **2:35 - 2:45** "Sprints with running sticks"
- **2:45 - 2:55** "4,3,2,1"

3:00 - 3:25 Throwing - Fielding

- **3:00 - 3:05** Explain today's concept
- **3:05 - 3:15** Warm up throwing & "partner throws for time"
- **3:15 - 3:25** "No throws ball blast"

3:30 - 3:55 Hitting - Slapping - Bunting

- **3:30 - 3:35** Explain today's concept or objective
- **3:35 - 3:55** "6 Part Bunting Series"

4:00 - 4:25 Pitching - Catching

- **4:00 - 4:10** Warm up
- **4:10 - 4:20** Practice Location
- **4:20 - 4:25** "First one to 10" game

4:30 - 4:55 Game Situations - Team Def. - Team Off.

- **4:30 - 4:35** Explain today's concept or situation
- **4:35 - 4:55** "Throwing Game"

4:55 - 5:00 Wrap Up

This is a 2 1/2 hour practice that involves five different skills groups and seven different drills. As you can see it's a well organized practice that allows some teaching and drill time without allowing you to get stuck on one certain drill doing it 100 times until "they get it right". It's that type of obsessing that usually leads to an injury in addition to preventing you from ever having enough time to get to the other skills your team needs to practice that day.

Once you make a practice schedule then do your best to stick to it! Otherwise, don't waste your time making one!

Bright Idea:

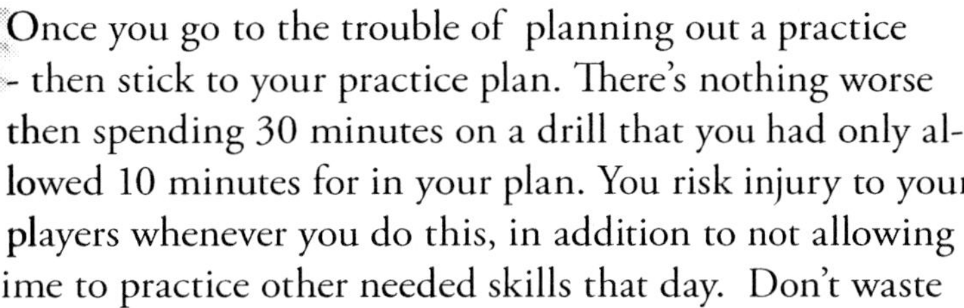

Once you go to the trouble of planning out a practice - then stick to your practice plan. There's nothing worse then spending 30 minutes on a drill that you had only allowed 10 minutes for in your plan. You risk injury to your players whenever you do this, in addition to not allowing your players time to practice other needed skills that day. Don't waste your time making a practice plan if you aren't going to stick to it!

Where Do You Find Drills?

This is a great question that I'm asked all the time. Coaches are always looking for drills and that's why I offer so many different drill products on my website (www.softballexcellence.com). I'm always working to add more drills in various formats so that you can get drills in either a downloaded paper format, a downloadable drill video clip (called eDrills), or a drill book.

Those of you that attend coaching clinics - these are another great place to learn new drills. Talk to your coaching friends and ask them to share drills with you. Most coaches are very willing to share their knowledge since there's usually a very helpful attitude among coaches. I suggest that if you live near a college or university with a softball program that you call up the coach and ask if you could go out and watch one or more of their practices. Most coaches will welcome you out there and once you're there, you'll be able to learn a ton of great drills along with seeing different ways to practice the same things your team is working on. Ask opposing coaches how they practice certain skills, or what their favorite drills are. Coaches love being asked things like that and I think you'll find they'll be willing to share.

Just make sure that if you're asked you also share your drills and tips with others - that has to work both ways!

Don't Forget the Game Part of Softball

As we get going in the practice planning mindset it's easy to completely lose track of the only reason we're practicing to begin with - it's to do well in games. Softball games - not softball drills. We don't have drill-offs against other teams, we play "games" against them. And, whoever wins the "game" is the best team that day, nobody knows or cares which team did their drills the best. So, this is your big word of caution for your practices - "Don't forget about the GAME part of softball!"

What this means in regards to planning out our practices is that we must always have some game-like situations, games, drills, or exercises as part of our softball practices.

This is particularly true if you're coaching younger, more beginning level players. These players really are clueless about the game! I know for many of you that have grown up playing either softball or baseball that's almost impossible for you to imagine because you aren't even aware of how much you know about the game. I'm not just talking about the skills, I'm talking about things like what base to run to and when, what bases you can overrun and which ones you can't, where to throw the ball and when and why, where to position yourself on defense and why it can change. Things like these aren't really learned in drills and yet they're the really important things that players need to know in order to fit all those skills they did learn in drills into the game itself.

When kids are left alone to play (I'm not talking about playing video games - although these are also called "games" but rather left alone to play outside) they will play some type of game, even if they have to make it up themselves. Why don't they just sit and drill themselves? Ever wonder about that? (Probably not). The reason is that drills are usually pretty boring and games are a whole lot more fun!

In softball, we never want our players to become robots because the game requires players to perform various skills based upon ever changing scenarios. Robots can perform something over and over and over, but they can't alter that something based on a change in their environment. Softball's a game of changing environments – this batter's left handed and slaps, the last batter was right handed and a power hitter. It's windy in right field but not in left, the umpire just changed his strike zone. There was 1 out with no runners on and now there's 1 out with the bases loaded...softball is always changing so our athletes can't just walk out onto the field and perform the skill, then leave – like they do in gymnastics, or diving, or figure skating. Softball players have to constantly adapt their skills to the changes in the game.

Your softball team will do much better in their games if your practices include some way for them to slowly learn all the complicated rules, situations and decisions that come up in softball. Or, if your team is made up of older and more experienced players, they still need to work on making faster and better quality decisions during games, as well as working together better. All of these things take practice so unless we make time for it all in our practice plans when is it that we realistically think our players are going to learn all this stuff?

Luckily there is a pretty simple way to stick this important element into our practice plans so we can make sure we are always giving our players some type of game situation work in addition to all the drills that help our players improve their individual softball skills.

Remember the Sample Practice we just looked at, the one that looked like this:

SAMPLE PRACTICE - 2

2:30 - 2:55	Baserunning - Conditioning
3:00 - 3:25	Throwing - Fielding
3:30 - 3:55	Hitting - Slapping - Bunting
4:00 - 4:25	Pitching - Catching
4:30 - 4:55	**Game Situations - Team Def. - Team Off.**
4:55 - 5:00	Wrap Up

Well you'll notice that slotted into this practice from 4:30 to 4:55 is what I call "Game Situations - Team Defense - Team Offense". This is the part of practice where you can give your players time to work playing the actual game of softball instead of just drilling on the skills of softball.

While 25 minutes might not seem like a lot of time to help improve your team in this area, keep in mind it's not just 25 minutes onetime and that's it. It's 25 minutes each time your team practices. As we've already discussed, those minutes add up and they will in regards to improving your team during game situations.

Now, if you're wondering what in the world you should do during these 25 minutes - don't worry. Not only will I show you 20 different practice examples later on in the Sample Practice chapter of this book, but you can also go to my website: **www.softballexcellence.com** and find lots of what I either call Team Drills or Game Situation Builders.

If you look at the more detailed practice listed back on page 34 - you'll see that in the Game Situations segment of this practice I added 5 minutes to explain the concept we'd be focusing on that particular day and then the team will spend 20 minutes doing the "Throwing Game" which is a simple game to play and yet a great way for a team to better learn game-like skills and decisions.

SAMPLE PRACTICE - 2

4:30 - 4:55 Game Situations - Team Def. - Team Off.
4:30 - 4:35 Explain today's concept or situation
4:35 - 4:55 "Throwing Game"

I'll cover this in far more detail in the Sample Practices (particularly in the Whole Team Situations and Competition Chapters that follow.) For now - just remember "Don't forget the GAME part of Softball!" in your practices.

Prioritize

As the season rolls along you're going to see things in your team that you'll need to spend more time on in practice. Let's say they're hitting the ball really well except with runners on base. If that's the case then you're going to have to work this new issue into your practice or spend more time on this point if it's something you've already been practicing. During your next few practices you might choose not to spend so much, if any, time on bunting or throwing - things that your team is either doing very well right now, or else isn't needing at all in their games.

Basically what I'm saying is that you will need to start prioritizing what skills your team is going to practice. This will change during different parts of the season - for instance in preseason you might choose to make throwing, catching, pitching, hitting, bunting, fielding and conditioning your priorities.

THROWING - FIELDING
HITTING - SLAPPING - BUNTING
CONDITIONING - BASERUNNING
PITCHING - CATCHING
GAME SITUATIONS - TEAM DEFENSE - TEAM OFFENSE

Once the season starts you realize that your team needs to spend a great deal more time on throwing, fielding and bunting but that your pitching and hitting is pretty good. If that's the case then you're going to give throwing, fielding and bunting the priority in practice and give those three skills more practice time. Choices like that are up to you based upon how your team is playing at the moment.

SAMPLE PRACTICE - 2

2:30 - 2:55 Baserunning - Conditioning
3:00 - 3:25 Throwing - Fielding
3:30 - 3:55 ~~Hitting - Slapping~~ - Bunting
4:00 - 4:25 ~~Pitching - Catching~~
4:30 - 4:55 Game Situations - Team Def. - Team Off.
4:55 - 5:00 Wrap Up

To adjust our practice time based on our new priorities might look like this:

2:30 - 2:55 Baserunning - Conditioning
3:00 - 3:45 Throwing - Fielding
3:50 - 4:25 Bunting (Pitchers & Catchers pitch during this time)
4:30 - 4:55 Game Situations - Team Def.
4:55 - 5:00 Wrap Up

Keep in mind that any change you make like the one above doesn't have to be forever - you're simply making an adjustment to your practice plan based on what skills are priorities for your team right now. Priorities can change with an injury, a tough week in your schedule or a sudden hitting slump - don't be afraid to change your practice priorities based on what your team needs at the moment.

If your team needs to spend more time on getting along together and forming a better "team" unit than it does on conditioning and baserunning - then make Team Unity a priority and slot it into your practice. I'm not saying that you won't still work on baserunning and conditioning, but you haven't made it a priority so you're going to have to work those two skills into your hitting sessions by simply adding baserunners while you're working on hitting or batting practice.

SAMPLE PRACTICE - 1

2:30 - 3:00	Baserunning - Conditioning - Team Unity
3:00 - 3:30	Throwing - Fielding
3:30 - 4:00	Hitting - Slapping - Bunting - Baserunning
4:00 - 4:30	Pitching - Catching
4:30 - 5:00	Game Situations - Team Def. - Team Off.

The choices are yours based on what things you feel need to be priorities during the different highs and lows of your season - and that includes all three of the seasons: Pre-Season, In-Season and Post-Season. Things change throughout the year and so should you and your practices. Just make sure you don't completely forget the skills your team was able to do well, or else those will quickly become priorities as well.

BE A CONSISTENT YOU

Whoever You Are in Games - Be in Practice

Basically this means if you're a freak in games, then be a freak in practice. If you lose your mind and go crazy during games yelling at umpires and players and virtually making Linda Blair from the Exorcist look like Mother Teresa - first I'd advice you knock it off and get some help - but, you also need to be that person in practice too.

The problem that players have is that coaches are usually one thing in practice, and an entirely different animal in games. That might be OK for fully grown professional athletes to handle but how many of you coach that level of player?

Players can handle things if they know what to expect. If they know you're going to go ballistic once everyone shows up, because that's what you've done so far every day in practice, then when you start doing that in games they won't be as surprised.

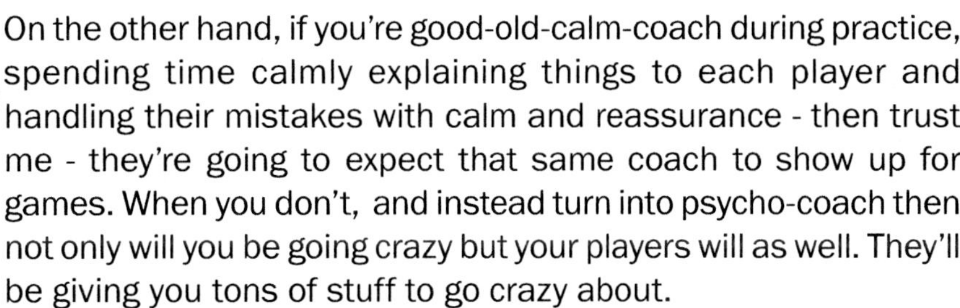

On the other hand, if you're good-old-calm-coach during practice, spending time calmly explaining things to each player and handling their mistakes with calm and reassurance - then trust me - they're going to expect that same coach to show up for games. When you don't, and instead turn into psycho-coach then not only will you be going crazy but your players will as well. They'll be giving you tons of stuff to go crazy about.

In the meantime, if you really want to help your players "play like they practice" then be a BIG part of that. Whoever your are in practice take with you and MAINTAIN during the games, or visa-versa.

Your players have enough on their hands trying to deal with all the challenges the opponents throw at them during games, they don't need changes in you as well.

Chapter Summary - Must-Haves for YOU

1. **Prepare Your Way:**
   - Whether you type it out, write it out or think it out just make sure it works for you.

2. **Plan Solidly:**
   - Know your total practice time for the whole season, know your needs for the whole season, know your needs by your first game, as well as your position and individual needs
   - All your practices revolve around knowing these things.

3. **Make Good Choices:**
   - Combine skills when possible to maximize your time, but always spend your practice time on what's going to happen most in your games.
   - And don't forget to include game situations in all of your practices!

4. **Be A Consistent You:**
   - Whoever you become in games is who you need to be in practice - no surprises for your players.

MUST-HAVES for PRACTICE

The last chapter dealt with things that YOU Must Have as a coach in order to organize good practices. Those things involved preparation, planning, making good choices and being consistent. Even though each concept dealt with practice in some way they were all things that really dealt more specifically with YOU than with a practice concept.

Well now we're going to look at those practice concepts - those elements that you need to have in each of your practices in order to prepare your team to succeed in games. That's why I've called them Must-Haves for Practice - because in order for your team to work in practice to win in games - they Must Have these elements present:

"*MUST-HAVES*" for PRACTICE :

1) SKILL BUILDING

a. Young Kids vs. Older Kids
b. "Everydays"
c. Putting the "Everydays" Into Practice

2) COMPETITION

a. Against Yourself
b. Against Time
c. Against Your Teammates
d. Competitive Challenges

3) ACCOUNTABILITY & CONSEQUENCE

a. Posting Results
b. Winners and Losers
c. "Just One More" & "End on a Good One"

4) PACE

a. Game Pace vs. Practice Pace

As you read through this chapter keep in mind that all of these elements need to be present in some form, in each one of your practices. Now I know that might sound pretty overwhelming to you right now, but I'm going to show you some pretty cool ways that you can easily include each of these 4 elements into your daily, weekly or monthly practices.

SKILL BUILDING

Every single practice you ever hold, no matter what level of athlete you coach or how long you stay in coaching - every practice will involve some type of skill building. One of your responsibilities as a coach is to help your players get better, and getting them to improve their individual skills is one of the areas that will need constant time and effort in practice.

Kids Learn by Doing

Before we get ahead of ourselves and start building their skills, we've first got to know how players learn skills to begin with. Players learn softball skills the same way they learned their major life skills - things like "DO NOT TOUCH!" Or, "Cindy, Don't go in there!", or "That's HOT!".

Kids generally DO NOT learn things simply by hearing someone give them instructions. For instance, let's take the That's HOT! example. Ever been told that before? I'm sure you have, as we all have. Well, did simply hearing DON'T TOUCH THE STOVE - IT'S HOT! was that enough information for you to really understand what the word HOT meant?

Nope! Oh you probably knew that touching the stove was something that you shouldn't do just by the way all the adults made such a big deal about it. But you still didn't really know why, did you? That is, until you did what? Touched the hot stove for the first time! Once you actually tried it yourself - then suddenly all those warnings and words you'd been told before - well they all made sense. Until you tried it yourself, you had no real association with what the word HOT meant!

Now, think about your softball coaching and how many times you've told players things before - particularly in practice - and yet they've acted like they've never heard you. Just like a kid who touches the stove, or opens the DO NOT OPEN door, or hits their brother after they've been told a million times not to do it. Until they try it, the words don't really have any meaning.

So, how can we put this information into practice with our players?

We've got to allow our players time to experience things for themselves, to try and put actual meaning to all those words we use. As adults, we know that telling kids NOT to do something is pretty much a guarantee that at some point, they're going to try it. Right? That DO NOT GO IN HERE sign posted on the door of your big brother's room only made you constantly think about what was in there that was so important it had to be protected by a sign. And more importantly, how you were going to figure out a way to get in there and see it.

So, to take your players from throws that look like this,

to throws that eventually look like this ,

involves some instruction - but more importantly, it involves lots and lots of actual throwing. Players aren't going to be able to simply hear your instructions and transform them into solid fundamentals.

You might be telling them that they need to make a circle with their arm, but as you've probably noticed - those verbal instructions aren't enough. Players need to experience what an arm circle feels like so they can learn to repeat it on their own. Make sure your practices allow time for your players to experience all the instructions you've given them.

Relax when they start trying things and get them all messed up. Allow them chances to work through their skills on their own. Try and put them in situations where they've got to make their own corrections in order to win the competition or to simply finish the drill. These types of self-corrections are far more powerful for the players than you telling them every-single-thing they should do.

Remember - when your parents told you "Don't touch the stove - it's hot!", you knew it was something you shouldn't do only by the way your parents told you - but you still weren't really sure why. That is until you touched the hot stove for yourself - and then suddenly all that previous instructions sunk in and make sense.

Try to allow your players time to "touch the stove" themselves during your practices so that they can really learn and understand the skills for themselves instead of avoiding the stove simply because that's what you've told them to do.

Young Kids vs. Older Kids

While all players need to have skill building present in some form in their practice there will be some obvious differences brought on by age and talent level.

Younger Kids need to spend the majority of their time practicing the basic skills mixed in with FUN ways for them to learn the strategies and decision-making skills needed in a softball game.

Most of your practice time with younger players will be spent going over the very basic fundamentals with fun and positive-type drills. You'll spend some time teaching them how all these skills actually fit into a softball game, but even the games will need to be an altered version of the real thing to make them a lot more fun, provide more action, all with a much shorter time frame. Remember with small kids to keep your words small, your concepts short and your excitement high (pretty much like the kids themselves). Think about it from their point of view, when you're young and don't really have any skills it can get pretty bad and boring going to a practice where you stand around the whole time practicing things you aren't very good at.

BRIGHT IDEA:

Make things FUN and Fast-Paced for younger kids and they'll want to practice and want to come back!

Older Players, while different in size and experience are also different in their attention span which allows you to spend more time on smaller details that would not be possible with the younger players. You'll still work on fundamentals with your older players, but you'll also be able to mix in more complex combinations of these skills along with decision-making skills, competitive situations and conditioning.

	Younger Kids	Older Kids
Fundamentals	✓	✓
Decision Situations	*very small doses*	✓
Competititve Challenges	*small doses*	✓
Game Situations	✓	✓✓
Positive Feedback	✓	✓
Fun	✓✓	✓

The box above shows what skills and concepts Older Players should have present in their practices compared with those of Younger Kids. The basic difference between the two isn't their age as much as it is their difference in attention span, skill level, experience, knowledge of the game, or overall maturity level.

There's a much easier way to understand how to successfully progress with your players as they try to learn and master any of the softball skills. While I'm sure this concept has an official name I've no clue what it is so I'm going to refer to it as the Skill Improvement Path.

Skill Improvement Path

This is nothing more than a four-step process that everyone goes through whenever they learn any new skill. You went through it when you learned how to type, or run a computer, or drive, or any of the things you probably now take for granted. There's a process that anyone learning any skill must go through in order to eventually perform it successfully under pressure. That process looks like this:

Let's take the skill of "learning to throw a ball" and see how it looks going through these four phases:

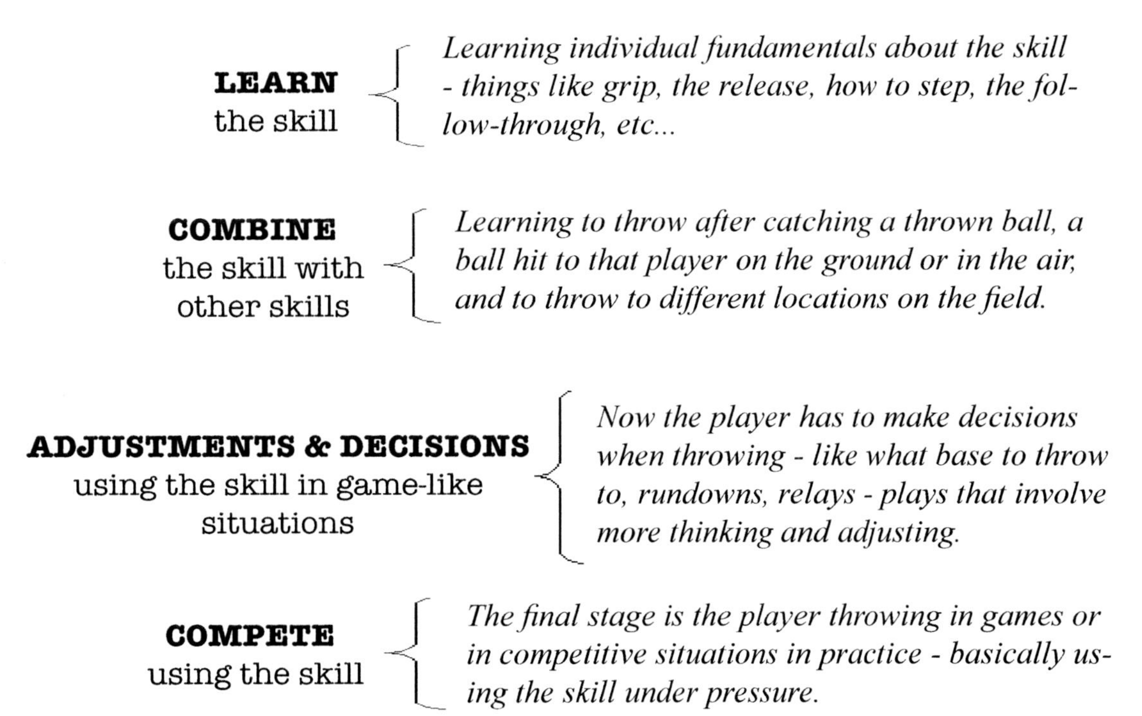

Now, not all players will advance successfully with each of their skills through all four stages. That's why you'll often see players that can do a certain skill well in practice (like hitting or pitching) but they can't do it in a game. Why? The difference is that 4th and final stage - competition. Most of us don't have enough competitive situations in our practices to allow players to get used to it, so when they get under this type of pressure in a game they don't do so well.

I have a whole section on competition later on in this book with lots of examples to help you put your players in more competitive situations in practices - for now, let's look at what these four stages of skill building look like in regards to Offensive and Defensive skills.

We're going to look at these four stages as if they were an upside-down pyramid - with the 1st stage as the largest stage since everyone goes through this one leading all the way up to the 4th and final stage - Competing - which everyone tries to get to but not always successfully.

The first one we'll look at is for DEFENSE - let's see how various defensive skills progress through these four stages of learning:

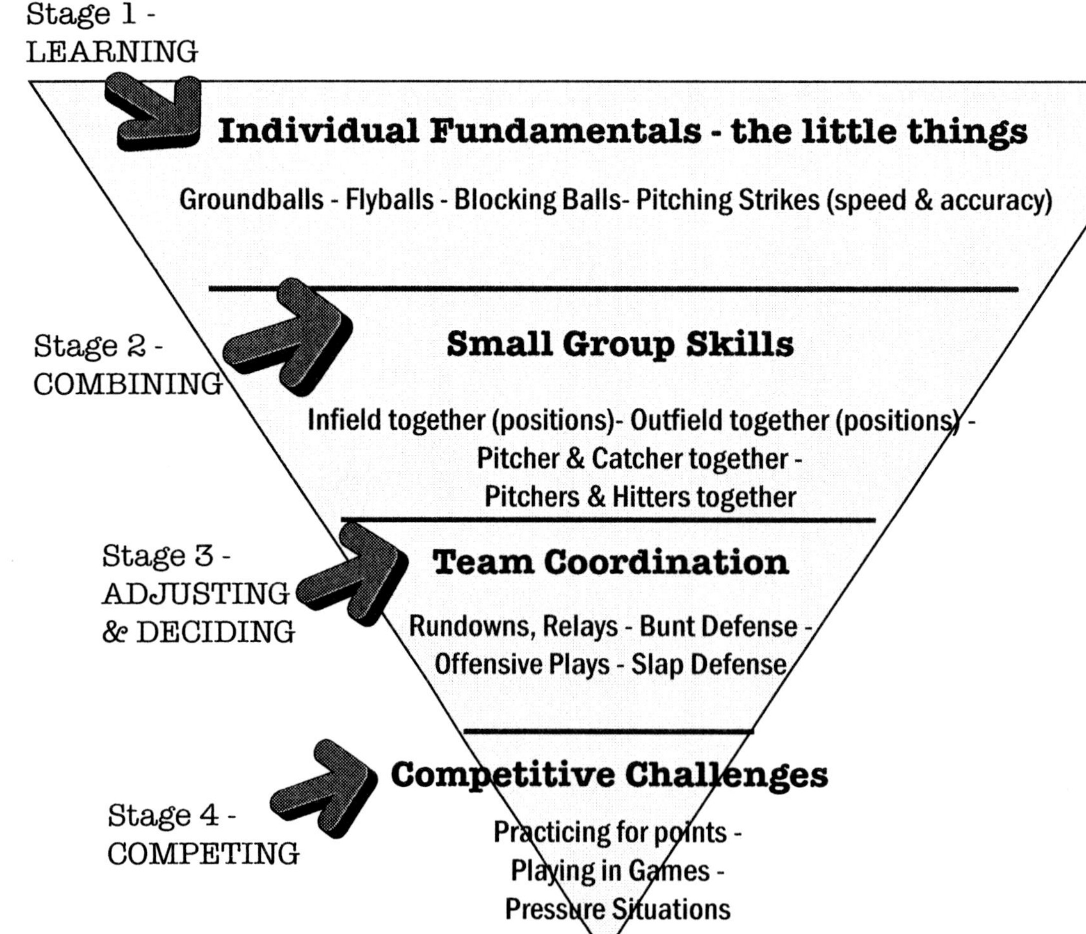

This same pyramid has a slightly different look when you stick the Offensive skills in it:

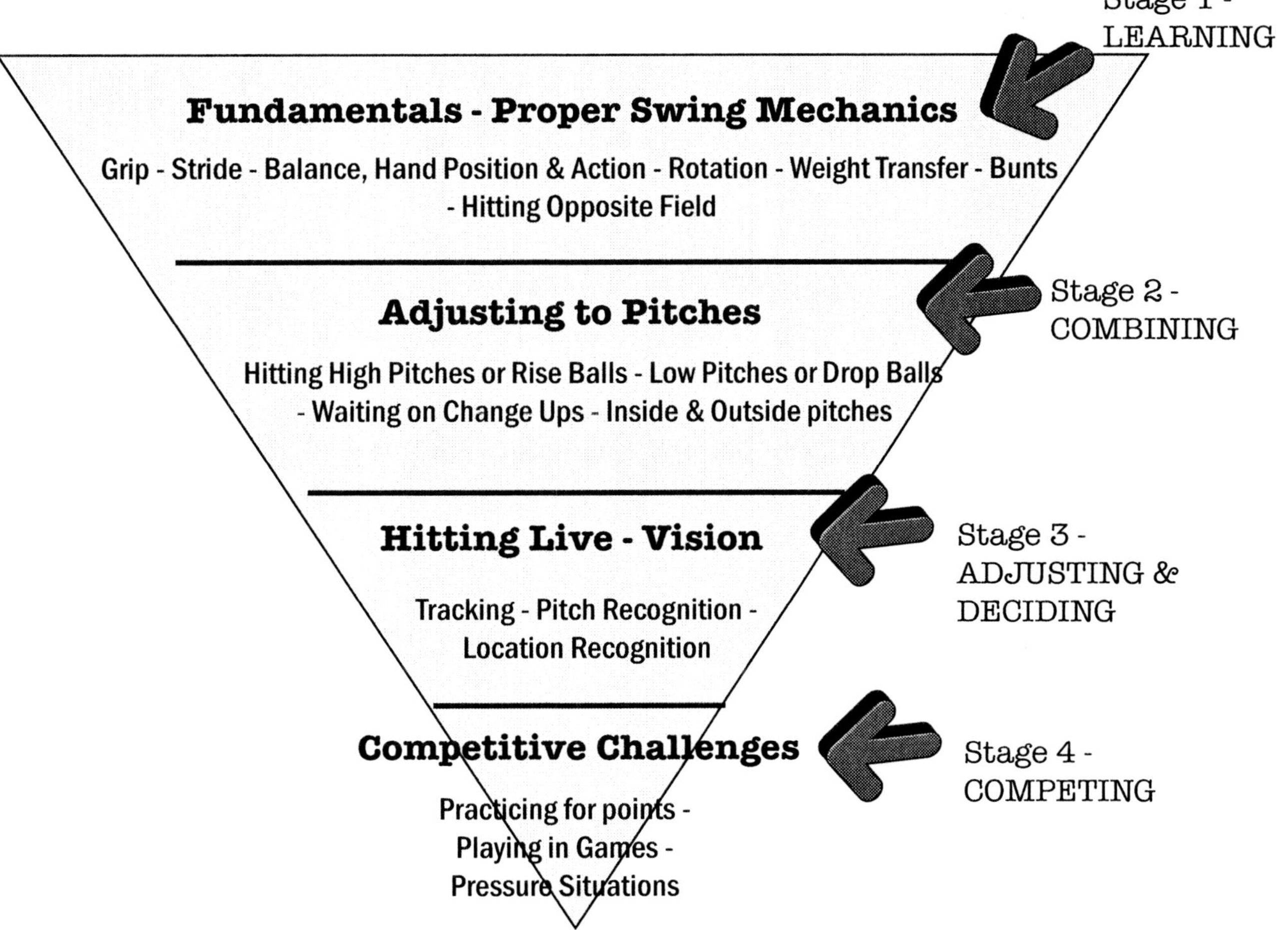

The idea here isn't to confuse you but rather to let you see the natural progression that players make when learning skills. All players at all levels go through these same four stages, the difference is that the really skilled players like the Lisa Fernandez's and the Michele Smith's (both multi-Gold Medalists for the USA), don't stay in any stage very long - they zoom through the first three stages on their way to stage four where they successfully perform the skills under pressure.

Me, on the other hand, and probably many of you and/or your players - spend a lot of time bobbing back and forth between all four stages with the goal of being successful under pressure (in stage four) but never really landing there for too long.

Be careful not to rush your players through any of these stages - doing so will only make you crazy and cause a lot of animosity. Kids will go through these stages at their own pace - the key words for us as coaches is to give them opportunities and be patient!

Some Big Ideas to Help Players Speed Up Their Skill Building

There are some things you can do as a coach to help your players build their skills faster and progress through these various skill building levels:

Video

Allowing your players to see themselves doing a skill is THE BEST thing you can do to help them improve their skills! Video your players whenever you can and play it back so your players can see what you see.

Dartfish is a GREAT software program to help you analyze your video by allowing you to play it back in slow motion, draw lines, circles or other marking right on the screen or put your players side-by-side with either their past performances or with elite level college or Olympic softball players. Check out my website for more information on how to purchase your Dartfish software.

Exposure to Better Talented Players (in-person if possible)

Take your team to a local college softball game whenever you can. When your players can watch better skilled athletes in person they get a clearer picture in their mind how to do all the things they spend time practicing, and yet they don't always know exactly how the skill should be done. Opportunities like this will really help motivate your team!

Camps/Clinics

Check out your area for the local college softball camps and clinics and let your players know them. Encourage your players (and their parents) to attend as many as they can as these are great opportunities for your players to learn from excellent coaches and players how to play softball on a higher level.

Watch College Teams Practice

Call your local college softball coach and ask if you can bring your team out to watch one of their practices - most of them will welcome you to attend and it will be a terrific opportunity for both you and your players learn through watching.

Everydays

This is an individual sport played in a team setting
- Joe Torre, Manager, NY Yankees

This is a fantastic term that I first heard from my good friend Mona Stevens. "Everydays" are things that each of our players need to work on "everyday" in practice. They're the basic fundamental skills each player needs to be successful at their position. They're the stage one skills we just talked about in the Skill Improvement Path - and the ones that players need to successfully perform without even thinking about them.

A good way to think about everydays is to think of them as the basics that player has to do everyday they go out to play their position.

For instance, a list of everydays for Infielders would involve lots of different types of glove work on ground balls - forehands, backhands, and shorthops. Let's look at a sample list of everydays for all the position groups on a softball team:

BRIGHT IDEA:

Split your players up into groups of 2 to make it easier for them to work on their "everydays". Grouping them up by position works best for both your planning and for their practicing.

INFIELDERS:
(NOTE: all involve glove and footwork & NOT throws)

Short Hops - *3 sets of 5*
- Center
- Forehand
- Backhand

Push Throughs (groundballs) - *3 sets of 5*
- Center
- Forehand
- Backhand

Drop Step Overhead Catches
- Left - 3 times
- Right - 3 times
- Center - 3 times

OUTFIELDERS:
(NOTE: all involve glove and footwork & NOT throws)

Short Flys - *2 sets of 5*
- Center
- Forehand
- Backhand

Groundballs - *3 sets of 5*
- Center
- Forehand
- Backhand

Drop Step Overhead Catches
- Left - 3 times
- Right - 3 times
- Center - 3 times

PITCHERS:

Wrist Snaps - *2 sets of 8 each*
(if pitcher has pitches)
- Fastball
- Dropball
- Riseball
- Curveball
- Screwball
- Changeup

Groundballs - *3 sets of 5*
- Center
- Forehand
- Backhand

Bunts - 3 sets of 5
- Center
- Left
- Right

CATCHERS
(NOTE: all involve glove and foot-work & NOT throws)

Framing - *3 sets of 5*
- Low Inside
- Low Outside
- High Inside
- High Outside

Blocking - *3 sets of 5*
- Center
- Leftside
- Rightside

Bunts - 3 sets of 5
- Center
- Left
- Right

You'll probably run into a need to have certain players have additional things to work on each day. When you do, you can call those *individuals* and then tack them onto the list of whatever position that person plays.

Let's say for instance you have a couple of infielders that need some extra work (maybe they're really outfielders but sometimes act as backup infielders) - simply list their names at the bottom of your INFIELD everydays list followed by whatever they need extra work on.

INFIELDERS:
(NOTE: all involve glove and foot-work & NOT throws)

Short Hops - *3 sets of 5*
- Center
- Forehand
- Backhand

Push Throughs (groundballs) - *3 sets of 5*
- Center
- Forehand
- Backhand

Drop Step Overhead Catches
- Left - 3 times
- Right - 3 times
- Center - 3 times

Individuals
- Megan - fielding bad throws (5x)
- Asia - turning shoulders on forehand (5x)

Putting "Everdays" Into Practice

If you're reading this and thinking to yourself that these everydays are a great idea but how could you possibly stick them into your practices when you already have more than enough things to work on? Well, that's where the easy part comes in. You've already figured that part out without even realizing it.

Let's first look at a few concepts that will help make it easier to stick everydays into your practices:

Grouping Your Players - the more skilled your players the more specific your everyday groups can be. For instance -

- ***Beginners*** *- Since it's very common for these players not to really have positions its still good for all of them to be grouped together and go through a short list of everydays that covers both infield, outfield, pitching & catching skills. This would help them build overall glove work for groundballs and flyballs, plus help you have more than one player that could eventually throw strikes - all in a short amount of time at each practice.*

- ***Intermediate*** *- These players have more specific infield, outfield, pitching and catching skills so you'd want to break your team up into pairs within these groups to work on their everydays.*

- ***Advanced*** *- These are the players you need to get even more specific with so instead of having just a group of "infielders" working on their everydays, you would have them in two groups; middle infield and corners, plus outfielders, pitchers and catchers. This just allows the two different parts of the infield to work on things more specific to their positions. Yet it's something that for sure, the Beginners couldn't handle and depending on the skill level of the Intermediates, they probably couldn't either.*

Everydays are nothing more than basic skill work done in a fairly quick amount of time, but done everyday (or every practice - depending on your situation). So depending on the number of skills you include in your everydays and the number of repetitions and sets, everydays should take between 5 and 15 minutes each practice.

If you remember back to our Sample Practice 2 when we added more detail to the 25 minutes per skill group, you could easily slip the everydays into the Throwing -Fielding part of practice.

Let's see how you might insert your everydays into one of our already existing practices-

SAMPLE PRACTICE - 2

2:30 - 2:55 **Baserunning - Conditioning**
2:30 - 2:35 Explain today's concept
2:35 - 2:45 "Sprints with running sticks"
2:45 - 2:55 "4,3,2,1"

3:00 - 3:25 **Throwing - Fielding**
3:00 - 3:05 Explain today's concept
3:05 - 3:15 Warm up throwing & "partner throws for time"
3:15 - 3:25 "No throws ball blast"

3:30 - 3:55 **Hitting - Slapping - Bunting**
3:30 - 3:35 Explain today's concept or objective
3:35 - 3:55 "6 Part Bunting Series"

4:00 - 4:25 **Pitching - Catching**
4:00 - 4:10 Warm up
4:10 - 4:20 Practice Location
4:20 - 4:25 "First one to 10" game

4:30 - 4:55 **Game Situations - Team Def. - Team Off.**
4:30 - 4:35 Explain today's concept or situation
4:35 - 4:55 "Throwing Game"

4:55 - 5:00 **Wrap Up**

You can slot your everydays into one of your drill time slots

3:00 - 3:25 **Throwing - Fielding**
3:00 - 3:05 Explain today's concept
3:05 - 3:15 Everydays
3:15 - 3:25 "No throws ball blast" Drill

Another common method of adding everydays into a practice is to put them in right at the very beginning of practice immediately following warmups. Here's a 25 minute everydays session slotted into an actual practice plan. Let's see what it all means:

3:30 - 3:55	**Warm-up / Cardio / Throw**			
3:55 - 4:20	**EVERYDAYS** (EDays)			
P's	**C's**	**Corners**	**Middles**	**OF's**
EDays	EDays	EDays	EDays	EDays
Line GB's	Feed	Line Gb's	Line GB's	LineGB's &FB's
← PB coverages & flips →			Relays	Sliding Fence Catches

In this practice plan, your team would do their everydays along with a few other defensive skills within the 25 minutes set aside from 3:55 - 4:20. This practice is from an actual Division I College team so they've broken their infield up into corners and middles - keep in mind that you wouldn't have to do that if your team wasn't that skilled.

Notice that following their everydays, all of the groups except the catchers then get into lines and have groundballs hit to them by the coaches. (Outfielders also get flyballs as well) The catchers break up and feed the coaches since their position doesn't require them to field groundballs, much.

The last part of this everday session involves defensive work that's more specific to each of the position groups. For instance, the Pitcher's (P's), Catcher's and Corners (1st and 3rd basement) will work on balls past the catcher and flips back to the player covering home.

The Middle infielders (Shortstop and 2nd base) are working on their positioning and mechanics for relays.

And the Outfielders are working on catching balls close to both the outfield and side fences by sliding feet first.

It doesn't take much room to do the everydays. Use your entire field if you can but you don't have to since most of the everydays don't require a lot of room - the outfielders probably require the most and they don't need an entire outfield for their everydays.

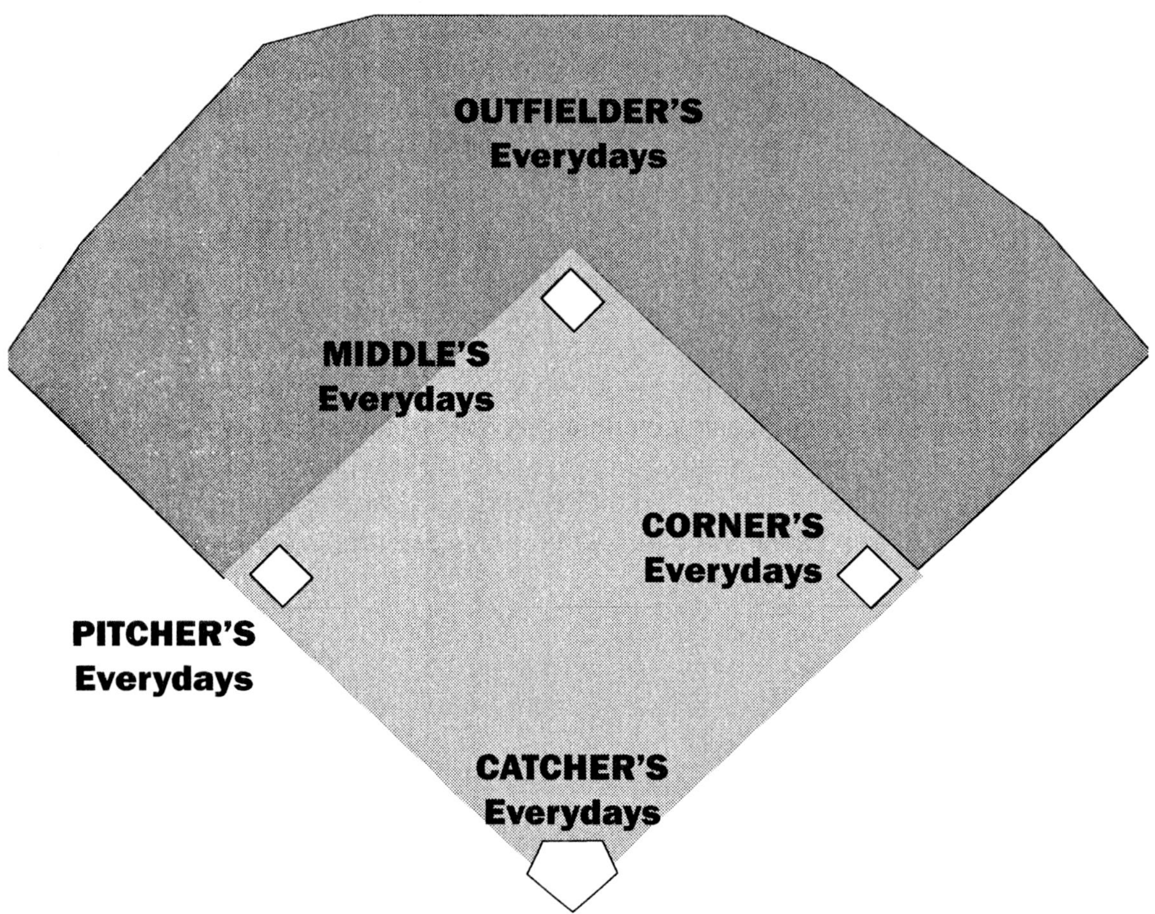

Everydays are just another way to help your team work on skill building during each practice. Remember that some part of practice must be set aside to help your players work on their individual skills - the less skilled your players the more time you will allow for their skill building (and the less you will put into team things like team defense).

Bright Idea:

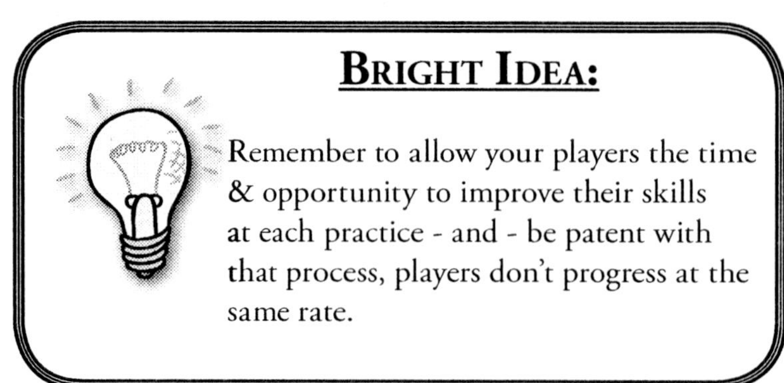

Remember to allow your players the time & opportunity to improve their skills at each practice - and - be patent with that process, players don't progress at the same rate.

- Skill Building Reminders -

They've Got to Try It Themselves -
Telling your players what to do won't cut it. Kids MUST try things themselves to really learn.

Be Patient with Their Progress -
Just because your team is practicing their skills doesn't mean they'll master them immediately. Or, that they'll learn them well enough to execute successfully in games. It's crucial that you stay patient and positive with each player as they work to constantly move their way up the skill building scale. Remember that skills take time to learn well enough to be done successfully in games - and our bodies can't read the schedule. Our bodies have no idea that they need to have the backhand, or drop ball, or running slap mastered by Tuesday's game. Sorry, but it doesn't work that way. Each player has a completely different time table inside themselves that determines when they'll "get it". Your job is to be patient and keep putting them in positions to improve!

Don't Nitpick Them to Death -
Along the same lines as being patient with their progress is this - "Don't nitpick them to death". When your players practice or play try to be supportive in your observations and don't pick apart everything they do. I hear coaches at a 10 and Under practice talking to their players as if they were the New York Yankees. And if they were the Yankees, the guys would laugh the coach out of the ballpark because he's just trying to show off with what he knows - and he doesn't really know that much. Keep in mind that kids don't get impressed with adults so help them, encourage them and be patient with them - don't nitpick them!

Teach Them to Fix Things Themselves
Instead of always telling the players what you think they need to fix or change or repeat - ask them to tell you what they think. Most of them will at first tell you that they don't know. So ask them to guess. Get your players involved in their own improvement so it can stay with them anytime they need it - like in the middle of a big game in a tough situation. The kind when you can't go out there and do it for them. Teach your players to fix things on their own by asking them to think out loud through the process.

Skills Make Plays - If They Don't Have Skills You Won't Have Plays
Don't fall victim to the trick play mentality. Remember that it takes skills to make plays, even trick plays, so spend your time practicing skills that happen all the time instead of plays that happen once-in-a-while.

Remember How Old YOU Are - They Aren't You!
They're kids. They like LOTS of things and softball may, or may not even be on that list, so don't coach them as if they're all mini-yous. They're kids, so have fun with them and allow them their kid-like wanderings and wonders...it might do you some good!

COMPETITION

Pressure Makes Diamonds

~ General George S. Patton

...or, it can crumble a bunch of rocks in the process. What we're trying to create in our practices are players that become diamonds during games, and games are tough because of that pressure. The inability to execute under the pressure of competition is the single biggest reason that players do well in practice but can't do well in games. How many times have you asked that same question? "Why can she do it in practice and not in a game?" Well COMPETITION is the reason why.

While there's no magic potion to sprinkle on your players to suddenly get them to do well in games, there are some things you can do in practice to help them get used to being under the pressure of competition. The good news is that these things also make practice a whole lot more fun for you and for your players!

Against the Clock

Adding competition against a clock (or time) is a really fun way to not only get your players more competitive, but to perform skills at a faster speed than they normally do in practice (which is important for those games when you will be playing against faster runners and pitchers and stronger hitters).

All you need is a stopwatch of any kind (it can be a hand held one like the one shown here, or the stopwatch function on a sports watch) and a clipboard to keep track of your results. I'll go into greater detail about how to track results and what you can do with them later on in this chapter, but for now simply know you will need to record all the various times you come up with.

You can have your players compete against the clock in almost every skill, and in some very creative ways. I'm going to give you a few examples that I've used with lots of success, but don't be afraid to make up your own.

In order to determine if you should time the speed of your players doing a certain skill, ask yourself if the ability to do that skill faster will help them succeed in games. If the answer's YES, then time it. Now, there are a few skills that the actual time either isn't a factor or else happens so fast it's too hard to measure with a stop watch. Let's take pitching for instance. While it's great for your pitcher to throw fast, it's hard to time that speed with a stopwatchand it's not important to time anything else about pitching so that's a skill we won't really use against a clock.

But here are quite a few ways we can add competition and it's pressure to your practices simply by having your players compete against a clock:

Infielder's Release Times:

Glove-to-Glove: You'll time your infielders from glove-to-glove, which means - when you're hitting your infielders ground balls start the clock when the ball touches the infielders glove and then stop it when their thrown ball touches the glove of the receiver (usually the 1st baseman).

Bat-to-Glove: An average 18 yr. old (and older) baserunner runs from home to 1st base in 3.0 seconds (a right handed batter on 60 foot bases) - and what that means is that your infielders can use this bat-to-glove timing as a competition against an imaginary baserunner. You can use this bat-to-glove method when you hit grounders to your infielders by simply starting the clock when the bat hits the ball and stopping it when the thrown ball hits he glove of the 1st baseman (or whoever the infielders are throwing to). ***NOTE*** *- the one thing to keep in mind if you're using this as a competition is to make sure the infielders position themselves in the same place. For instance, you might have them put a cone beside them to mark where they start when they're back, and another cone to mark where they play when they're in. Then time them from bat-to-glove from both locations and keep track of the results from both a "back" and an "in" position.*

Keep in mind that infielders will play IN against slappers as well as weak hitters and bunters. We'll discuss bunt coverage next so for now, know that we're talking about the IN position for your infielders against either weak hitters or slappers.

Infielder's Bunt Coverage

This is pretty similar to the "in" position I just mentioned for infielders. When you're practicing your defensive Bunt Coverage you can pull out the stopwatch and keep track of how quickly your infielders are getting to the ball and getting rid of it by tracking the bat-to-glove times.

Bat-to-Glove: An average 18 yr. old (and older) baserunner runs from home to1st base in 3.0 seconds (a right handed batter on 60 foot bases) - and what that means is that your infielders can use this bat-to-glove timing as a competition against an imaginary baserunner. You can use this bat-to-glove method when you hit grounders to your infielders by simply starting the clock when the bat hits the ball and stopping it when the thrown ball hits he glove of the 1st baseman (or whoever the infielders are throwing to).

Since the following competitions against the clock have to do in some way with baserunning times - either for outfielders and catchers trying to throw out runners, or for baserunners themselves trying to compare themselves to themselves, their teammates or other quick runners - it's helpful to know what good times are for baserunners. Here's a table to show a variety of times from SLOW all the way up to GREAT. Please keep in mind these times are for college softball players so you will have to scale back for younger players accordingly:

Baserunning Times

	Home-1st *(righty)*	Home1st *(lefty)*	2nd-Home	1st-2nd	Home-Home
Slow	Above 3.1	Above 3.0	Above 6	3.30 sec.	Above 12.5
Average	3.0	2.7 - 2.8	5.75		11.50 - 12.00
Good	2.8	2.5 - 2.6	5.3 - 5.5	2.99	11.00 - 11.3
Great	2.6	2.3 - 2.4	5.2 or lower		10.8 or lower

NOTE: all times are from a standing start and not from a swing. If you have your players swing first before they run then all times will be about .5 seconds slower.

Team Baserunning Times:

Foot speed is such an advantage in softball since it forces the defense to throw and catch faster than they can do so successfully. As a result, tracking your baserunner's progress in this department can really help. Using the chart below you can help your players get really competitive when they practice their baserunning by tracking their times every time they run the bases.

Touch to Touch: You'll time your runners from touch-to-touch which means - you'll start your watch as soon as their first step hits the ground and stop the watch when their foot hits the base. Or, "touching" the ground to "touching" the base.

One thing you'll start to notice is that technique starts to play a BIG part in their times once they start running multiple bases. The fastest runners can run Home-1st the fastest, but sometimes they can't control their speed in the turns and end up taking too big of a turn between bases which slows them down on their times.

	Home-1st *(righty)*	Home1st *(lefty)*	2nd-Home	1st-2nd	Home-Home
Slow	Above 3.1	Above 3.0	Above 6	3.30 sec.	Above 12.5
Average	3.0	2.7 - 2.8	5.75		11.50 - 12.00
Good	2.8	2.5 - 2.6	5.3 - 5.5	2.99	11.00 - 11.3
Great	2.6	2.3 - 2.4	5.2 or lower		10.8 or lower

Outfielder's Release Times:

You can time your outfielder's releases the same way you would your infielders by using the glove-to-glove method. Release time is really important for outfielders and is also one of the most overlooked outfielder throwing qualities. Most people concentrate on arm strength and accuracy, which are both important, but if your players have really strong and accurate arms but take forever to get rid of the ball then it won't do you much good at all.

Glove-to-Glove: You'll time your outfielders from glove-to-glove, which means - when you're hitting flyballs to your outfielder start the clock when the ball touches the outfielders glove and then stop it when their thrown ball touches the glove of the receiver .

Catcher's Release Times:

Release time is critical for your catcher's and an excellent indicator of ability to throw out somebody stealing. Well, release time combined with accuracy.

Glove-to-Release: You'll time your catchers from glove-to-release, which means - you start the clock with the ball touches your catcher's glove and stop it when the catcher releases the ball. NOTE - this happens pretty fast so it's going to take a pretty quick hand to get the timing on the watch down.

Times: 1.00 seconds = OK
.8 seconds = Good
.6 seconds = Excellent

Throwing - quick throws for time:

Throwing is also a skill that we usually practice at a fairly slow speed and yet it happens pretty fast during games. To help our players throw better during games we need to add a timed throwing competition to our practices.

Unlike the other things I've mentioned so far, this competition won't involve timing their releases, but instead, will involve seeing how many throws they can throw within a certain period of time. Let's see what I mean:

- *Split your teams up into pairs, each pair has their glove on and one ball - (this works really well during warmups when we usually have our team warm up throwing while facing each other in pairs.) This setup is just like the one for warm up throwing.*
- *Have all the balls start at the same side of the line of players and all the players be the same distance apart.*
- *When you say "GO" start the clock and see how many times each pair can throw back & forth within a 10 second period of time (you can make the time period anything you want but 10 seconds is pretty long for a play in softball).*
- *Each time a person touches the ball it counts as "1" and if they throw it away they need to chase it and keep going.*
- *Pair with the most points in 10 seconds win.*
- *If there's a tie, have the winning pairs have another 10 second throw-off.*

Throwing - quick throws for numbers:

Set up is the same as above, the difference is that this is a competition to see which pair can make X amount of throws first, instead of who can make the most throws in a certain amount of time.

- *We always used "10" as the number to get to on quick throws.*

Against Yourself

Having your players compete against themselves (not against each other as that's our next category) is another method of helping your players get better in practice to compete successfully during games.

So, how do your players compete against themselves in practice? Well, one simple way is to keep track of all scores and times for all of your players and then anytime you do that same drill or contest tell each player what score or time they're trying to beat.

For instance, let's take one of the competitions against the clock that we just talked about - let's take *Infielders Release Times*. This exercise not only becomes a competition against the clock for each of your infielders, but if you record everyone's time then the next time you do this same thing each infielder is competing against themselves as well as competing against the clock.

Pitcher's Practice Games

The easiest group I've found to compete against themselves in practice is the pitchers. This works out great for coaches since many coaches aren't pitching coaches and aren't really sure just what to do with their pitchers during practice - so they send them off to the bullpen to do their "spins" and whatever else on their own, while the coach works with the rest of the team.

Well, I don't know what kind of players you have, but the kind I'm familiar with aren't the greatest at pushing themselves hard without some type of direction and adult supervision. So, if you're not in a position to be with your pitchers during their practices them you've certainly got to have some type of competition going on with them so they'll push themselves in some manner that will help prepare them for games.

NOTE: *I cover far more details about pitching and even how to properly practice pitching in my book, The Complete Book of Pitching, which is available on my site:*

<u>www.softballexcellence.com.</u>

Pitcher's Practice Games, continued

For now let's look at a few examples of how pitchers can compete against themselves during practice:

"Runs & Outs" Game -

The catcher puts up a target & all scores are based on the pitcher hitting the target (based upon skill level - if the pitcher is a really young beginner then the target becomes simply throwing a ball or a strike. If the pitcher is advanced, then hitting the target means the catcher does not move her glove - make sure to set the strictness of this appropriately for the skill level of the pitcher.)

- *if the pitcher hits the target = 1 strike*
- *If the pitcher misses the target = 1 ball*
- *3 strikes = 1 out*
- *4 balls = 1 bases and 4 bases = 1 run*
- *Pitch a certain number of innings (usually 2-4) and each pitcher should work to hold the runs to less than 2. (less than 1 if an elite level pitcher)*

"Points" Game -

This is a great game for younger pitchers who are simply working on throwing strikes. If you have older and more talented pitchers then you can use this game to work on one or more of the pitches they're developing (like their change up).

- *Select a certain score the winner needs to get (10 is a great number for most pitchers). Determine this number before the game starts.*
- *This game has the pitcher playing against the catcher - and on every pitch one or the other gets a point.*
- *The catcher puts up a target (or for younger and less skilled pitchers the target is simply the strike zone) - if the pitcher hits the target the pitcher gets 1 point (or a strike = 1 point.)*
- *If the pitcher misses the target (or throws a ball if they're a younger aged pitchers) then the catcher gets a point.*
- *The first player to 10 (or whatever score they agreed to before hand) WINS.*

Against Your Teammates

Adding competition between your players is a great way to get them tougher and more battle-tested to do well in games. Plus, it's something that you can add pretty easily to the things you're probably already doing at your practices.

Batting Practice -

Putting players against each other in batting practice is a great way to make what is usually a very boring part of practice have a lot more interest and excitement, but to also help your players learn to hit better under pressure.

Before we look at a method for turning batting practice into a competition among your hitters let's first talk about some steps you can take to make your batting practice carry over better to game at-bats:

- Batting Practice Tips -

1) *Divide a player's total number of swings (or pitches) into smaller groups of 4-5 swing/pitches. This will more closely resemble the number of pitches a player gets during a game at-bat instead of the usual number (like 15 or 20) we give them in practice.*

2) *Split your team up into groups of 2 and let each group move together through your hitting practice. This will get them used to helping each other more during practice.*

3) *Take batting practice in the batting order when possible. This just helps them get used to hitting after a certain person and gets them comfortable.*

4) *Your batting practice can be taken off of any type of pitching (live or machine pitch), off of a Batting T, and off of either side or front toss. The main thing about batting practice is that your players get practice swinging at a ball so don't let how that ball gets to them be a huge factor for you in creating your practices.*

Bright Idea:

If you're having trouble figuring out who is going to record all these points during your player-against-player competitive practices, try having your players do it. Simply add a "points tracking" station as the station right before the batting station - and for the pitchers points tracking, have the pitchers not currently pitching on the field keep track of the points. Also, injured players can record points.

Let's look at a simple Batting Practice and see how we can get our players to compete against themselves:

Hitter's Competition in Batting Practice (BP)

- *Divide your players into groups of 2 for BP.*
- *Each pair (group of 2) will have a combined score that they will use to compete against all other pairs.*
- *Each player takes their designated number of swings & a point is given for the result of every swing based on the point values listed below.*
- *Decide ahead of time how you want to score foul balls...they can either be scored as if they were fair and therefore based on the type of hit in the point box below - or - if you're working on hitting fair balls that day in practice then you would create a negative point value for foul balls (say, -2 points for foul balls). You should create a point value based on the type of hit ball you are trying to encourage your players to have (your +points) with the negative points for the type of hits you're trying to discourage.*
- *The point value should not be based on whether batting practice is taken off of live pitching, front toss, side toss, machine or Batting T.*

Hitting Points	
Groundball	+1
Flyball	-3
Line Drive	+3

Pitching Batting Practice -

Batting Practice is also a great time to help your pitchers get some much needed work in against real batters. Remember that most of the time pitchers are pitching only to a catcher - they don't usually have batters standing in down in the bullpen or where ever they're usually pitching, so putting your pitchers into batting practice can be very helpful to both the batters as well as the pitchers.

First, let's talk about a few issues that always come up whenever the concept of pitching batting practice is mentioned:

- Pitching Batting Practice Tips -

1. Many people say that pitchers should never throw batting practice. That's a pretty tough statement and one that I never followed since the main thing pitcher's do is throw to batters. But, every coach is certainly allowed to have their own opinion. What I did with my pitchers, both in coaching college and in the professional league, was to have my pitchers throw in 3 different types of pitching situations:
    - *One, was down in the bullpen to work on their various pitches and locations. This was their skill building time.*
    - *Two, the other thing I did was have them throw simple fastballs to hitters to allow our hitters time to work on their skill building off of live pitching. Our pitchers actually liked this as it allowed them to pitch at a pretty easy pace - about 60% to 75% of their max. speed - and allowed them to stretch out their arms. We would often have our pitchers do this the day after they had pitched and since we had 3 pitchers we were able to do this often in practice.* ***Note****: They* *<u>always</u>* *used a protective screen when doing this!*
    - *Three, we had our pitchers pitch to batters while they worked on either certain pitches, certain combinations of pitches, or certain counts. This was much tougher for the hitters but was great game-like practice for our pitchers (and for our hitters).*

NOTE *- I'll show you specific practice examples of just how I mixed in these types of pitching practice later in the book under Sample Practices.*

2. If you work in pitcher's during batting practice make sure that only the pitcher actually doing the pitching is standing out on the field - have the other pitcher's off the field near the dugout while they wait their turn to pitch.

3. Have one pitcher throw to a pair of hitters at least twice before switching with another pitcher (remember how I talked about the hitter's going through batting practice in pairs and taking their x number of swings in groups of 4-5 swings instead of all x at one time?). This makes it much more game-like in regards to pitching to 3-5 hitters and then taking a break (while your offense bats), then pitching to 3-5 hitters and taking a break so another pitcher can pitch. Too often, our pitching practice is too many repetitions for too long a period of time - and none of it translates to actually pitching in a game.

4. Your batting practice can be taken off of any type of pitching (live or machine pitch), off of a Batting T, and off of either side or front toss. The main thing about batting practice is that your players get practice swinging at a ball so don't let how that ball gets to them be a huge factor for you in creating your practices.

Just like I talked about counting points for the hitters during batting practice we can do the same thing for the pitchers. Remember that the point system is based on rewarding the player (in this case a pitcher) with more points for doing the things that will help them be successful in games, and less points for the things that will hurt them.

So, based on that let's see what our pitching points for batting practice looks like:

Pitcher's Competition in Batting Practice (BP)

- *This point-counting-system is going on at the same time as the Hitter's Competition and Point Counting during batting practice.*
- *Pitcher's will throw their workout just like they would over in the bullpen, the difference is there is a live batter in the batters' box (who is also trying to earn points).*
- *Points are counted for result of every ball put in play (NOTE: you might decide to give the same points for foul balls based on how they were hit - or else you might not give any points for a foul ball and let it simply be a "no play".*

Pitching Points	
Groundball	+1
Flyball	+1
Line Drive	-3

Here are some suggestions for workouts that pitchers can throw while pitching batting practice to hitters:

1. **High-Low:** This involves the pitcher throwing only high and low pitches, which for younger pitchers might simply be pitching high and low fastballs. As the pitchers get more advance a workout like this might involve a riseball or screwball for the high pitch and a dropball, curveball, or changeup for the low pitch. The pitches do not have to be alternated, meaning the pitcher does not have to throw a high pitch, then low pitch and then high pitch. Rather, they can throw these in any combination but they can only throw something high or low.
2. **Inside-Outside:** Same idea as the High-Low workout except this involves only inside and outside pitches. So again, for the younger and less skilled pitchers this might only involve fastballs on the inside and outside corners, but as the pitcher gets more advanced she'll be able to use her different pitches to throw only inside or outside pitches during this workout.
3. **Opposites:** This workout involves the pitcher only throwing pitches that are opposite of each other. For instance, for a younger pitcher it might simply be throwing a fastball and then it's opposite which is a change up. More advanced pitchers might work on opposite locations such as something High-Inside and something Low-Outside. Or, something Low-Inside and something High-Outside. Another form of opposites for advanced pitchers also involves a Fast pitch (any of them) and then their change up for the Slow pitch.

Competitive Challenges

Competitive challenges are drills or situations you create in practice that really force your players to be competitive with each other. They differ from the competitions against their teammates that we just discussed because they usually will involve either the whole team in one activity or drill, or else a large number of players. The same idea of creating an extremely competitive environment still applies to this concept as it has for the ones I've already mentioned.

Remember that even though I'm going to list some examples of drills and exercises you can use for Competitive Challenges, I have tons more drills available on my website: **www.softballexcellence.com.**

7 UP (focuses on defense under pressure):

- *Place all of your players out on the field on defense. They won't really be in positions but rather just scattered all over the field as shown below.*
- *Balls will be hit to the defense by either one coach or two coaches (coaches will fungo the balls they hit to the fielders - which means they toss the balls up and then hit them themselves.) Coaches will alternate hitting balls so they don't injure or confuse the players.*
- *A player is "out" after they bobble a ball for the 2nd time, or they avoid even trying to field a ball because they might bobble it.*
- *All players that are "Out" must leave the field - the last player standing wins!!*

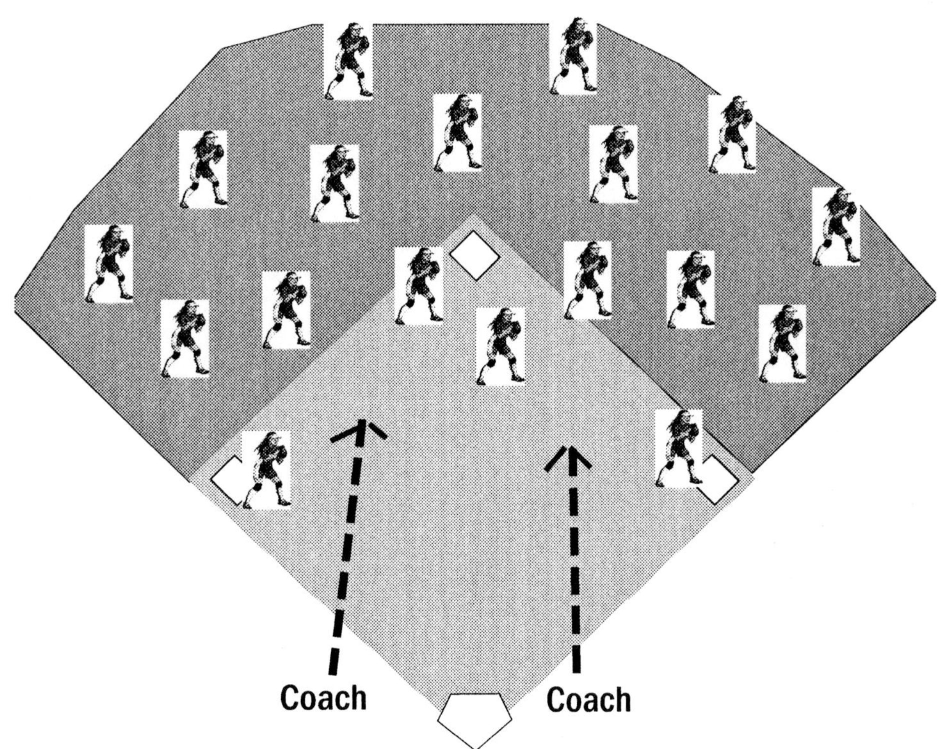

8 IN A ROW (focuses on defense under pressure):

- *This drill will involve all of your infielders and your pitchers (IF's & P's) working on their defense while the outfielders and catchers (OF's & C's) hit them grounders ad catch their throws.*
- *The IF's & P's get into 3 to 5 lines of 4 to 5 players each line.*
- *The OF's & C's will be the ones hitting balls and catching the thrown balls to and from the IF's & P's.*
- *Each line has a ball, a catcher or an outfielder with a bat and a catcher or an outfielder with their glove.*
- *Each line is a separate line from all the others and works separately from all the other lines.*
- *The first player in each line goes (⟶) until they get to 10 in a row. If they miss a ball completely, give up on a ball they bobble, or throw the ball away, their score goes back to 0 and they start over.*

Here's how this drill works:

- *A C or OF hits a groundball (⟶) to the first player in their line who tries to do everything possible to either field the ball cleanly, keep it from going past them, or make a play on the ball if they first bobble it while fielding it.- Once they field the ball the IF or P then throws the ball to the catcher in their line (····>).*
- *If the fielder makes a good throw to complete the play they get "1", and they go again. The object is to get "8" in a row.*
- *If the IF or P fielding the ball totally misses the ball, doesn't make an effort for it, bobbles it and doesn't pursue the ball, or throws it away - they start all over at "1" and must stay in the front of the line fielding balls until they get "8" in a row, then they move on to the next line.*
- *All IF's & P's must get 8 in a row in EACH LINE and then they're finished and can go sit down while they wait for the rest of their teammates to finish.*

This drill really helps players rebound from making an error and get their head right back into the next play. Sometimes a player will be struggling at the front of a certain line, when this happens players coming from other lines just skip that line and go to another line until

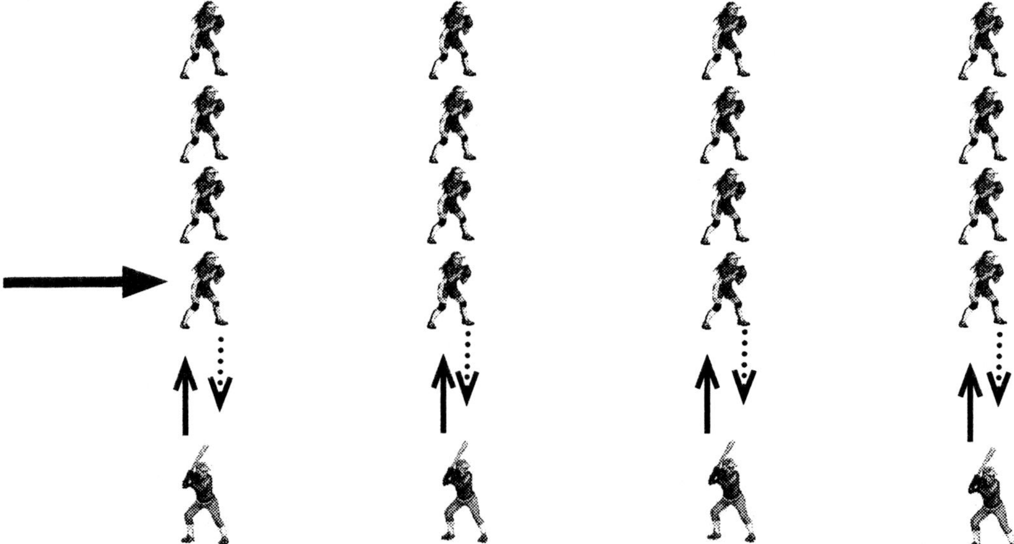

BUNT FOR SPRINTS (focuses on bunting under pressure):

- *This drill pits one bunter against one pitcher (just like in a game) with the only object for the bunter being to bunt a ball FAIR and ON THE GROUND. Period. The bunter does it one time and they're finished and can go down to the end of the line with the first player in line moving into the batter's box to take her place bunting.*
- *The rest of the team lines up in a straight line down the right field foul line (without their gloves).*
- *If the bunter gets the bunt down and fair, then she goes to the end of the line and the first person in lines moves into the batter's box to bunt.*
- *If, however, the bunt is either foul, or popped up, or both - then the entire line sprints down to 2nd base and back - while the bunter stands in the batter's box and watches her teammates run.*
- *The bunter then tries another bunt, and stays in the batter's box until she gets one bunt on the ground and fair.*
- *The drill is over when everyone in the line has bunted.*

Just a word of caution - if you don't have lights on your field you might want to start this drill earlier in your practice!

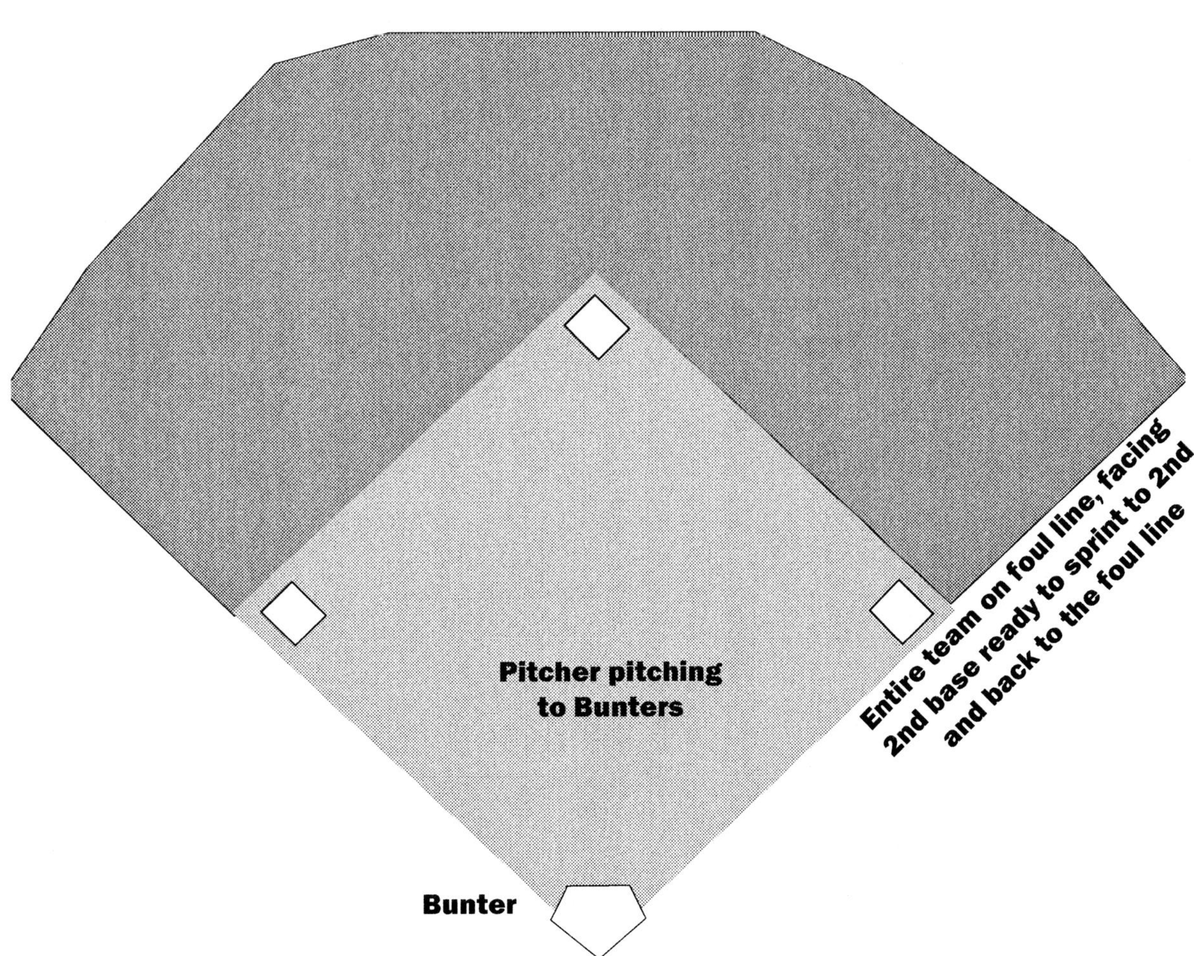

SHORT GAME (focuses on bunting, slapping and defense under pressure):

- *This drill works on your short game defense against your short game offense.*
- *Split your team up into two teams each with a pitcher and catcher and infielders. If you don't have enough infielders then put your best pitcher with your weakest infield for awhile (and then switch so your whole first team can get some defensive work in).*
- *Or, you can also play this short game using a pitching machine or someone throwing batting practice.*
- *Play two innings on defense before switching into offense.*
- *Play it out as a game, counting points for both the offense and the defense just like before with the Batting Practice Points game.*

SCORING:

Offense:
1 point for each base touched

Defense:
1 point for each strike out
1 point for each pick off
1 point for getting lead runner out

HOME TO 2nd FOR SPRINTS (focuses on bunting under pressure):

- *This drill also works on bunting under pressure.*
- *This can be used as a station within your practice instead of a drill for your entire team since it doesn't require more than 5-6 players at a time.*
- *This drill involves a pitcher and a catcher, each with their gloves along with 4-5 bunters with their helmets and bats.*
- *The pitcher and catcher get into their defensive positions while the bunters will get into the batter's box one-at-a-time.*
- *The first bunter simply has to bunt the pitch fair and on the ground. If she does then she goes to the end of the line, if she doesn't then she must SPRINT to 2nd base and then jog to the end of the bunting line and continue.*
- *Ask each player to put down 5 successful bunts before the line switches to another station.*

ACCOUNTABILITY & CONSEQUENCE

What's the difference between Accountability and Consequence? Well *accountability is what you're responsible for.* For example, the firstbase player is accountable (or responsible) for catching all balls thrown or hit near her. *Consequence*, on the other hand, means *the result of your actions.* So, if the firstbase player misses a thrown ball the consequence (or result of her actions) is that the batter-runner can usually take an extra base and get into scoring position. In this example the firstbase player is accountable (responsible) for catching or stopping all balls either thrown or hit to her and the consequence (or result) is that the batter-runner can advance on to secondbase and into scoring position if she misses a ball.

Games do this - they hold us responsible for our plays (accountability) and no matter what kind of plays we make there are definitely consequences (results). Games hold us accountable for our actions, our inactions, our judgments, our decisions, our lapses, our hustle, for all of our play, both good and bad. And, there is no place to hide from your mistakes in a game. Softball is unique from most other sports (other than baseball) in that it's an individual sport in a team setting. One player pitches the ball to one other player, who then hits the ball to one other player, who then hopefully fields it and throws to one more player. Each of those actions either helps or hurts that team and yet each are performed singularly while everyone watches just that one player. And, if a mistake is made it's almost impossible to get lost in the crowd as can easily happen in soccer and basketball.

What's important about all this is that it isn't the way that most of us practice. In practice, our players are usually allowed to make lots of attempts at plays in order to make that one good result. That's something that games don't give us - the ability to try something over and over until we get it just the way we want it. Games are unforgiving. Games demand that we play our best but if we don't, however we play counts anyway.

In addition to the play counting in a game, no matter how good or bad it actually was, there is also the matter of a consequence. In games, when you make a mistake the result (or consequence) is that the other team benefits from that mistake. Period. It doesn't matter that the player didn't mean to make the mistake, or that they're a "really good kid", or that the player works really hard, or that they've never made a mistake like that before - none of that matters - there's still going to be a result from the mistake.

As a result of all of this accountability and consequence our players feel a ton of pressure in games. Pressure that they don't feel in practice, which is another reason our players usually do well in practice and not so well in games.

Posting Results

One way that I've found really helps work on accountability and consequence is to post your practice times, scores and results. You might be wondering what in the world you'd post, or what I'm even talking about but think back for a minute, to all the things I've mentioned so far that require some type of timing, or scoring or results. There have been a bunch so far and in fact I just mentioned five of them on the previous two pages.

Posting your practice results is simply a matter of listing each drill or activity by name and then listing the individuals or pair times and scores and listing them in order of first to last. I know this might sound harsh, but games do this. Games declare a winner and a loser and even post the score. Remember that we're trying to learn how to hold better practices so our team will do better in games, so you can't be afraid of results and competition and accountability.

That's really all a list like this is - it's an open declaration of accountability for everyone to see just how everyone did in practice. But it's something your team will not understand the real purpose for at first and will probably cause them to accuse you of being harsh or cruel for posting it. So you're going to have to remind them that you aren't doing this to embarrass anyone but rather to help everyone get comfortable with owning their results so we can all have better results in games.

So, here's what a practice results list would look like:

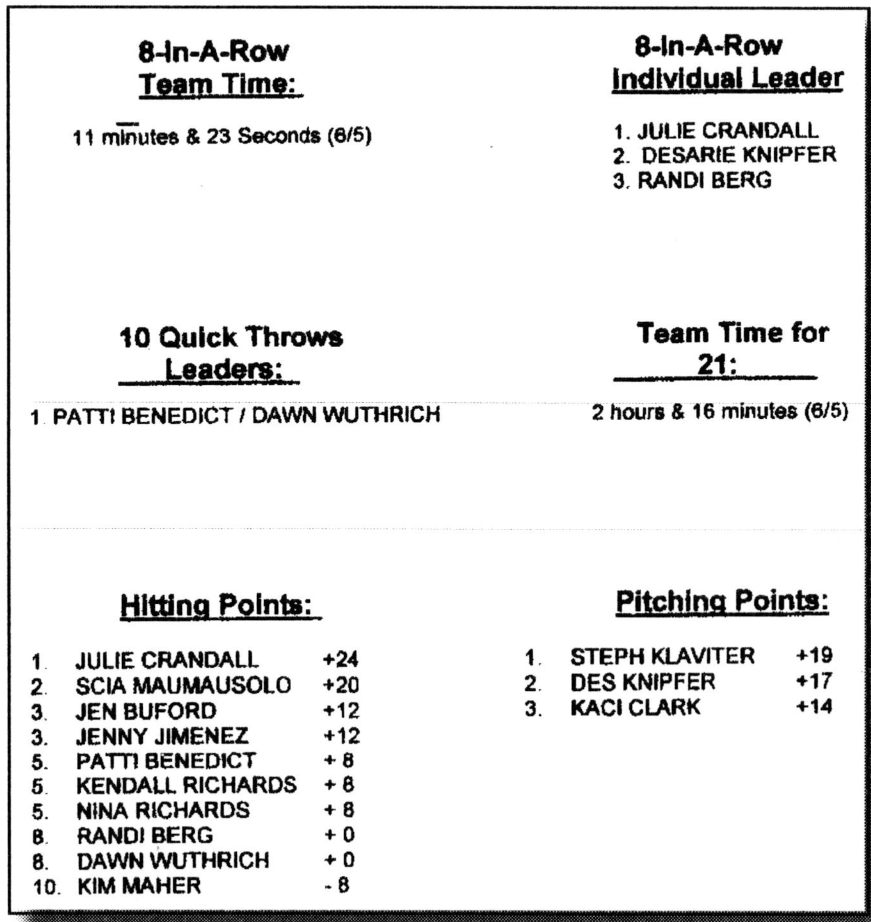

8-In-A-Row Team Time:

11 minutes & 23 Seconds (6/5)

8-In-A-Row Individual Leader

1. JULIE CRANDALL
2. DESARIE KNIPFER
3. RANDI BERG

10 Quick Throws Leaders:

1. PATTI BENEDICT / DAWN WUTHRICH

Team Time for 21:

2 hours & 16 minutes (6/5)

Hitting Points:

1.	JULIE CRANDALL	+24
2.	SCIA MAUMAUSOLO	+20
3.	JEN BUFORD	+12
3.	JENNY JIMENEZ	+12
5.	PATTI BENEDICT	+ 8
5.	KENDALL RICHARDS	+ 8
5.	NINA RICHARDS	+ 8
8.	RANDI BERG	+ 0
8.	DAWN WUTHRICH	+ 0
10.	KIM MAHER	- 8

Pitching Points:

1.	STEPH KLAVITER	+19
2.	DES KNIPFER	+17
3.	KACI CLARK	+14

Let's dissect the list and see what we can find:

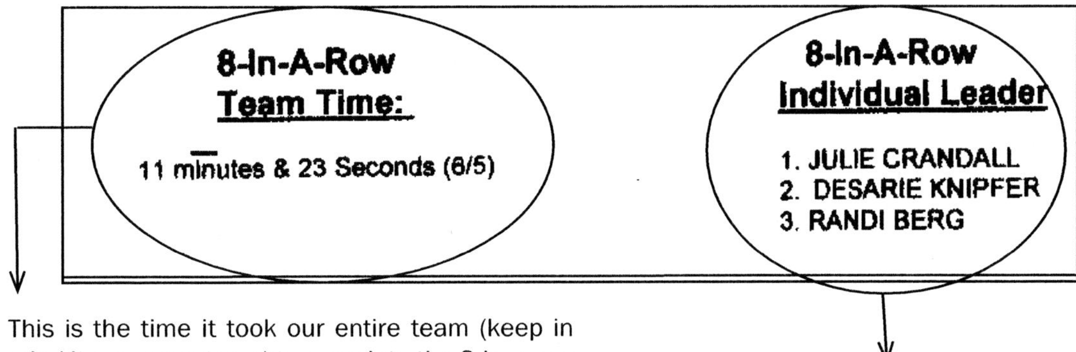

This is the time it took our entire team (keep in mind it was a pro team) to complete the 8-in-a-row drill I talked about on page 70. I simply started a stopwatch when the drill began and then stopped it when the last person completed their 8th in a row in the last line. While this drill is mainly targeted at improving individual players skills, it also tells us all how good we're getting as a team at our defensive skills. The 6/5 is the date we did this time so I could track how long our progress would take.

This shows the top 3 players from our most recent 8-in-a-row. While this is not an individually timed drill the people you list here will be the top 3 from your most recent attempt at this.

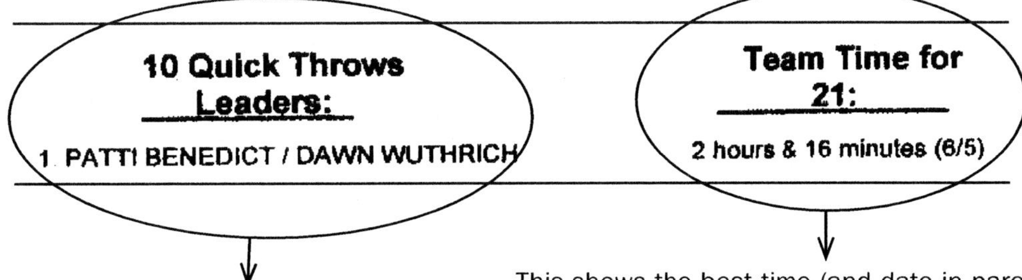

This shows who the winning pair was for the most recent 10 quick throws competion we held (listed on page 62). It shows that Patti and Dawn were the winning pair.

This shows the best time (and date in parenthesis) for our team when doing the drill 21. This is a very tough drill designed to create tension and adversity within your defense so that the players will have to work through it in practice instead of blowing up from it in games. While this drill is not listed in the this book it is available on my website: **www.softballexcellence.com**

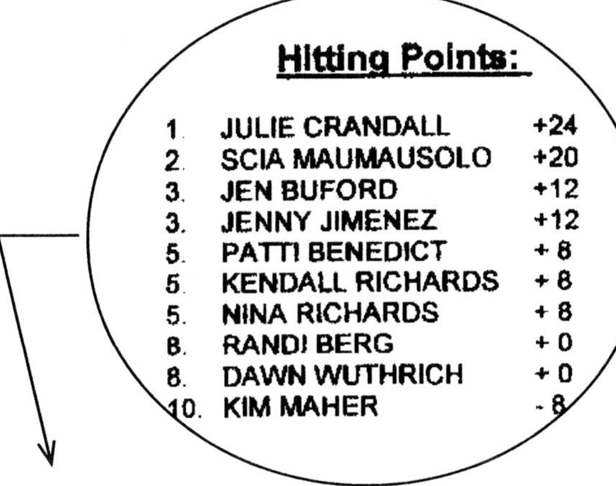

This is the list of all the points our hitters had during the Batting Practice for points listed on page 66. I list all the players instead of just the top 3. I add their newest point total to whatever their current value is.

Pitching Points:

1. STEPH KLAVITER +19
2. DES KNIPFER +17
3. KACI CLARK +14

These are the points our pitchers got during the Pitching Points portion of batting practice. Our drop ball pitcher was the point leader since she threw balls that were hit mostly for ground balls, and our rise ball pitcher was in last place because her balls were hit more for fly balls and line drives.

***NOTE**: All of these players were professional athletes & outstanding softball players.*

Winners and Losers

Since games have winners and losers our practices need to as well. Certainly not every part of every practice should as there is a time for skill building that won't involve so much competition. But if you're serious about helping your players do better during games then you've got to start to involve the concept of winners and losers during practice. Accountability and consequence can create a lot of pressure for your players because the thought of making an error and possibly causing your team to lose is a lot for players to deal with.

So let's try and help them deal better with this by putting our players in a position during practice to win or lose. Let's revisit the drills we just mentioned in our previous section on competition and see how they can now be used to help our players learn to be comfortable with the pressures the accountability of winning and losing creates.

All of the following drills create winners (and therefore losers) and can be used to work on more than one thing at-a-time (not to mention the physical skills the player is also working on).

7 UP (focuses on defense under pressure):

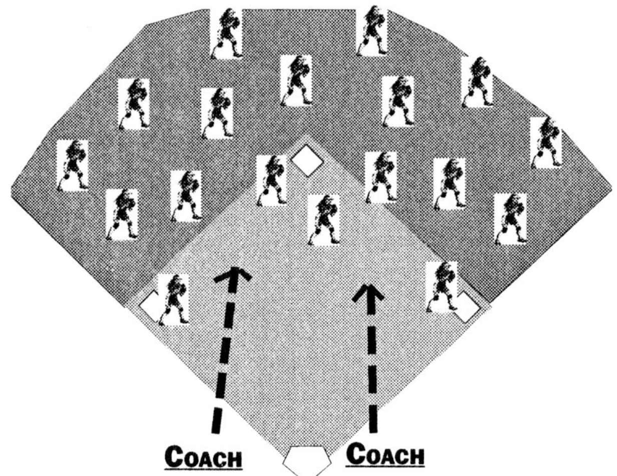

SHORT GAME (focuses on bunting, slapping and defense under pressure):

SCORING:

Offense:
1 point for each base touched

Defense:
1 point for each strike out
1 point for each pick off
1 point for getting lead runner out

8 IN A ROW - sometimes called 10-in-a-Row (focuses on defense under pressure):

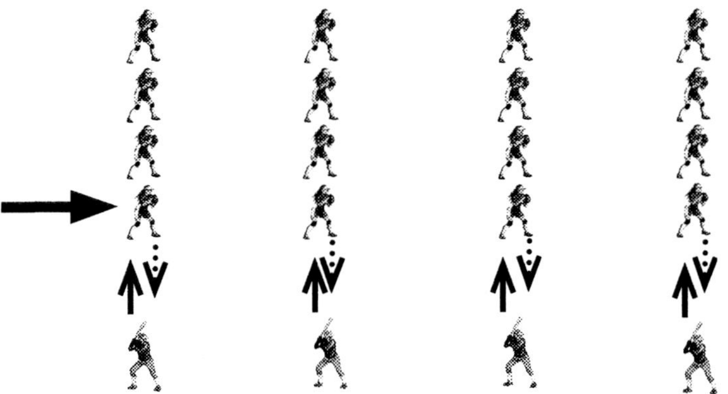

BUNT FOR SPRINTS (focuses on bunting under pressure):

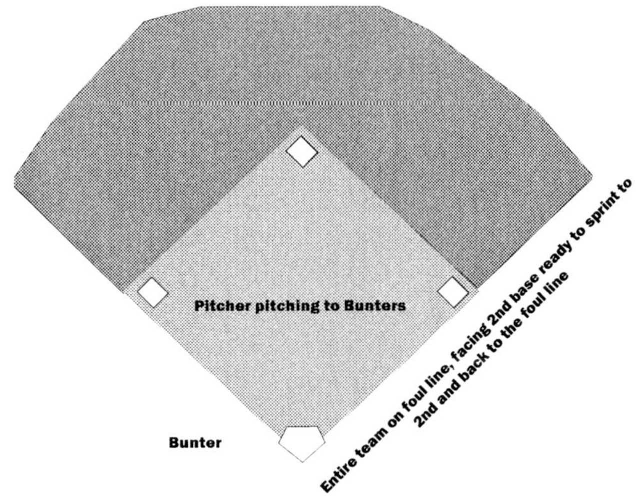

HOME TO 2nd FOR SPRINTS (focuses on bunting under pressure):

5 PITCHES - 5 TIMES BP (focuses on pitch selection under pressure):

This is a new drill I haven't mentioned before that's great for working on pitch selection (which is the batter learning to choose good pitches to swing at and letting the balls go by). Here's how the drill works:

- *Regular live batting practice off of a toss or a pitcher*
- *Batter gets a maximum of 25 pitches in groups of 5*
- *Batter doesn't swing at a strike - THEY'RE DONE*
- *Batter swings at a ball - THEY'RE DONE*

"Just One More" & "End on a Good One"

I know I'm going to sound harsh here but I can't stand either of these two statements! I think - with the exception of really young kids just learning to play softball - both of these statements help ensure mediocrity and prevent players from excelling during games!

I know I'm really going against the grain of sports by saying all of this since doing *"just one more"* in practice has become a way of proving we're tough enough and that we really care about improving. But, keep in mind that practices are supposed to get our teams ready for games, and how many games have you or your teams played in that allowed you to have *"just one more"*, or to *"end on a good one"*? None I'd guess.

That's my point. Games don't let your pitcher *"end on a good one"* when she just walked in the winning run. Games also don't allow you to have *"just one more"* swing and continue swinging until you eventually hit the ball even though you really struck out about five swings ago.

Games don't allow these kinds of "re-do's" as my nephew used to call them, but our practices usually do. Games are pretty harsh and final. That's one major reason that players don't do so well in games even though they are pretty good in practice - they can't handle the game pressure that comes with the finality of their actions.

A major thing we can do as coaches to help our players use practice time to really get better during games is to limit (and eventually eliminate) our use of these two phrases - *"end on a good one"* and *"just one more"*.

But, keep in mind that with skilled players of any age that these statements are limiting. What you can say instead that will help your players learn to make their last play a good one is to say something like, "***let's do 3 more of these, so make them good***". Do you see how that challenges the player to make her last ones good if in fact she wants to end on a good one? But, either good or bad, she's done after 3. If she get's all disappointed and tries to talk you into "just one more" (that you always end up doing far more than one) just tell her if she's that disappointed or mad, then think about how to fix it and next time we work on it let's see you do better!

This type of coaching is far more challenging to the player and forces the player to make the adjustment instead of forcing you to stay out at practice as the player tries "just one more" about 150 more times.

Coaching Younger & Less-Skilled Players

Now, I'm going to add a disclaimer to this and say that all of this applies to players that have some degree of skill. If you're coaching really young kids or kids that are just learning how to play softball then they're going to need the safety-net type of feeling that these two statements provide. If players can leave the field believing in their skills and knowing that they improved that day, then it helps build their confidence for the future. I know that and that's why I think using these statements with younger and newer skilled players is OK. I use both of these statements with many of the 9 and 10 year olds that I work with, but when I'm dealing with the 16 year olds up to the college-aged pitchers, I change my approach.

PACE

Game Pace vs. Practice Pace

There's a definite difference between the pace of a softball game and the pace of most of our practices. The pace - or speed - of a game is basically something like this: slow, slow slow, FAST. Slow, slow, slow, FAST. Etc... There are lots of times during a softball game when nothing, or next to nothing is happening. That's when the pace is pretty slow, like in between pitches, or after a foul ball, or in between innings, or right after a play. These are all pretty slow paced times with not much going on.

Now, there are also a few times during games when things happen pretty FAST - like when your player is in the batter's box and the pitch is on it's way. Or, when the ball is being hit directly to one of your players, or the runner is coming your way, or your runner is on 2nd base and the ball is hit. These are all times that the play happens really FAST and sometimes it seems as though it's happening faster than you can think, or than your players can think. But for the most part the pace or speed of games is pretty darn slow.

Let's look at a table that shows the difference between the pace - or speed - of one at-bat during a game, and one at-bat during practice:

	Pitches	**Swings**	**Time**	**(in 1st 22 seconds)**
GAME	6	5	*2 minutes 14 seconds*	*(1 swing)*
PRACTICE	5	5	*22 seconds*	*(5 swings)*

You'll notice that both batters get almost the same number of pitches; the game batter gets 6 and the practice batter gets 5. They each take 5 swings (which is usually high for the number of swings a batter will take during one at-bat in a game). The BIG difference between the two types of at-bats is how long they take - the at-bat in practice takes 22 seconds while the at-bat during the game lasts for 2 minutes and 14 seconds. In fact, during the first 22 seconds, the batter during practice got all 5 of her pitches and swings, while the game batter only got 1 swing in her first 22 seconds!!!

To me this is HUGE! If we're going to help our players prepare themselves in practice to succeed during games, then the speed at which we do things must come as close to game speed as possible!

What this told me, when I looked at the time and numbers of pitches and swings, was that as a coach, I needed to be clearer with my team on when to hustle and when it's OK not to. In games, there are times when we don't need to hustle or rush. During an at-bat is one of those times. We need to teach our players how to take their time and really focus when they're at-bat, but how can our players learn how to do that when most of our practices are set up to rush?

Someplace along the way we've all mixed up hustling with rushing and as coaches we've become freaks about our kids hustling. In games, the way we require it is for our players to run on and off the field and while it looks good that our players do it, it doesn't give our teams any more runs on the scoreboard, and it won't get us out of a bases loaded jam.

Doing so simply helps us feel better as coaches by giving us the impression (and hopefully the opposing coach as well) that if our team hustles on and off the field it will transfer over to hustle at the right time, on the right play during the game. Are there any of you out there that have been coaching for a long period of time that really believe this happens? Hey, I'm just like you - I like my players to hustle on and off the field too, but I no longer believe this either helps or hurts our ability to hustle properly during games.

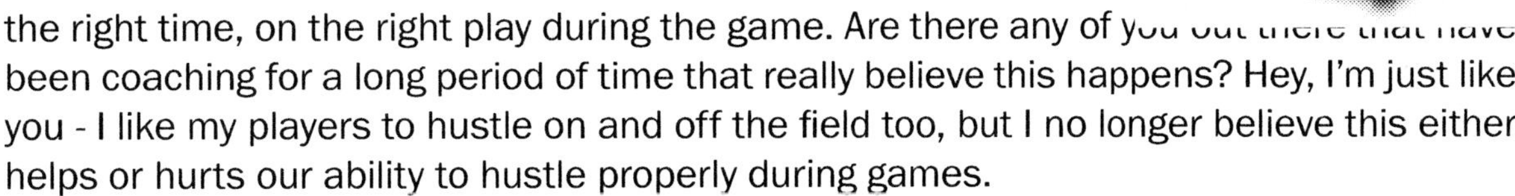

Here's what I do believe though about hustle and pace. I think that what kills our players during games is their inability to properly handle the boring pace of a game because we all rush our players through practice as if we're afraid they'll forget how to hustle.

What we need to learn about the pace of a game is that there are what I call 3 different speeds during games:

1. **Jogging Speed** - this happens in-between innings when we jog out to or in from our positions, and anytime when we don't need to be thinking about anything - we can just relax for a bit.
2. **Thinking Speed** - this happens in between all the pitches in a game either on defense or offense, and it's when we think about what we need to do on the next pitch and at the speed we need to think it. COACHES - this is also our thinking speed. We must use the short time in-between pitches to calmly think about what we need to do now based on the current situation and not on the previous play or whatever has gone wrong in the immediate (or sometimes distant) past!
3. **Action Speed** - this is the speed of the pitch, or the swing, or the run to catch the ball, or the decision to hold or send a runner, or to determine the batter is bunting, or to take the next base as a runner... all the speeds involved with the various actions within a softball game.

To help our practice be more game-like we need to have our practice pace be more game-like. Try slowing down your batting practice to more closely imitate the time a batter takes in the box during a game. Try slowing down the time in-between hits, or pitches or tosses in practice and give your players more time to think about what they need to either repeat or fix. And if you find that you're having the hustle withdrawals, then have your players run from station to station but once they get there, have them relax and settle into a realistic game-like tempo. Teaching your players how to positively handle all the downtime in softball that allows players to think and rethink about their bad plays, or else not think at all is the biggest reason that softball (and baseball) are such difficult sports. Neither one have constant activity as a means of occupying a players mind, so help teach your players what to do with their "thinking speed" time.

Remember, when dealing with your practice pace have your players hustle from station to station and then once at their stations work on game speed in order to help ensure more success during games!

Chapter Summary - Must-Haves for PRACTICE

1. **Skill Building:**
   - Young kids require more time for building skills and less for conditioning, while older players can condition more and skill build a little less.
   - Creating a core group of skills for players to do "everyday" is a great way to improve their main skills.

2. **Competition:**
   - Finding creative ways for your players to compete against the clock, themselves, their teammate and in groups is a terrific way to help them do better in games.
   - These competitive type drills and games also add a lot more fun to your practices.

3. **Accountability & Consequence:**
   - Hold your players accountable for their decisions, skills, actions and inactions in practice by posting results, having winners ad losers in drills and getting rid of saying "just one more" and "end on a good one"

4. **Pace:**
   - You don't have to rush your practices to show that your players hustle - be smart about your practice pace and make it much more game-pace-like.

BE CREATIVE

"Never Minimize Your Ability to THINK Your Way Through Any Situation!"

~ Norman Vincent Peale

Being able to "use your head", as my Mom used to tell us all the time, will not only save you some money in this whole coaching process, but it will also give you some very clever solutions to many of the problems you're going to encounter as a coach.

Norman Vincent Peale was right when he made the above statement - your ability to think your way through any situation you come across as a coach is going to determine not only your ability to solve that problem, but ultimately your team's ability to be successful.

You might not think of yourself as a very creative person and that's OK. I'm going to share with you some examples of coaching creativity so you can get the idea and ultimately be able to start thinking in a more open and creative way. Another thing my Mom always used to tell us has remained one of my favorite sayings to this day:

"If You Can't Raise the Bridge, Lower the River"

~ Liz Bristow (my Mom)

While I'm not sure that my Mom actually invented that saying, I'm attributing it to her since she's the first person I ever heard it from, and I heard it from her a lot! So, what does it mean? Basically, there's always more than one way to do things, so if the first thing you try doesn't work out, like possibly trying to raise the bridge higher, then try something else, like lowering the river so the bridge seems like you've raised it.

In softball, an example of this type of thinking would be, let's say you're trying to keep a pitcher from snapping her hips so much. Instead of telling her to not snap her hips try instead to tell her to move her hand faster than her hips. It accomplishes the same thing in a different way.

You'd be amazed at how this type of thinking keeps you calmer in a situation that might seem frustrating or impossible. And once you're calm you're more likely to think of something that will help you instead of thinking about how frustrated you are. Plus, a calm coach helps keep players calm - translation - they aren't as likely to freak out!

Equipment Creativity - What Gadgets Matter?

There certainly are a ton of softball gadgets on the market and more coming out all the time. Everyone seems to be pushing their solution to your coaching problem - everything that is, except better players...but anyway. So, how much of this stuff do you need and how do you know what's good and what's just junk?

Some of that will be up to you. I'm not a gadget person so I don't really like much of that stuff. Not only is most of it expensive, but you've got to haul it with you (since most of us don't have equipment sheds at our fields) and then use it often enough to set it up. I'm not saying that there aren't some very creative and useful products out there but just put your thinking caps on and see what things you can come up with to solve some of your own problems or challenges.

5 gallon Bucket :

- *Put a Batting Tee on it to practice hitting the riseball and staying on top of the high pitch.*

Protective pitching screen with hole:

- *Have your pitchers throw rise balls through it. This will help make sure their pitch doesn't rise too early. Gives them the visual idea of throwing the ball out and then making it go up. Also good for fastpitch accuracy.*

Shuttle cocks, miniature footballs:

- *Use to help your pitcher work on their riseball spin.*

Ice Chest

- *Place this in front of a hitter's front foot if she tends to open up her front foot too soon (or steps in the bucket). The ice chest will keep her front foot from flying open and still allow her to swing.*

Popcorn Kernels

- *Use to help your hitters work on their pitch tracking skills. The hitter stands in the batter's box, without a bat and with a popcorn kernel in her mouth. The pitcher throws regular speed (and pitches) to the catcher. The batter swings at the strikes and lets the balls go by. When she swings at a strike, she spits the kernel trying to hit the ball with it. This makes the hitters follow the pitch the entire way.*

Spongy-soft Jugs Lite-Flite Softballs

- *While these are often used by hitters for hitting into fences (so they won't dent the fence) we use them with our infielders to keep their hands aggressive and not allowing their weight to settle back on their heels. We'll start out by rolling these balls at the infielders and then progress to hitting them at them. The infielders start without their gloves (to get the idea of fielding the ball with their hands instead of their gloves) and eventually allow the players to use their gloves.*

Training gloves (boxing) or Karate kickgloves

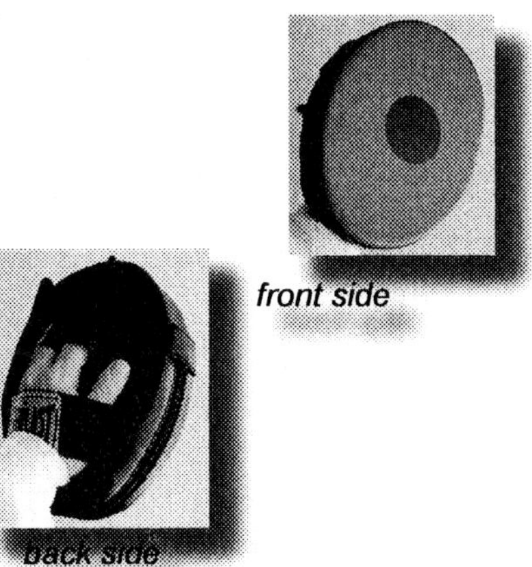

- *These are heavily padded, flat gloves that fit over both hands. I use these to work on bunting and slapping. I'll have the bunters put the glove on their top hand, and practice bunting balls from either the pitcher, a machine or a tosser (no bats). You can do the same thing with slappers to work on keeping their hands high.*

Folding Table

- *You can take this table, fold out the legs, put it on it's side, and place it parallel to the outside batter's box line – behind the hitter. Then use it to help your slappers keep moving straight toward the pitcher, before contact, instead of pealing off toward 1st base. This works great!*

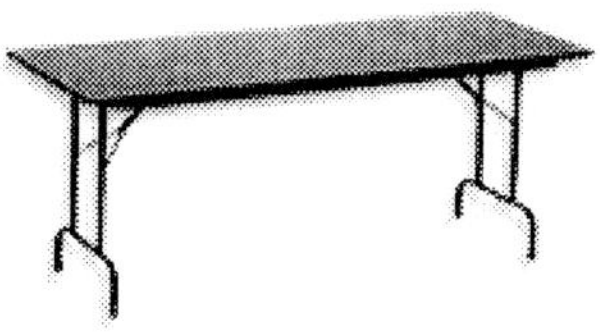

Archery Target

- *This is a great way to protect your catchers from getting beat up when your pitchers are practicing their drop balls. It's an archery target that you can get from either a sporting goods store or an outdoor-hunting store. It's about 3 feet square and is filled with straw so it's light enough to move easily and yet strong enough to protect you. Plus, if you get the 3' x 3' one it's short enough for the catcher to position themselves behind it and still catch the ball (particularly great when the catcher happens to be Mom, Dad or Coach sitting on a bucket).*

Batting T and Plunger

- *This is a simple and inexpensive way for you to keep a basketball or soccerball on top of a batting T (in case you use these for hitting to help build up the power of your hitter's swings and follow-throughs). If you simply try and place a bigger ball on top of a regular batting T it will fall off constantly. By placing a plunger upside down in the T, so the wooden handle goes down the shoot of the batting T, you can place the basketball or soccerball on the larger head plunger without the ball falling off.*

Indoor Practices

Practicing indoors is all about ADJUSTMENTS and CREATIVITY! Because your space will be limited to some degree you're going to have to make adjustments to a few areas of your practices and be creative in how you still accomplish everything you need to.

If you're reading this from your home in Southern California or Arizona I'm not really talking to you. If you find yourself practicing inside it's so unusual it's fun - for a day. I'm talking to those coaches who live in either cold or wet climates when their season starts and know they're going to be spending a good part of their early season inside. If that's you, then here are some tips that might help you.

Adjust Your Time

Since you will usually have limited space inside, it makes sense to try and limit the number of people you're dealing with. The easiest way to do this is to use a staggered start practice that I explain in Sample Practice 4 listed below:

SAMPLE PRACTICE - 4

6:00 - 6:30	Infielders Only (go home at 6:45)
6:30	Outfielders Show Up (go home at 7:15)
6:30 - 6:45	Infielders & Outfielders Work Together
7:15 - 8:00	Pitcher's and Catcher's Only

Adjust Your Equipment

- *Use softer balls that do less or no damage on floors, walls and lights.*
- *Hang blankets or nets in front of walls or off the end of bleachers and hold batting practice.*
- *Use tennis balls for infield and outfield defensive work.*
- *Use tennis balls for hitting practice (if you have a tennis team with a tennis ball machine, see if you can use that for fielding and hitting practice).*
- *Hit basketballs or soccerballs for extra strength at and through contact.*

- *Put a sheet on the gym pads and with helmets on, have your players practice both sliding and diving for balls.*

Adjust Your Distances

- *Use shorter bases to help make your infielders and outfielders work on quicker releases.*
- *Make everything in the gym (walls and ceilings) live so you can hold scrimmages.*
- *Have your outfielders throw diagonally across the gym in order to get them throwing as long as possible inside.*

Use What You Have!

- *Use whatever indoor space you can get! Don't complain about what you don't have, instead, use what you have.*
- *Use hallways for rundowns, sliding and diving practice.*
- *Use classrooms for strategy sessions and teamwork/teambuilding opportunities.*
- *Have only half-a-gym? Then use it to practice with your pitchers & catchers, and on your bunting and slapping.*

And finally, probably the most important thing to remember is:

Know Your Opponents are Doing it Too!

SAMPLE PRACTICES

Up to this point you've learned various methods for organizing your practices, ways to write out and plan your practices as well as what things you should be doing during practices. Now you get to look at samples of practices for both beginning and advanced teams.

These practices will be broken up into Beginning and Advanced practices. The Beginning practices will focus on skill building and game awareness, while the Advanced practices will allow more specialized practice for defensive and offensive skills (sometimes even separating the practices completely).

Some of the drills I'll mention in the various practices you can find within this book, the rest of the drills you'll find on my website (along with tons of other drills): **www.softballexcellence.com.**

List of Sample Practices

PRACTICE INTRODUCTION

BEGINNING PRACTICES-

Practice 1
Practice 2
Practice 3
Practice 4
Practice 5
Practice 6
Practice 7
Practice 8

ADVANCED PRACTICES

Practicing with Small Groups
Whole Team Practice Situations

Defensive Only Practices -

Practice 09
Practice 10
Practice 11

Offensive Only Practices -

Practice 12
Practice 13
Practice 14
Practice 15

Combination Practices

(Offensive & Defensive)

Practice 16
Practice 17
Practice 18
Practice 19
Practice 20

PRACTICE INTRODUCTION

Each of the 20 Sample Practices that I explain in this chapter will all follow the same type of format to help make it easier for you to understand what each one is trying to accomplish and how.

I'm going to take up 2 pages per practice;

1. One page to show either the practice timeline (or schedule if that's what you like to call it) or the physical practice layout. This page will be called the Diagram page.
2. The other page will then explain what every thing means by an easy-to-follow number system. This page will be called the Explanation page.

It's all going to look like this:

Diagram

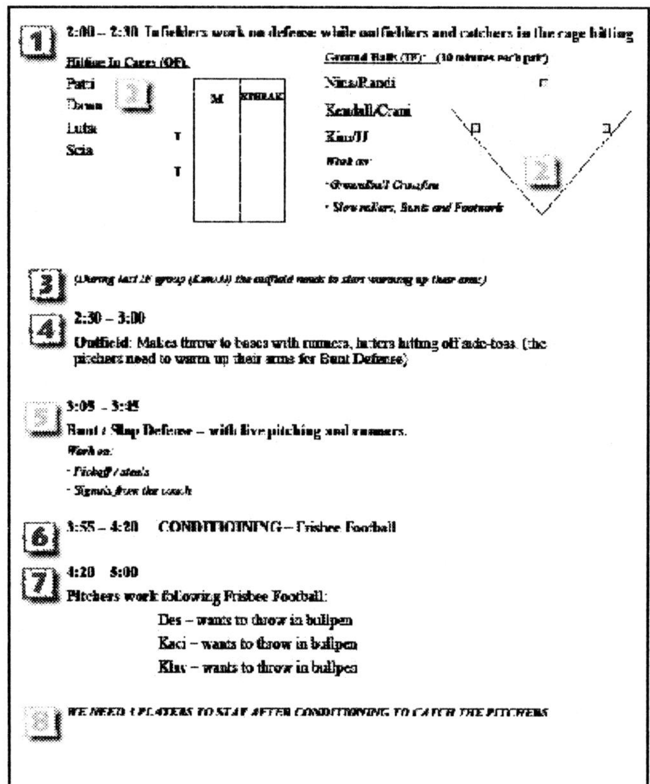

1 2:00 – 2:30 Infielders work on defense while outfielders and catchers in the cage hitting

Nina/Randi

Kendall/Crami

Kim/JJ

M

T

T

2

2

3

4 2:30 – 3:00

Outfield: Makes throw to bases with runners, hitters hitting off side-toss. (the pitchers need to warm up their arms for Bunt Defense)

5 3:05 – 3:45

Bunt / Slap Defense – with live pitching and runners.

Work on:

6 3:55 – 4:20 CONDITIONING – Frisbee Football

7 4:20 5:00

Pitchers work following Frisbee Football:

Des – wants to throw in bullpen

Kaci – wants to throw in bullpen

Klay – wants to throw in bullpen

8

Explanation

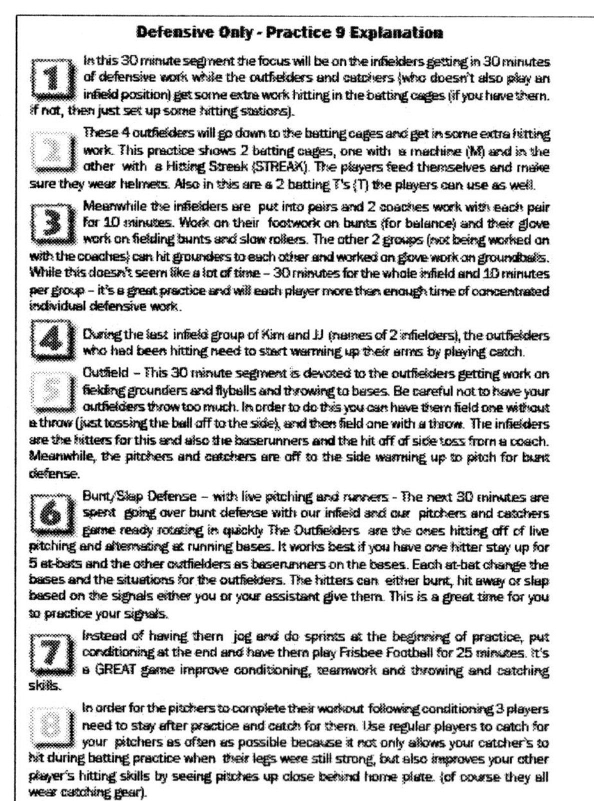

Defensive Only - Practice 9 Explanation

1 In this 30 minute segment the focus will be on the infielders getting in 30 minutes of defensive work while the outfielders and catchers (who doesn't also play an infield position) get some extra work hitting in the batting cages (if you have them. if not, then just set up some hitting stations).

2 These 4 outfielders will go down to the batting cages and get in some extra hitting work. This practice shows 2 batting cages, one with a machine (M) and in the other with a Hitting Streak (STREAK). The players feed themselves and make sure they wear helmets. Also in this are a 2 batting T's (T) the players can use as well.

3 Meanwhile the infielders are put into pairs and 2 coaches work with each pair for 10 minutes. Work on their footwork on bunts (for balance) and their glove work on fielding bunts and slow rollers. The other 2 groups (not being worked on with the coaches) can hit grounders to each other and worked on glove work on groundballs. While this doesn't seem like a lot of time – 30 minutes for the whole infield and 10 minutes per group – it's a great practice and will each player more than enough time of concentrated individual defensive work.

4 During the last infield group of Kim and JJ (names of 2 infielders), the outfielders who had been hitting need to start warming up their arms by playing catch.

5 Outfield – This 30 minute segment is devoted to the outfielders getting work on fielding grounders and flyballs and throwing to bases. Be careful not to have your outfielders throw too much. In order to do this you can have them field one without a throw (just tossing the ball off to the side), and then field one with a throw. The infielders are the hitters for this and also the baserunners and the hit off of side toss from a coach. Meanwhile, the pitchers and catchers are off to the side warming up to pitch for bunt defense.

6 Bunt/Slap Defense – with live pitching and runners - The next 30 minutes are spent going over bunt defense with our infield and our pitchers and catchers game ready rotating in quickly The Outfielders are the ones hitting off of live pitching and alternating at running bases. It works best if you have one hitter stay up for 5 at-bats and the other outfielders as baserunners on the bases. Each at-bat change the bases and the situations for the outfielders. The hitters can either bunt, hit away or slap based on the signals either you or your assistant give them. This is a great time for you to practice your signals.

7 Instead of having them jog and do sprints at the beginning of practice, put conditioning at the end and have them play Frisbee Football for 25 minutes. It's a GREAT game improve conditioning, teamwork and throwing and catching skills.

8 In order for the pitchers to complete their workout following conditioning 3 players need to stay after practice and catch for them. Use regular players to catch for your pitchers as often as possible because it not only allows your catcher's to hit during batting practice when their legs were still strong, but also improves your other player's hitting skills by seeing pitches up close behind home plate. (of course they all wear catching gear).

Beginning Practices

The key to everything is PATIENCE. You get the chicken by hatching the egg, not by smashing it!

~ Arnold H. Glasgow

Practicing with young kids that are in the beginning stages of their softball lives is a challenge, to put it mildly. It takes TONS of **patience**, and even then there will be times when you'll need more!

To me, this quote by Arnold Glasgow hits the nail on the head in regards to coaching younger players - it actually fits for all coaches, period, no matter the age or skill level. Your beginning level players are going to improve by you "hatching" their softball skills, not by you "smashing" them. I know that sounds easy to say and is much, much harder to do. But, try to keep in mind that the real purpose of a coach is to help their players get better and not for the players to help elevate the level of the coach!

Holding softball practice with younger aged players takes a lot of patience and, as we've already discussed, a lot of planning. I'm going to show you eight examples of different types of practices you can hold with beginning level teams and players, and each practice is based on the steps we discussed in Chapters I and II.

BRIGHT IDEA:

Keep in mind, to find the DRILLS mentioned within these practices, look through this book as many are listed within - or else check out the website: **www.softballexcellence.com**

Beginning Practice 1 - Diagram

The first Sample Practice we're going to look at in greater detail is the one I listed earlier in the book on page 32. This is an example of a practice that is segmented out to allow time for all the major skill blocks - basics like throwing & fielding, hitting & slapping & bunting, pitching & catching, and the game situation skills - all of these skill are given time blocks in which you can do whatever drills within each one that fit into the time allowed and that emphasize the skills you're focusing on that day.

SAMPLE PRACTICE - 1

1

2:30 - 2:55 Baserunning - Conditioning

2:30 - 2:35 Explain today's concept
2:35 - 2:45 "Sprints with running sticks"
2:45 - 2:55 "4,3,2,1"

2

3:00 - 3:25 Throwing - Fielding

3:00 - 3:05 Explain today's concept
3:05 - 3:15 Warm up throwing & "partner throws for time"
3:15 - 3:25 "No throws ball blast"

3

3:30 - 3:55 Hitting - Slapping - Bunting

3:30 - 3:35 Explain today's concept or objective
3:35 - 3:55 "6 Part Bunting Series"

4

4:00 - 4:25 Pitching - Catching

4:00 - 4:10 Warm up
4:10 - 4:20 Practice Locations
4:20 - 4:25 "First one to 10" game

5

4:30 - 4:55 Game Situations - Team Def. - Team Off.

4:30 - 4:35 Explain today's concept or situation
4:35 - 4:55 "Thunderball

6

4:55 - 5:00 Wrap Up

Beginnng Practice 1 - Explanation

1 Baserunning and Conditioning will happen from 2:30 to 2:55, and within that time frame the first 5 minutes will be spent on explaining to the team what they're trying to accomplish today in this part of the practice. For the next 10 minutes (2:35 - 2:45) you'll take your team through a drill called "sprints with running sticks" which helps teach them how to use their arms properly while running. Then for the last 10 minutes of the Baserunning/Conditioning segment of this practice will be spent on the "4,3,2,1" drill - which will involve your whole team and will pretty much wear them out.

2 After a 5 minute break to get some water and change stations and equipment, the Throwing/Fielding is the next 25 minute segment of this practice. You'll spend the first 5 minutes, again, going over what you're trying to get them to work on and why. Then for the next 10 minutes (3:05-3:15) you'll have your team warm up and then do the drill "partner throws for time". This will help them work on catching and throwing at game-like speed and is also a competition so you can keep track of everyone's time to post it later. The last 10 minutes of this segment of practice will work on their fielding skills with the "No throws ball blast" drill (without any throwing, which allows them to get tons more balls since you're not worried about the stress on their arms since they aren't throwing).

3 Another 5 minute break to get some water and change stations and equipment, and it's on to the next segment of practice which will be the Hitting-Slapping-Bunting part of practice. This 25 minute segment will be spent on bunting (but you could switch it out each practice and focus on another part of one of these 3 offensive skills). After the usual 5 minutes (or less if possible) to explain the goal for this segment and to give them any important skill tips, it's on to the only drill we'll do in this segment - the "6 part bunting series" which will last about 20 minutes (since it has 6 parts). This is a great drill series to really help your players learn to master their bunting skills, plus it's fun too!

4 After the usual 5 minute between-segments break, the next practice segment is pitching and catching. While this segment will deal mainly with your pitchers and catchers, the rest of your players should have their batting helmets on and their bats and be standing in the batter's box watching pitches as the pitchers practice pitching. Your hitter's can rotate from one pitcher to another and then to a break station so that all your hitter's get to watch pitches but also so all of your pitchers can pitch to both right and left handed batters. In the first 10 minutes of this segment the pitchers can start warming up to each other while the catchers put on their catching gear. Once their gear is on the catchers can then move into place and help the pitchers finish their warm up. Batters can stand in the batter's box during warmups too - it only helps the pitchers do better in games by getting comfortable with having hitters in the box. The next 10 minutes (4:10-4:20) will be spent on the pitchers working on pitching to different locations whether it's up and down, or in and out. The catchers will give a target and the pitchers will work on hitting that location. The last 5 minutes will be spent playing the "First one to 10 game" - again, keep track of winners and losers so you can post them as we discussed.

The final segment will start at 4:30 after a 5 minute break. This segment will work on Game Situations-Team Defense-or Team Offense. After explaining the drill and concept for this segment the team will play the "Thunderball". A fun game to help the players work on all of their game skills.

The last 5 minutes of practice is a wrap-up and time for any announcements about the next practice or game.

Beginning Practice 2 - Diagram

This is the same practice format as the previous practice (practice 1) - except I'm just slotting in different drills. I'm doing this to show you how easy it can be to create completely different practices by keeping the same shell and simply inserting new drills. The hardest part for you as the coach, if you do your practices this way by simply swapping out drills, is to make sure you've done your drill homework ahead of time and can explain each one to your players without wasting time. Write them down in your practice notes/plan if you have to - there's nothing wrong with that. As you'll see later on with many of my advanced practices, I had to draw out where everyone went and where the equipment went or else I'd forget. Use whatever system works best for you!

SAMPLE PRACTICE - 2

1 **2:30 - 2:55 Baserunning - Conditioning**

2:30 - 2:35 Explain today's concept
2:35 - 2:45 "Clap and Go"
2:45 - 2:55 "3,2,1"

2 **3:00 - 3:25 Throwing - Fielding**

3:00 - 3:05 Explain today's concept
3:05 - 3:15 Warm up throwing & "partner throws for #'s"
3:15 - 3:25 "Throw and Go"

3 **3:30 - 3:55 Hitting - Slapping - Bunting**

3:30 - 3:35 Explain today's concept or objective
3:35 - 3:55 Hitting Stations:

- Soccerball hit off T
- Soccerball hit off bounce
- Pizza throw
- Popcorn spit
- Front arm frisbee throw

4 **4:00 - 4:25 Pitching - Catching**

4:00 - 4:10 Warm up
4:10 - 4:15 Practice Locations
4:15 - 4:25 "2 inning game" game

5 **4:30 - 4:55 Game Situations - Team Def. - Team Off.**

4:30 - 4:35 Explain today's concept or situation
4:35 - 4:55 "Gladiator"

6 **4:55 - 5:00 Wrap Up**

Beginning Practice 2 - Explanation

1 Baserunning and Conditioning will happen from 2:30 to 2:55, and within that time frame the first 5 minutes will be spent on explaining to the team what they're trying to accomplish today in this part of the practice. For the next 10 minutes (2:35 - 2:45) you'll take your team through a drill called "Clap and Go" which helps teach them when to leave the base when baserunning. Then for the last 10 minutes of the Baserunnng/Conditioning segment of this practice will be spent on the "3,2,1" drill - which will involve your while team and, like the 4,3,2,1 drill will pretty much wear them out.

2 After a 5 minute break to get some water and change stations and equipment, the Throwing/Fielding is the next 25 minute segment of this practice. You'll spend the first 5 minutes, again, going over what you're trying to get them to work on and why. Then for the next 10 minutes (3:05-3:15) you'll have your team warm up and then do the drill "partner throws for #'s". This is like the "partner throws for time" except this time you they don't compete against the clock - just the first pair to whatever number you picked wins. This also helps them work on catching and throwing at game-like speed and is also a competition so you can keep track of everyone's time to post it later. The last 10 minutes of this segment of practice will work on their fielding, throwing & baserunning skills with the "Throw and Go" drill.

3 Another 5 minute break to get some water and change stations and equipment, and it's on to the next segment of practice which will be the Hitting-Slapping-Bunting part of practice. This 25 minute segment will be spent on hitting by using different hitting stations. After the usual 5 minutes (or less if possible) to explain the goal for this segment and to give them any important skill tips, break your team up into groups of two's (pairs) and have the pairs go through the following stations: soccerball hit off t, soccerball hit off bounce, pizza throw, popcorn spit and front arm frisbee throw. 5 stations in 20 minutes - that's about 2 pairs per station, 4 minutes per station - 2 minutes per pair which is 1 minute per player - then rotate.

4 After the usual 5 minute between-segments break, the next practice segment is pitching and catching. While this segment will deal mainly with your pitchers and catchers, the rest of your players should have their batting helmets on and their bats and be standing in the batter's box watching pitches as the pitchers practice pitching. Your hitter's can rotate from one pitcher to another and then to a break station so that all your hitter's get to watch pitches but also so all of your pitchers can pitch to both right and left handed batters. In the first 10 minutes of this segment the pitchers can start warming up to each other while the catchers put on their catching gear. Once their gear is on the catchers can then move into place and help the pitchers finish their warm up. Batters can stand in the batter's box during warmups too - it only helps the pitchers do better in games by getting comfortable with having hitters in the box. The next 5 minutes (4:10-4:15) will be spent on the pitchers working on pitching to different locations whether it's up and down, or in and out. The catchers will give a target and the pitchers will work on hitting that location. The last 10 minutes will be spent playing the "2 inning game" - again, keep track of winners and losers so you can post them as we discussed.

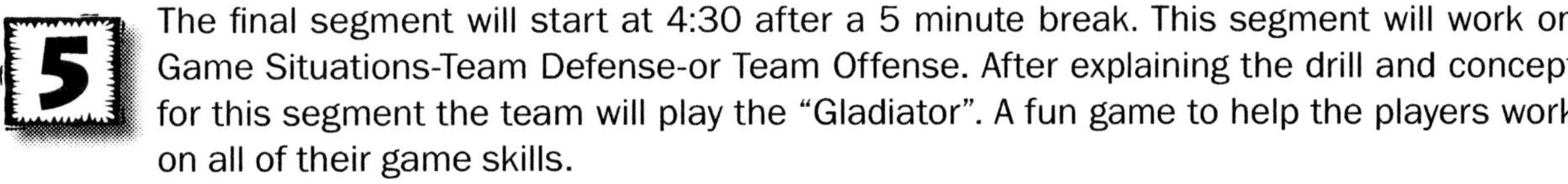

5 The final segment will start at 4:30 after a 5 minute break. This segment will work on Game Situations-Team Defense-or Team Offense. After explaining the drill and concept for this segment the team will play the "Gladiator". A fun game to help the players work on all of their game skills.

6 The last 5 minutes of practice is a wrap-up and time for any announcements about the next practice or game.

Beginning Practice 3 - Diagram

This sample practice is listed on page 33 and follows a similar format to Practice 1 but combines the Pitching & Catching segment with the Throwing & Fielding segment while allowing more time for the Game Situations segment. This would be a practice you'd want to follow if your team was struggling with, or needing more time to work on the situations or coverages that come up during games.

SAMPLE PRACTICE - 3

1

2:30 - 2:55 Baserunning - Conditioning

2:30 - 2:40	1/2 at rice buckets and 1/2 at bat wiper stations, switch
2:40 - 2:45	"2 and Stop" drill
2:45 - 2:55	"Whistle Leads" with pitchers warming up

2

3:00 - 3:25 Throwing - Fielding & Pitching - Catching

3:00 - 3:15	"6-in-a-row" drill for all
3:15 - 3:25	Pitchers throw to catchers while players step in with helmets and bats - no swings but watching pitches and calling out "swing" (for strikes) and "take" (on balls).

3

3:30 - 4:07 Hitting - Slapping - Bunting

3:30 - 4:07	Hitting, slapping, bunting stations scattered all over the field. 3 hitting stations, 1 slapping station and 2 bunting stations. 5 total stations and 4 players per station (grouped in pairs) - 5 minutes per station which is 2 1/2 minutes per pair, or 1 minute 15 seconds per person per station. Everyone rotates by pairs to the next station.

4

4:12- 4:48 Game Situations - Team Def. - Team Off

4:12 - 4:48	"Throwing Game"

5

4:48 - 5:00 Wrap Up

Beginning Practice 3 - Explanation

1 The Baserunning and Conditioning segment will still happen first from 2:30 to 2:55, but this practice will introduce a 10 minute hand and forearm strengthening session. The team will be split in half and will go to one of 2 stations for 5 minutes each and then rotate. One station will be the Rice Buckets which are 3 gallon paint buckets filled with rice where the players will put their throwing arms in and draw the alphabet. The other station has all players with their bats and doing "Bat Wipers" where they hold the bats at the knob straight out in front of them and move them back and forth like windshield wipers while keeping their arms straight - both arms. The next 5 minutes is the "2 and Stop" drill, followed by the "Whistle Leads" drill with the pitchers warming up easy one-at-a-time on the mound. This drill works on timing lead -offs.

2 After a 5 minute break to get some water and change stations and equipment, the Throwing/Fielding is the next 25 minute segment of this practice. You'll go right into a 10 minute "6-in-a-row" drill to work on fielding under pressure (a shorter version of the 8-in-a-row). The last 10 minutes (3:15-3:25) you'll have your pitchers throw to your catchers while the rest of your players put on their helmets and get their bats and take turns standing in the batters box against each pitcher and calling out "swing" on a strike and "take" on a ball. This helps the hitters to recognize good pitches to hit (and helps you see if they can really tell balls from strikes) and also helps the pitchers learn to block out distractions and concentrate.

3 Another 5 minute break to get some water and change stations and equipment, and it's on to the next segment of practice which will be the Hitting-Slapping-Bunting part of practice. This 25 minute segment will be spent on hitting, slapping and bunting using 5 different stations (3 for hitting, 1 for slapping and 2 for bunting) - you pick the drills to do at each station from your drill list (from my website: www.softballexcellence.com). 5 stations with no more tan 4 players per station if you can help it (grouped in pairs). That comes out to 2 1/2 minutes per pair per station or 1 minute 15 seconds per player per station. Everyone rotates by pairs to their next station.

4 After the usual 5 minute between-segments break, the next practice segment is Game Situations. This entire time will be spent playing the "Throwing Game" and keeping score. If you've already played this before in practice then keep those same teams and continue the score from where you left off. Remember to post the winners on your Practice Leaders sheet each week. Your team will enjoy playing a game and having some fun instead of always just doing drills in practice.

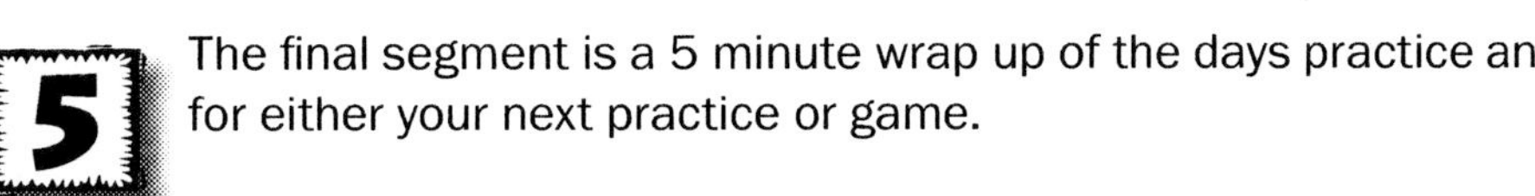

5 The final segment is a 5 minute wrap up of the days practice and any announcements for either your next practice or game.

Beginning Practice 4 - Diagram

(Single Coach or Individual Player Practice)

Intent:

- *Help one-coach teams*
- *Give you more time with your individual players*

This practice is intended to help those of you Lone Rangers out there, that coach by yourselves - or, if you have more than one coach working with the team - this practice will help you spend more time with individual players, something you don't usually get to do in a typical practice.

SAMPLE PRACTICE - 4

1 **6:00 - 6:45 Infielders Only Show Up**

6:00 - 6:30 You work on fielding, throwing or whatever these players need to work on. There should only be about 4 to 6 of them so the numbers of you-to-them are small enough to help you really accomplish something in 30 minutes.

2 6:30 - 6:45 Infielders work with Outfielders (who just showed up) on Team Defensive things that require the entire defense.

3 6:45 Infielders go home

4 **6:30 - 7:15 Outfielders Only Show Up**

5 6:30 - 6:45 Outfielders overlap with Infielders to work on team defense

6 6:45 - 7:15 Infielders have gone home and now you can work with just the outfielders on whatever fielding and/or throwing things they need work on. There should only be about 3-6 of them again so the numbers are good.

7 7:15 Outfielders go home

8 **7:15 - 8:00 Pitcher's and Catcher's Only Show Up**

9 7:15 - 7:30 Pitcher's warm up to themselves while you work with the catchers on blocking and receiving.

10 7:30 - 8:00 You work with the pitchers and catchers

11 8:00 Pitchers and Catchers and YOU go home!

Beginning Practice 4 - Explanation

1 The basis of this whole practice is to split your team up into smaller, more manageable groups so you can work with them more one-on-one...or at least, closer to it. First split your team up into 3 groups; infielders, outfielders and pitchers/catchers and then ask each group to come for only 45 total minutes - 30 of those minutes will be just those position players and you. The last 15 minutes of the infielders and the first of the outfielders will be spent together working on team defense. Let's see how it goes...

2 After you've worked exclusively with just the infielders for the first 30 minutes of this practice (from 6:00 - 6:30) then the Outfielders show up and for the next 15 minutes (from 6:30 - 6:45) you get to work with both groups together on some type of team defensive issue. Maybe you work on some communication problems you've been having, or else you simply hit them balls and have them make throws to bases. It's your choice what to do with these 15 minutes but have both groups together will help solve some defensive issues.

3 At 6:45 the Infielders go home - but the Outfielders stay so you can now work with them alone for 30 minutes.

4 5 From 6:30 - 7:15 the Outfielders show up - remember that the first 15 minutes of that time the Outfielders will overlap with the Infielders so you can work with both groups together on some type of defensive issues.

6 At 6:45 the Infielders go home - but the Outfielders stay so you can now work with them in a much smaller numbered group for 30 minutes. This time will be spent however you feel it necessary in order to help each individual outfielder with their particular needs.

7 At 7:15 the Outfielders go home and the Pitchers & Catchers now show up.

8 The last group for you to work with are the Pitchers & Catchers who show up from 7:15 and stay until 8:00.

9 From 7:15 to 7:30 the Pitchers will warm up to themselves which gives you time to spend working with the catchers on their skills like blocking, receiving, special conditioning things - anything you feel the catchers need work on. Since the Pitchers are just warming up and not yet throwing hard, they should be able to catch for each other. This is a good way to get the pitchers to work together better and to also increase some of the catching and throwing skills of your pitchers. It's amazing how tough people can become when they aren't allowed to be babied!

10 From 7:30 - 8:00 you get to work with both the Pitchers and the Catchers on their control, their location, both - whatever work they need you're now able to be there with them instead of being off working with another group of players.

11 At 8:00 everyone goes home - INCLUDING YOU! This type of practice only keeps players there for 45 minutes (which is great during times like exams). You're the only one who has to be there the entire time - and you're only there for 2 hours. It's amazing how much more you can accomplish with smaller groups in shorter time frames!

Beginning Practice 5 - Diagram

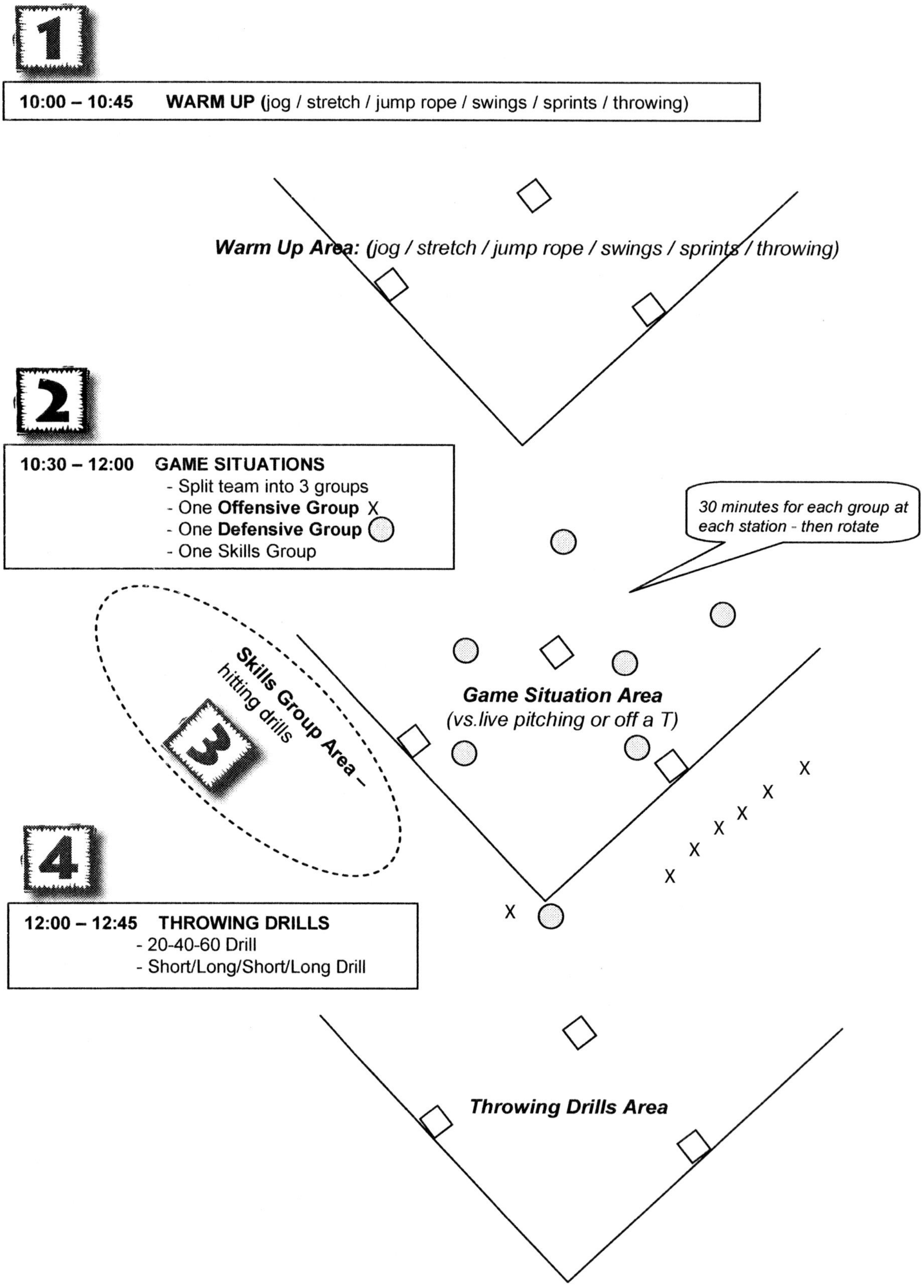

10:00 – 10:45	**WARM UP** (jog / stretch / jump rope / swings / sprints / throwing)

***Warm Up Area:** (jog / stretch / jump rope / swings / sprints / throwing)*

2

10:30 – 12:00 GAME SITUATIONS
- Split team into 3 groups
- One **Offensive Group** X
- One **Defensive Group** ○
- One Skills Group

30 minutes for each group at each station - then rotate

Skills Group Area – hitting drills

3

Game Situation Area
(vs.live pitching or off a T)

4

12:00 – 12:45 THROWING DRILLS
- 20-40-60 Drill
- Short/Long/Short/Long Drill

Throwing Drills Area

Beginning Practice 5 - Explanation

The first part of this practice (from 10:00 until 10:45) will involve warming up, jogging, stretching, jumping ropes and sprinting for conditioning - and then going into throwing. All of this can be done on the infield as shown in the diagram. Once the throwing part begins, have the players first warm up throwing, and then pick 2 throwing drills to do.

The second part of this practice will focus on Game Situations for one hour and 30 minutes by splitting your team up into 3 different groups; one will be on offense first, one on defense and the third group will start over in the skills group area and will be working on hitting drills. The Game Situations can be done off of live pitching, off a batting T, or off of side toss and will occur on the field as shown in the diagram. Each group will stay in their position for 30 minutes before rotating to the next position.

The Game situations can be handled any way that works best for you. It's designed to have as many defenders in place as possible and to have your offensive team hit balls and actually run them out. Make this game-like so real plays and decisions can be made. Don't forget to put helmets on your hitters and baserunners. This type of situation allows you to stop play and explain things to your players so they can learn things correctly for games.

The Skills Area group that will be working on hitting drills should be located someplace off the field that gives them enough room to do their drills without being in the way of the two teams on the field.

Rotate as follows:

- *Offensive group moves to Defense*
- *Defensive Group moves to Skills Area*
- *Skills Area Group moves to Offense*

NOTE: If the 1 1/2 hours allotted for Game Situations is too long for your level of player, then feel free to shorten this time to whatever will work best for your team!

The last 45 minutes of practice will be spent on Throwing Drills. They can be done using the entire field as shown. The 2 drills used in this practice will be the 20-40-60 drill that involves the entire team split up into competing teams of 4, and the short/long/short/long drill that can also be done in groups of 4.

Beginning Practice 6 - Diagram

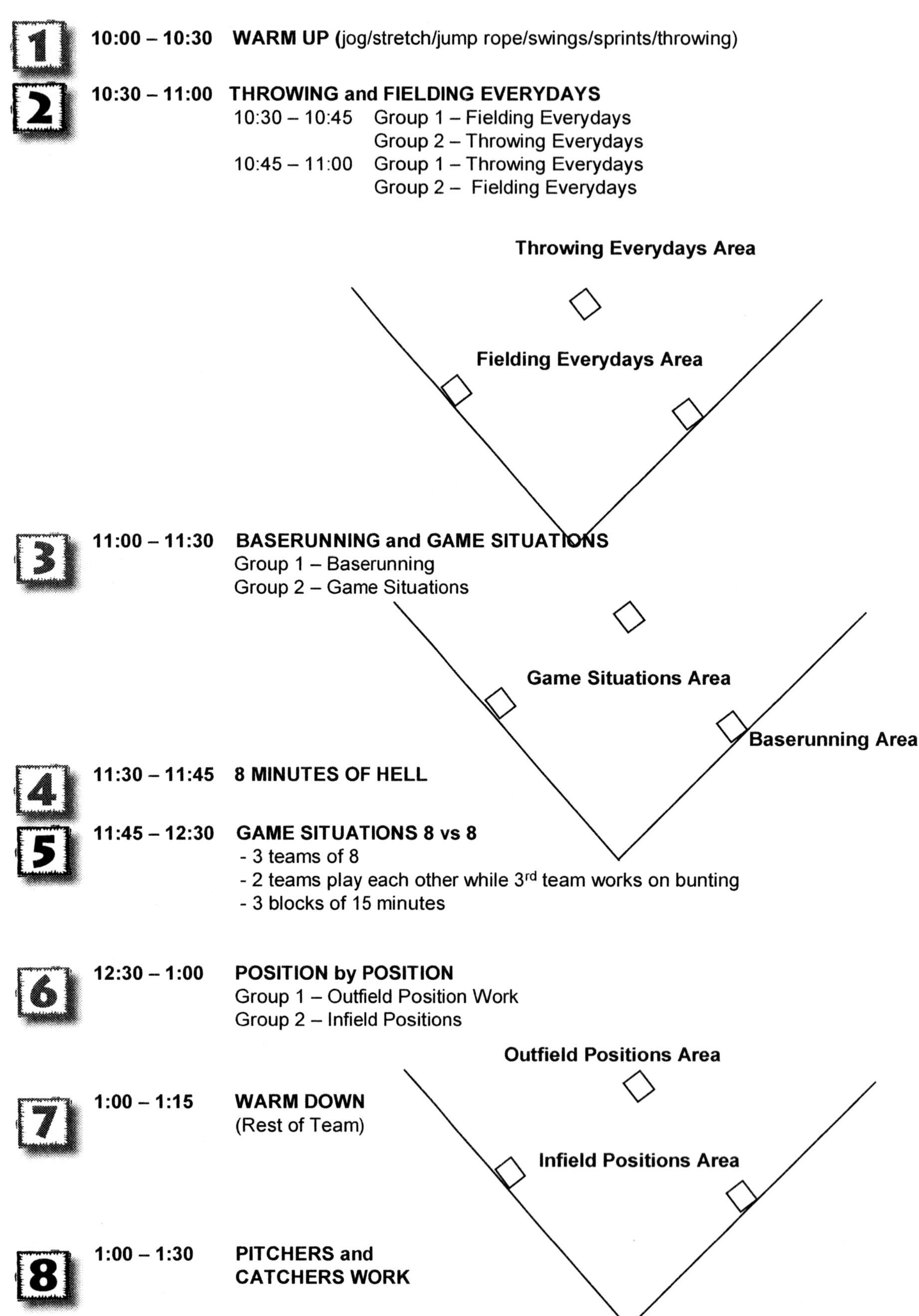

1 **10:00 – 10:30 WARM UP (**jog/stretch/jump rope/swings/sprints/throwing)

2 **10:30 – 11:00 THROWING and FIELDING EVERYDAYS**

10:30 – 10:45 Group 1 – Fielding Everydays
Group 2 – Throwing Everydays
10:45 – 11:00 Group 1 – Throwing Everydays
Group 2 – Fielding Everydays

3 **11:00 – 11:30 BASERUNNING and GAME SITUATIONS**

Group 1 – Baserunning
Group 2 – Game Situations

4 **11:30 – 11:45 8 MINUTES OF HELL**

5 **11:45 – 12:30 GAME SITUATIONS 8 vs 8**

- 3 teams of 8
- 2 teams play each other while 3rd team works on bunting
- 3 blocks of 15 minutes

6 **12:30 – 1:00 POSITION by POSITION**

Group 1 – Outfield Position Work
Group 2 – Infield Positions

7 **1:00 – 1:15 WARM DOWN**

(Rest of Team)

8 **1:00 – 1:30 PITCHERS and CATCHERS WORK**

Beginning Practice 6 - Explanation

The first part of this practice (from 10:00 until 10:30) will involve warming up, jogging, stretching, jumping ropes and sprinting for conditioning. Followed by warming up everyone's arms for throwing - which happens next.

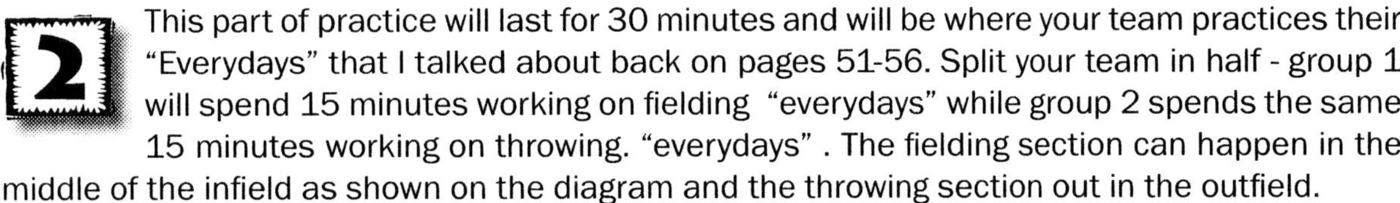

This part of practice will last for 30 minutes and will be where your team practices their "Everydays" that I talked about back on pages 51-56. Split your team in half - group 1 will spend 15 minutes working on fielding "everydays" while group 2 spends the same 15 minutes working on throwing. "everydays" . The fielding section can happen in the middle of the infield as shown on the diagram and the throwing section out in the outfield.

After 15 minutes the groups rotate and the fielders move to throwing and throwers move to fielder. Again, each group does the 2 drills selected and stays at their station for 15 minutes.

Let everyone get some water and then set up for the next 30 minute session.

3

This session will involve your infielders in group 2 - as they will be working on game situations, and your outfielders and pitchers in group 1 - working on their baserunning. If you have other players that play infield positions then switch them out after a few reps running bases. This session allows you to spend 30 minutes working with your infield on their infield coverage, throws and decisions again live baserunners (wearing helmets).

Next is 15 minutes of conditioning in the 8 minutes of Hell drill. Feed all of your players into this drill as it goes along and while it's only called 8 minutes - it will wear all of your players out. 15 minutes is allowed so you have time to set up the area and also to rest and get drinks following.

The next 45 minutes will be Game Situations involving 3 teams of 8 players each (or as close to it as your numbers allow); 2 teams will be playing each other while the 3rd team works on bunting at the bunting stations. Each game will last 15 minutes as follows:

11:45 - 12:00	Team 1 vs Team 2 Team 3 at Bunting Station
12:00 - 12:15	Team 2 vs Team 3 Team 1 at Bunting Station
12:15 - 12:30	Team 3 vs Team 1 Team 2 at Bunting Station

The next 30 minute session from 12:30 -1:00 allows you to split your team up into 2 groups; outfielders and infielders. The outfielders will go to the outfield and work on their skills for 30 minutes while the infielders work on their infield skills for 30 minutes in the infield.

Except for the pitchers & catchers, the team is finished and can warm down from 1:00 - 1:15.

From 1:00 - 1:30 you can work with the pitchers and catchers to finish practice

Beginning Practice 7 - Diagram

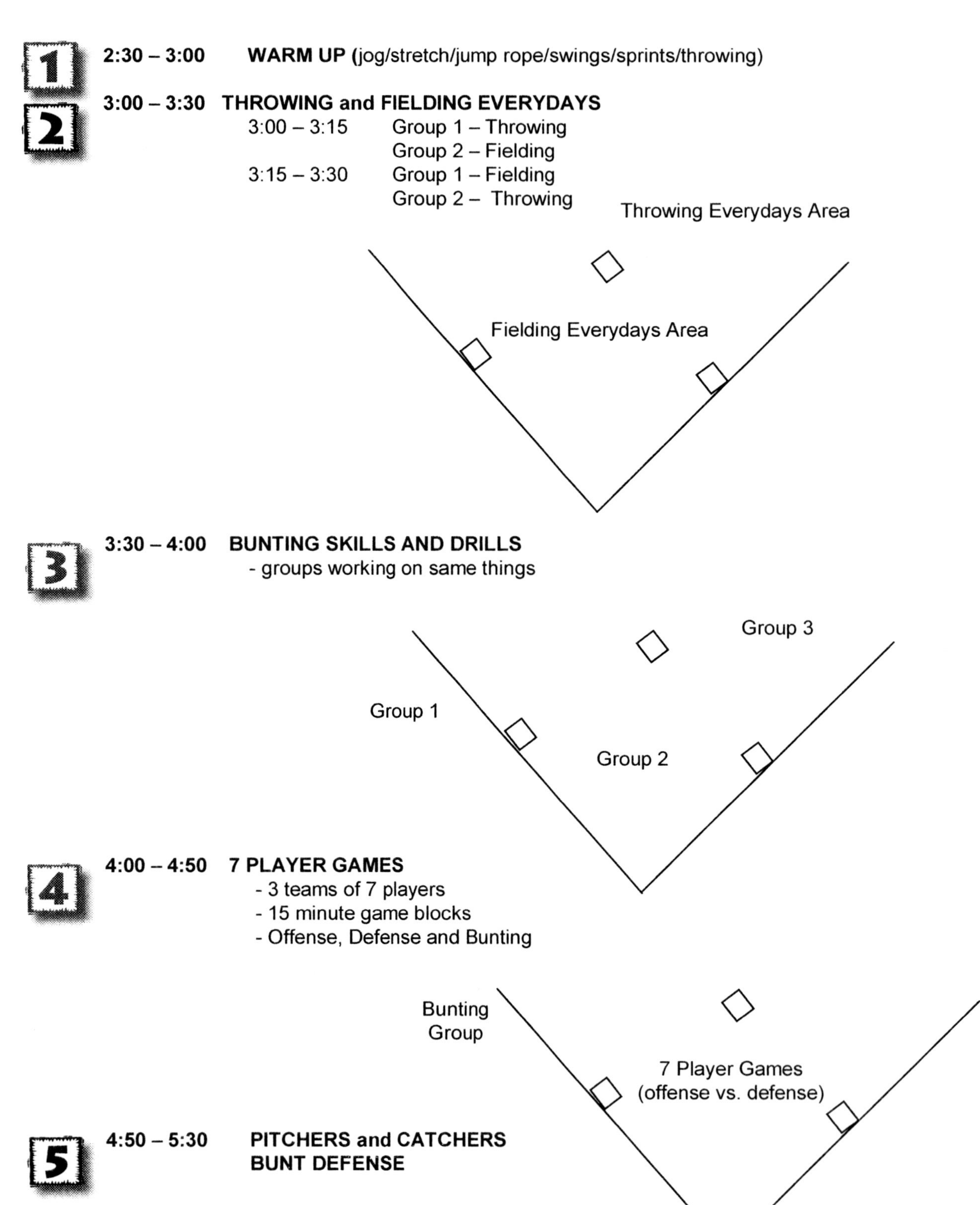

1 **2:30 – 3:00** **WARM UP (**jog/stretch/jump rope/swings/sprints/throwing)

2 **3:00 – 3:30** **THROWING and FIELDING EVERYDAYS**

3:00 – 3:15 Group 1 – Throwing
Group 2 – Fielding
3:15 – 3:30 Group 1 – Fielding
Group 2 – Throwing

3 **3:30 – 4:00** **BUNTING SKILLS AND DRILLS**

- groups working on same things

4 **4:00 – 4:50** **7 PLAYER GAMES**

- 3 teams of 7 players
- 15 minute game blocks
- Offense, Defense and Bunting

5 **4:50 – 5:30** **PITCHERS and CATCHERS**
BUNT DEFENSE

6 **5:10 – 5:30** **GAME SITUATIONS**
(twice through)

Beginning Practice 7 - Explanation

The first part of this practice (from 2:30 until 3:00) will involve warming up, jogging, stretching, jumping ropes and sprinting for conditioning. Followed by warming up everyone's arms for throwing - which happens next.

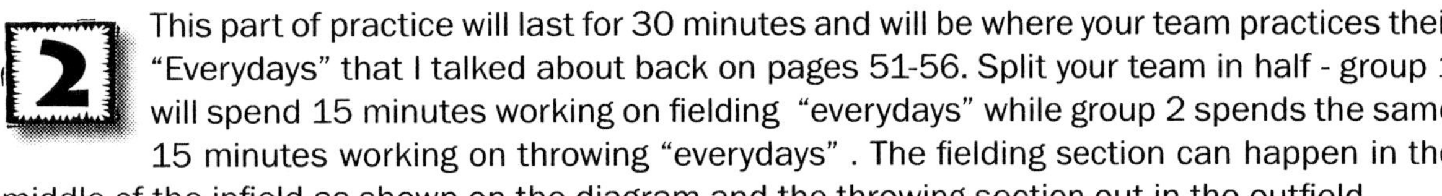

This part of practice will last for 30 minutes and will be where your team practices their "Everydays" that I talked about back on pages 51-56. Split your team in half - group 1 will spend 15 minutes working on fielding "everydays" while group 2 spends the same 15 minutes working on throwing "everydays" . The fielding section can happen in the middle of the infield as shown on the diagram and the throwing section out in the outfield.

After 15 minutes the groups rotate and the fielders move to throwing and throwers move to fielder. Again, each group does the 2 drills selected and stays at their station for 15 minutes.

Let everyone get some water and then set up for the next 30 minute session

3

This session will work on Bunting practice with your team split up into 3 groups, each one stationed at a different location on the field, and each one practicing the same skills. Pick 2 -3 different bunting drills (based on how well they can do each one and therefore how quickly they can do them) and you walk between each of the 3 groups observing their technique and skills.

In this 50 minute session your team will be split up into 3 teams - matched in skill and numbers as evenly as possible. If you can't make 3 teams of 7 then make 3 teams of as many as you can.

2 teams will be playing each other for 15 minutes on the field while the 3rd team is off the field working on more bunting for their 15 minutes. Since you won't have all positions filled in your game don't use a pitcher (instead, hit off of front toss, side toss, a Batting T or a pitching machine) and also designate one or more of the outfields as DEAD (where you don't have any outfielders) and anyone who hits the ball there is OUT.

After 15 minutes, rotate. The rotation can go as follows:

4:00 - 4:15: Team 1 vs Team 2, Team 3 Bunting

4:15 - 4:30: Team 2 vs Team 3, Team 1 Bunting

4:30 - 4:45 Team 3 vs Team 1, Team 2 Bunting

5

After a 5 minute break to let everyone get some water, the pitcher and catchers will work out on the infield (one at a time so the rest are pitching off to the side of the infield) for 50 minutes total. The first 20 minutes of that time (from 4:50 - 5:10) the defense will also be out on the infield practicing Bunt Defense (along with the pitchers and catchers).

For the last 20 minutes of practice, while the pitchers and catchers all work out off to the side, you can take the defense through various game situations (offensively and defensively).

Beginning Practice 8 - Diagram

6:00 – 6:05 WARM UP: Mix in conditioning as well

6:05 – 6:25 THROWING and FIELDING

6:05 – 6:15 Group 1 – Throwing Practice with Coach 1
Group 2 – Fielding Practice with Coach 2
SWITCH
6:15 – 6:25 Group 1 – Fielding Practice with Coach 2
Group 2 – Throwing Practice with Coach 1

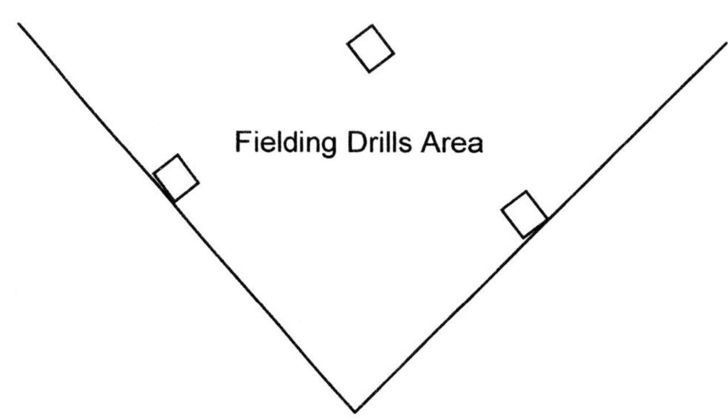

6:25 – 7:10 GAME SITUATIONS – Teams of 8 (if possible)

- 3 teams of 8 (if possible) in 15 minute blocks
- Offensive / Defensive / Bunting
- Coach 1 or Coach 2 pitching (or a T or machine)
- This format allows you to stop and explain things if needed

6;25 – 6:40: Team 1 – Offense, Team 2 – Defense, Team 3 – Hitting
6:40 – 6:55: Team 2 – Offense, Team 3 – Defense, Team 1 – Hitting
6:55 – 7:10: Team 3 – Offense, Team 1 – Defense, Team 2 - Hitting

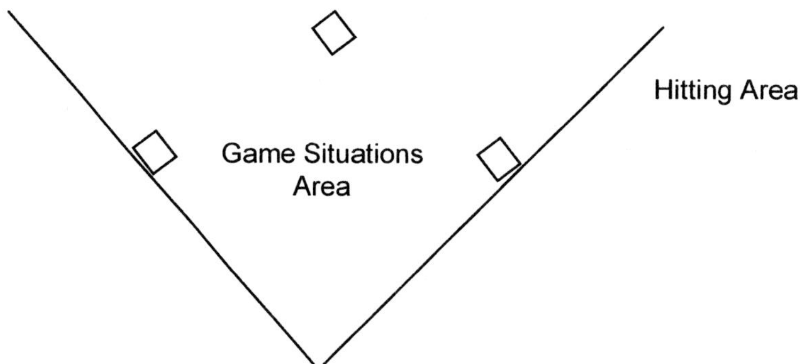

7:10 – 7:40 PITCHERS and CATCHERS with Coach 1
Rest of team taking flyballs off Coach 2

7:40 – 8:00 BASERUNNING / OFFENSIVE GAME SITUATIONS

- Group 1: 10 minutes with Coach 1 on Baserunning
- Group 2: 10 minutes with Coach 2 on Situations

SWITCH

- Group 1: 10 minutes with Coach 2 on Situations
- Group 2: 10 minutes with Coach 1 on Baserunning

Beginning Practice 8 - Explanation

5 minutes of warm-up that can also involve some conditioning (sprints or cone work)

25 minutes of Throwing and Fielding will occur in 10 minute sessions with half your team at the Throwing station for 10 minutes (with one coach) and the other half at Fielding for those same 10 minutes (with another coach).

Then switch, so the Throwing station group goes to Fielding for 10 minutes and the Fielding station group goes to Throwing. 10 minutes is about enough time to do 2 drills per skill with each group.

Throwing can happen in the outfield and the fielding can happen in the infield.

3

Game Situations will happen for the next 45 minutes. Break your team up into 3 groups of 8 or as close to that as you can get.

2 teams will be playing a game against each other on the field (actually keeping score) while the 3rd team is off to the side working on Hitting Drills.

Each game lasts 15 minutes and then rotate as listed. This is a great way to get your players a lot of game experience and make practice fun, in a relatively short amount of time.

The Pitchers and Catchers will practice for 30 minutes while the rest of the team takes fly balls from one of the coaches in the outfield. They don't have to throw every ball they catch - work instead on fielding skills and have each player throw about every 4th ball.

The final part of practice will involve Baserunning and Situations. Break your team up into 2 groups - for the first 10 minutes of this session one group will be on the bases with one coach working on baserunning while the other group works with coach 2 on various situations. Let the players ask questions and also question them during this session.

After 10 minutes then switch - the Baserunning group goes to Situations and the situations group goes to Baserunning.

Advanced Practices

"The country is full of good coaches. What it takes is a bunch of interested players."

~ Don Coryell

So how do you create and maintain interested players? That really is the question, isn't it?

Holding great practices that are helpful, fun, interesting, challenging, positive and competitive is one of the best ways to create a bunch of interested players. Doing this once isn't so hard, particularly right after some clinic you've been to where you learn a few new drills or heard someone speak about things to do at practice.

Nope, holding one or two good practices isn't hard at all, but continuing this through every single one of your practices all year long separates the good coaches from those that are excellent!

While "Beginning Practices" involve a majority of time spent on learning and practicing the basic softball skills mixed in with some game-like experiences, "Advanced Practices" will begin to focus much more on competition and practicing to succeed in competition - both individually and collectively as a team. Joe Torre, manager of the NY Yankees said it best when he said, "*this is an individual game in a team setting*".

And that's exactly what softball is - an individual sport played in a team setting. So, our practices have to prepare the individuals to play together in a team setting - under the pressure of competition - and that's the key!

The Advanced Practices that follow will allow time for the individual players to continue to improve on their fundamental skills, but you'll notice that they also begin to work more on the "team setting" situations that come up. There will be time set aside in some of these practices for the "everydays" we talked about, along with some smaller group settings plus more specialized practices that work only on either defense or offense. But the common thread among all of these Advanced Practices will be the introduction of more competition, accountability, and game-pace - which are all the factors I mentioned as crucial to game success in Chapter II.

Please keep in mind that the practices listed within this entire Sample Practice chapter are just that - samples. You can choose to use them exactly as the are listed, ignore them totally, or make whatever changes you feel might be necessary so they work better for your team and your situation - that's entirely your choice.

Most of the Advanced Practices are copies of actual practices I held with the women's professional softball team I coached - the Florida Wahoos. The idea is to share with you different ways to use your practice time to accomplish different things. You don't have to follow these practices exactly - you can take parts from different ones that you like and piece them together in your own practice. These are all presented to help get your mind going to find creative ways for you to practice the needs of your team, in a fun and game-like way!

The Advanced Practices will fall into the following categories:

Practicing with Small Groups

This section is not intended to give you samples of entire practices, but rather to show you how to mix in Small Group sessions within your practice. Small Groups is a term for combining various combinations of your defense that, within the course of a softball game have to work together. For instance, outfielders throwing to bases, double plays, bunt throws to 1st base, steal throws and coverage, passed balls and covering home, etc...Plays like these don't take the entire team but rather are best done with a "smaller group" of players.

Whole Team Practice Situations

Whole Team Practice Situations are again, not entire practices on their own but rather a way of organizing a segment, or part, of your practice to allow you to work on defense and offense at the same time. I will show you a few different examples of ways to organize your Whole Team Segment of practice to better utilize your time.

Defensive Only Practices

These 3 sample practices will be just that - Defensive Only. Of course you won't want to use these for every practice you hold all season long because you've also got to give your players offensive practice time as well, but there are times throughout a season when your offense is doing well and you simply need to spend an entire practice working on your defense.

Offensive Only Practices

These 4 sample practices, like the Defensive Only ones, will focus only on offensive skills. Again, you won't want to do this every practice all season long, but when your team is in an offensive slump it's a good thing to spend a little extra time in this area.

Combination Practices (Offensive & Defensive)

The last 5 sample practices involve Combination Practices. These involve both offensive and defensive skills throughout the practice.

Please keep in mind that these are all just *samples* of practices you can hold. You're free to use any of the ones I list in this book, change them slightly for your own needs or ignore them all completely. It's your choice, but I wanted to share different examples of practice plans to help you get better at creating your own. Best of luck in this area and let's look at some Advanced Practices.

Practicing with Small Groups

Using the “Small Groups” concept in practice allows you to take your larger defensive team and break it up into smaller groups that logically work together in certain situations - and to do all that plus get a lot of repetitions in a short amount of time. If you remember back to the basic practice plan concept that allowed a certain amount of practice time for defense, a certain amount for offense and a certain amount for game situations, think of the small groups concept as a short segment you can use to follow the “everydays” segment. Everydays work on individual defensive fundamentals and Small Groups work on defensive fundamentals involving a few players.

Here’s how it works:

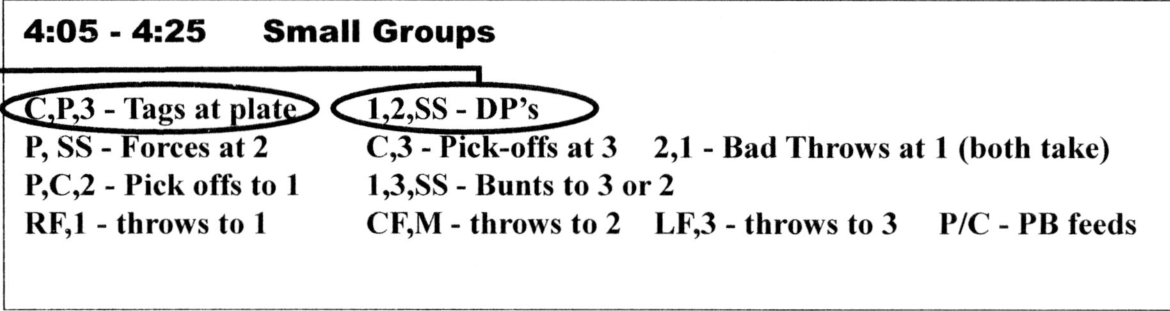

4:05 - 4:25 Small Groups

C,P,3 - Tags at plate 1,2,SS - DP’s
P, SS - Forces at 2 C,3 - Pick-offs at 3 2,1 - Bad Throws at 1 (both take)
P,C,2 - Pick offs to 1 1,3,SS - Bunts to 3 or 2
RF,1 - throws to 1 CF,M - throws to 2 LF,3 - throws to 3 P/C - PB feeds

Let’s look at a 20 minute Small Groups part of an advanced Practice Plan created by an excellent coach and friend of mine - Mona Stevens :

Each of these lines happen in the order they’re listed, and the two groups can happen at the same time. Also, each letter stands for a position. So, the first line is first and actually means the following:

Catcher (C), Pitcher (P) 3rd base (3) - work on Tag plays at the plate
A coach will hit grounders to the Pitcher and 3rd base who throw to the Catcher for a tag play at the plate (Diagram 1) X = the coach hitting and C = the Catcher

1 (1st base), 2 (2nd base), SS (shortstop) - work on Double Play Footwork
A coach will alernate hitting grounders to the Shortstop, 2nd baseman and 1st baseman who will work on their DoublePlay footwork - no throws back to 1st. (Diagram 2)

Since both of these plays do not involve throws to the same bases or hits to the same fielders or areas of the field - as long as the hitters can control their hits - these plays can be done at the same time.

The following diagrams show what the action of each segment looks like - you can do them together or separate them if you’re more comfortable that way. If so, just know this segment will take longer than the 20 minutes scheduled for it in this example.

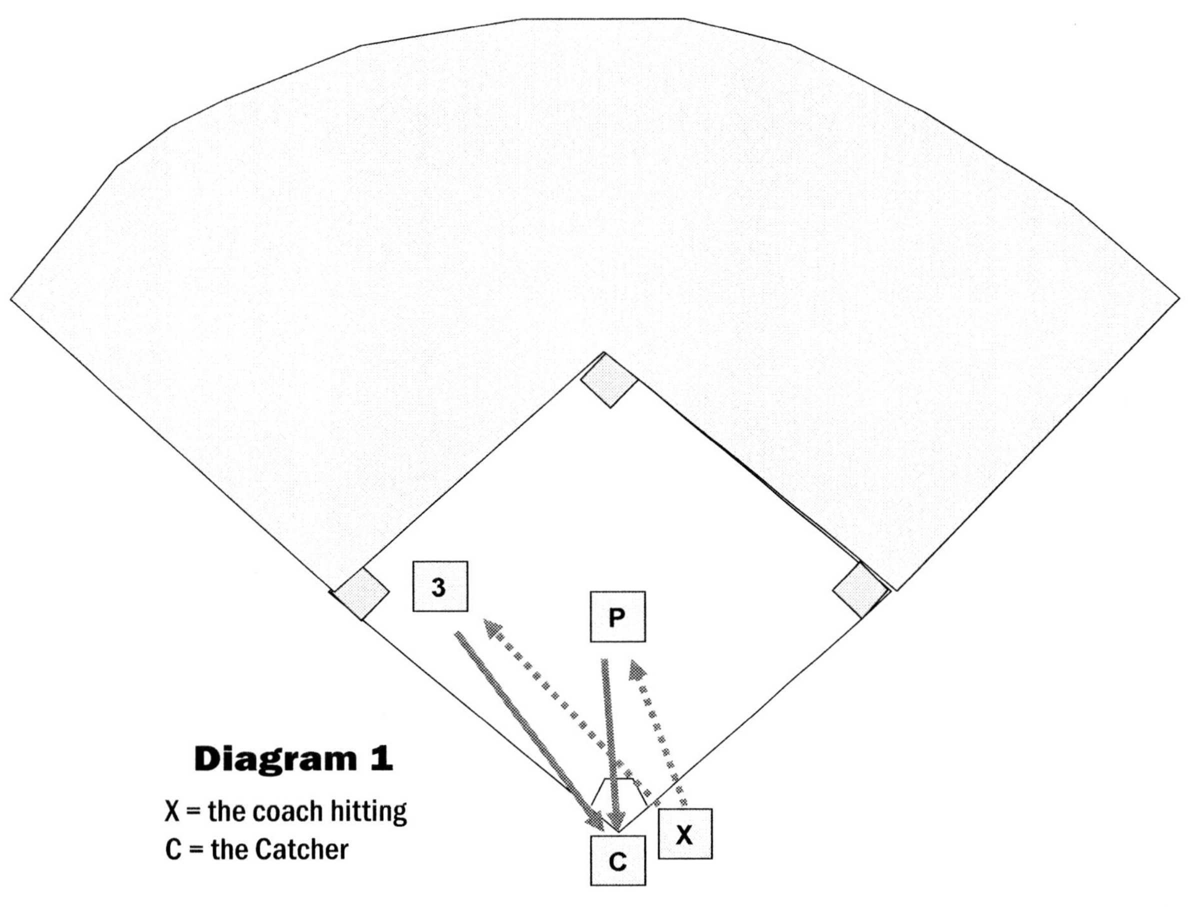

Diagram 1

X = the coach hitting
C = the Catcher

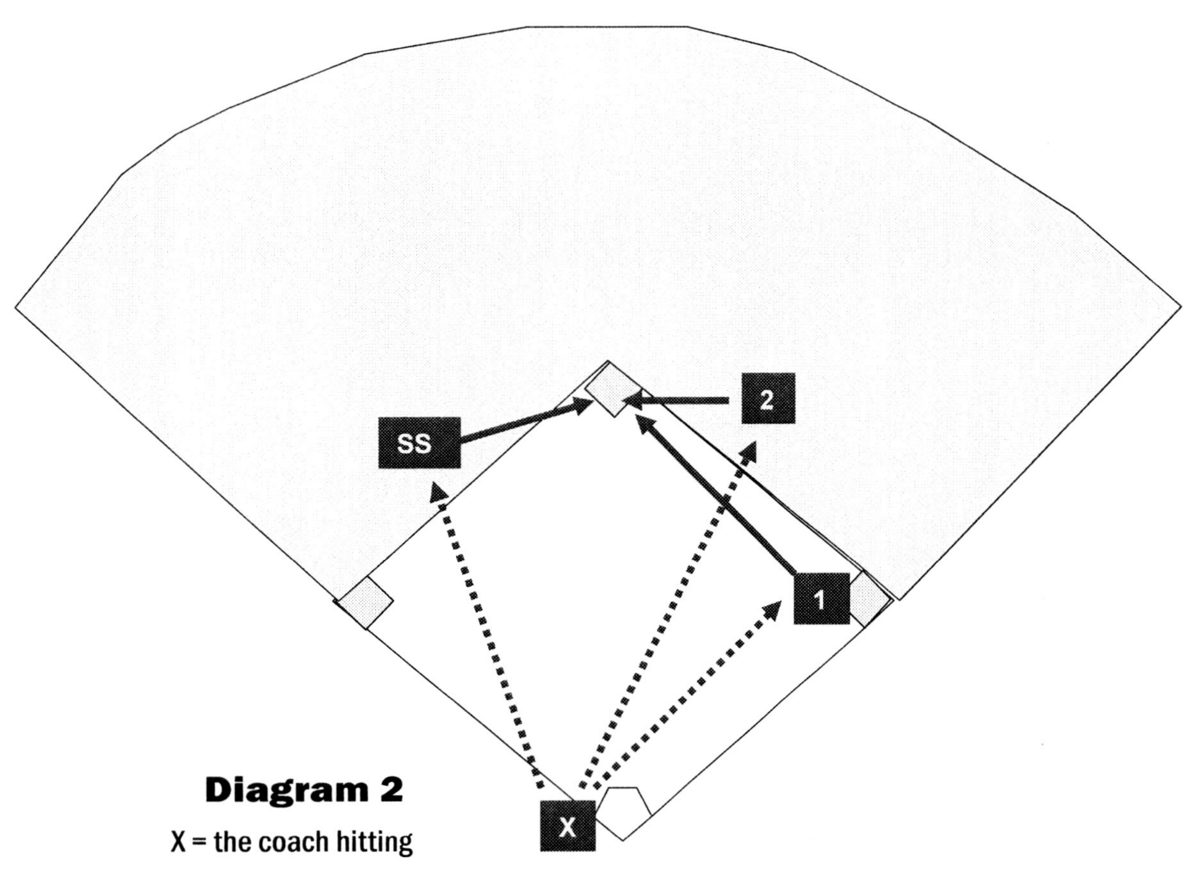

Diagram 2

X = the coach hitting

4:05 - 4:25 Small Groups

C,P,3 - Tags at plate 1,2,SS - DP's

Here's a look at how both of these groups can fit together, each doing their own Small Group activity, yet using the same field and taking up the same amount of time:

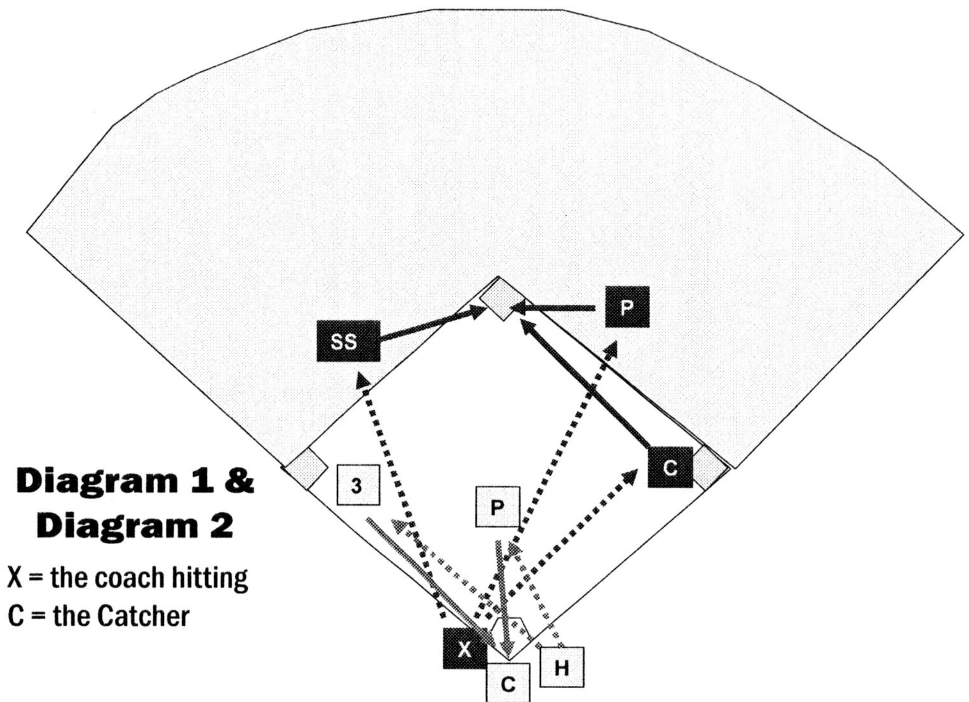

4:05 - 4:25 Small Groups

C,P,3 - Tags at plate 1,2,SS - DP's
P, SS - Forces at 2 C,3 - Pick-offs at 3 2,1 - Bad Throws at 1 (both take)
P,C,2 - Pick offs to 1 1,3,SS - Bunts to 3 or 2
RF,1 - throws to 1 CF,M - throws to 2 LF,3 - throws to 3 P/C - PB feeds

Pitcher (P), Shortstop (SS) work on Forces at 2nd base-
A coach will hit grounders to the Pitcher who throws to SS covering 2nd for force. (Diagram 3)

Catcher (C), 3rd Base (3) work on Pick-offs at 3rd base -
A coach stands near pitcher and tosses balls to Catcher who throws down to 3rd for pickoff. (Diagram 4)

2nd Base (2) and 1st base (1) work on handling bad throws at 1st -
2nd base has a line of balls infront of her on the ground and fields each ball (one-at-time) and makes a bad throw on purpose to 1st so 1st can practice making plays on bad throws (Diagram 5).

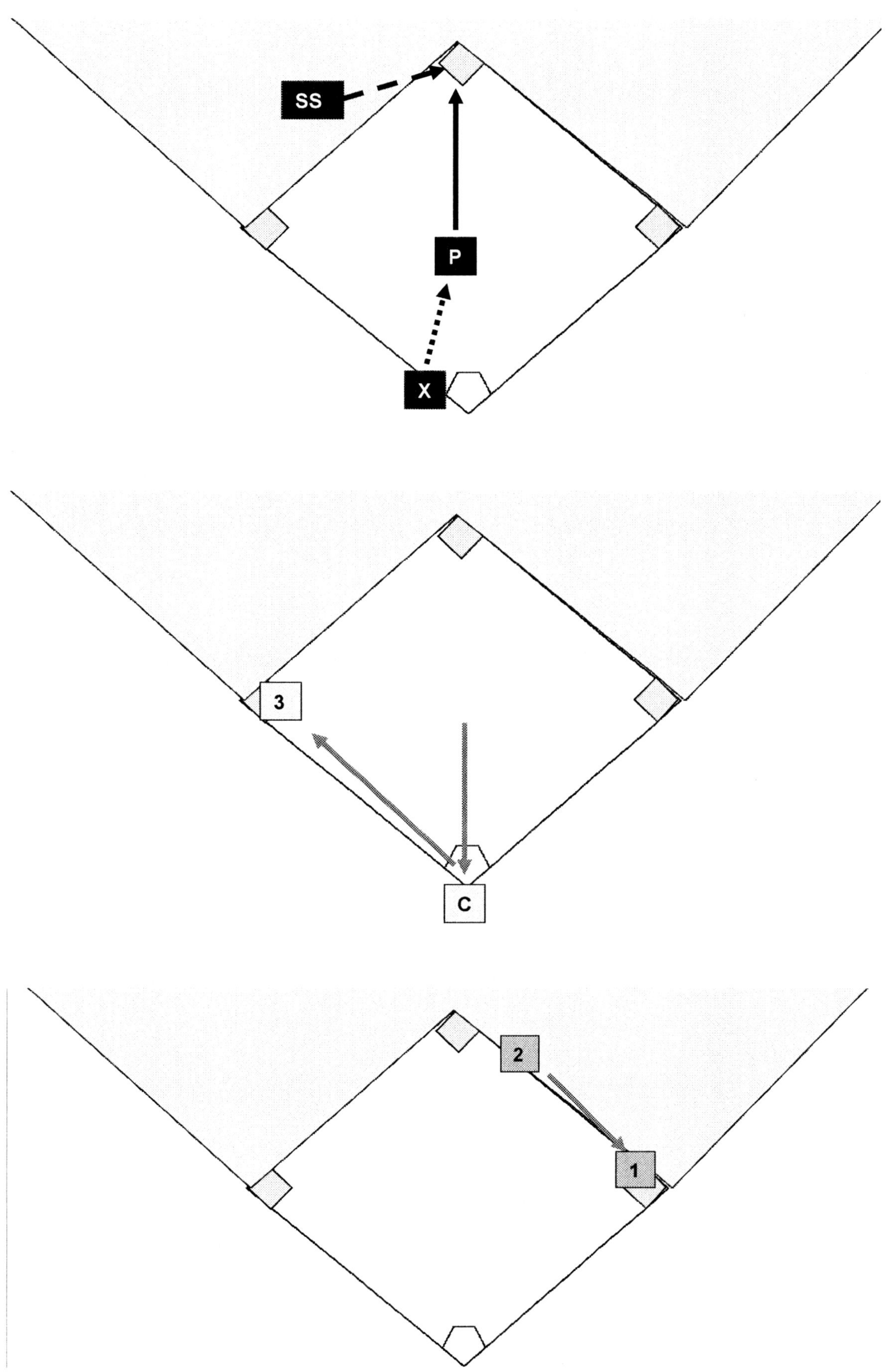
SS
P
X
3
C
2
1

4:05 - 4:25 Small Groups

P, SS - Forces at 2	C,3 - Pick-offs at 3	2,1 - Bad Throws at 1 (both take)

Again, here's a look at how this entire line of Small Groups will be able to work together:

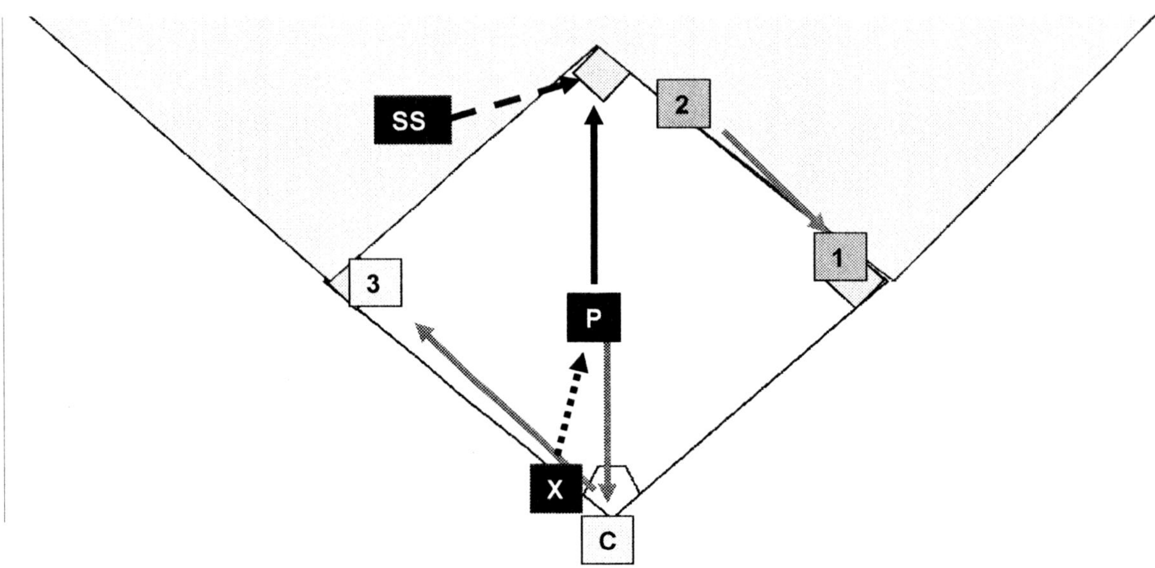

4:05 - 4:25 Small Groups

C,P,3 - Tags at plate	1,2,SS - DP's		
P, SS - Forces at 2	C,3 - Pick-offs at 3	2,1 - Bad Throws at 1 (both take)	
P,C,2 - Pick offs to 1	1,3,SS - Bunts to 3 or 2		
RF,1 - throws to 1	CF,M - throws to 2	LF,3 - throws to 3	P/C - PB feeds

Pitcher (P), Catcher (C), 2nd base (2) - work on pick offs at 1st -
The Pitcher will pitch to the Catcher who throws down to the 2nd baseman covering 1st base for the pickoff. (Diagram 7)

1st base (1), 3rd base (3) and Shortstop (SS) - work on bunts to either 3rd or 2nd base
A coach (X) tosses a ball out like a bunt and either the Pitcher, 3rdbaseman or 1st baseman field it and throw to either 2nd base or 3rdbase with the Shortstop covering - the base has been called out by the coach ahead of time. (Diagram 6)

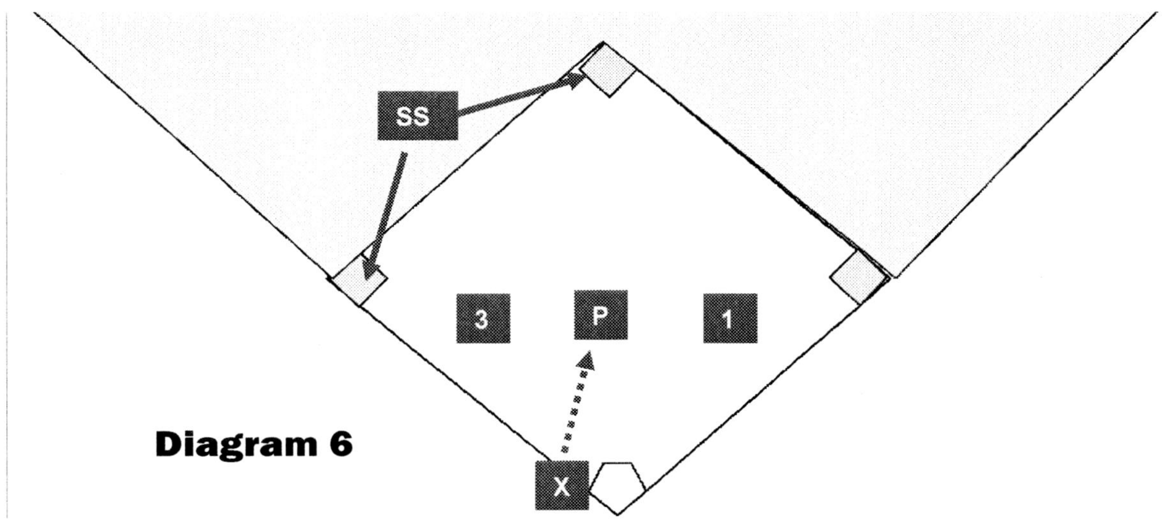

Diagram 6

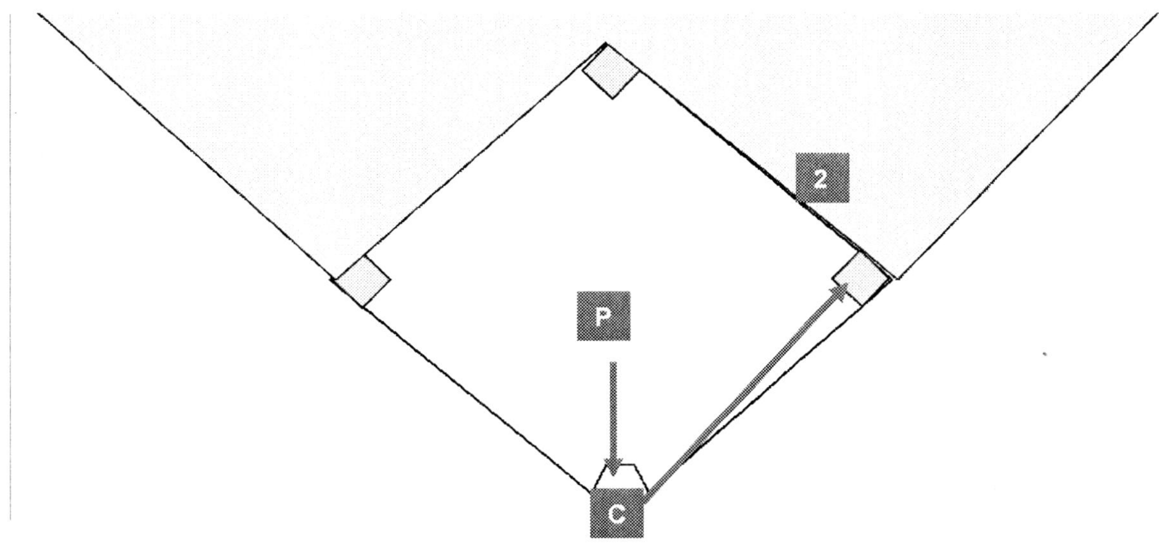

4:05 - 4:25 Small Groups

P,C,2 - Pick offs to 1 1,3,SS - Bunts to 3 or 2

Here's a look at how this line (Diagram 6 & 7) go together:

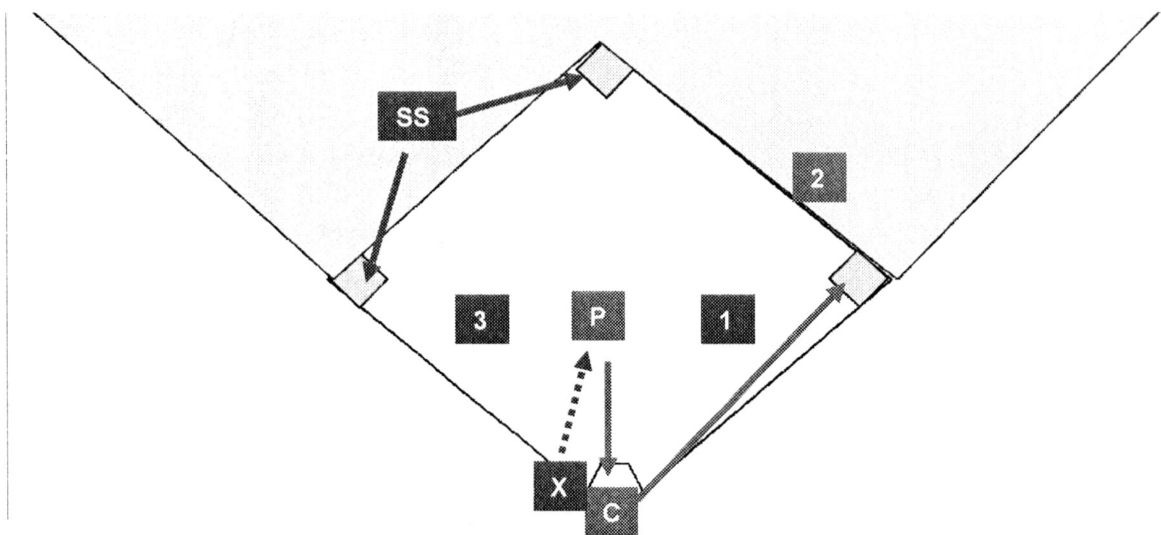

The last of this 20 minute Small Groups workout involves the outfielders throwing to a designated base and the pitchers and catchers covering home on passed balls.

4:05 - 4:25 Small Groups

C,P,3 - Tags at plate 1,2,SS - DP's
P, SS - Forces at 2 C,3 - Pick-offs at 3 2,1 - Bad Throws at 1 (both take)
P,C,2 - Pick offs to 1 1,3,SS - Bunts to 3 or 2
RF,1 - throws to 1 CF,M - throws to 2 LF,3 - throws to 3 P/C - PB feeds

Rightfielder (RF) throws to 1st -
Coach (X) stands out near pitcher and hits balls to Rightfield who throws to 1st. (Diagram 8)

Centerfielder (CF) throws to Middle Infielders (M) Short and 2nd -
Coach (X) stands out near pitcher and hits balls to Centerield who throws to 2nd. (Diagram 8)

Leftfielder (LF) throws to 3rdbase (3) covering 3rd -
Coach (X) stands out near pitcher and hits balls to Leftfielder who throws to 3rd. (Diagram 8)

Pitcher (P) gets tosses/feeds from Catcher (C) on passed balls -
Pitcher tosses balls against fence and covers home as catcher tosses to Pitcher covering. Diagram 8)

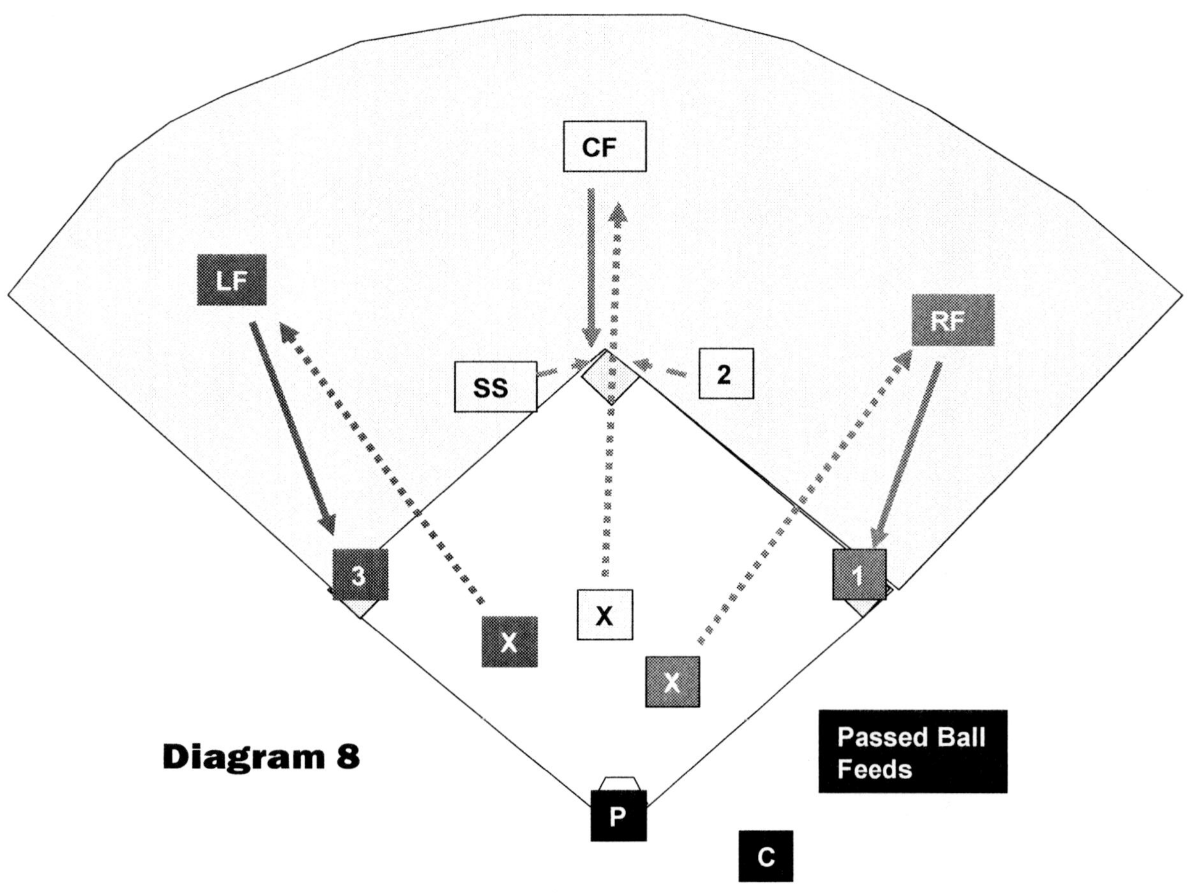

Diagram 8

Summary - Small Groups

By using a well-thought-out and planned list like the one below (that we've just gone through) I think you can see how a lot can get done in a short amount of time. In the span of 20 minutes this Small Groups plan is able to get your entire team a lot of work in different combinations of defensive coverage - work that's different than their individual everydays but just as critical.

4:05 - 4:25 Small Groups

C,P,3 - Tags at plate **1,2,SS - DP's**
P, SS - Forces at 2 **C,3 - Pick-offs at 3** **2,1 - Bad Throws at 1 (both take)**
P,C,2 - Pick offs to 1 **1,3,SS - Bunts to 3 or 2**
RF,1 - throws to 1 **CF,M - throws to 2** **LF,3 - throws to 3** **P/C - PB feeds**

Whole Team Practice Situations

Whole Team Practice Situations are not entire practices on their own but rather different ways of organizing a segment, or part of your practice to allow you to work on defense and offense at the same time or else to work on game-like situations. I'll show you a few different examples of ways to organize your Whole Team Situations portion of practice - each one will help you use your time better by practicing two things at once.

As you'll see in this section, Whole Team Situations are really just blocks of time that you designate during your practice to work on some more competitive situations (some of which we've already discussed in the Competitive Challenges section back on pages 69 - 72).

Let's take the following 30 minute section of a practice as an example and see how it

4:30 – 5:00

Bunt D and Slapper D (machine set up)
3 rounds – 3 teams (hit, defense, run)
1. **GD, MS, JW, IH, BD/KN** (D,D,O)
2. **LW, JT, DQ, KN, BD, P** (O, R, D)
3. **AA, CS, SL, TC, P** (R, O, R)

On the surface this might look pretty confusing and not too easy to understand, so let's look at this in greater detail to see what it really means:

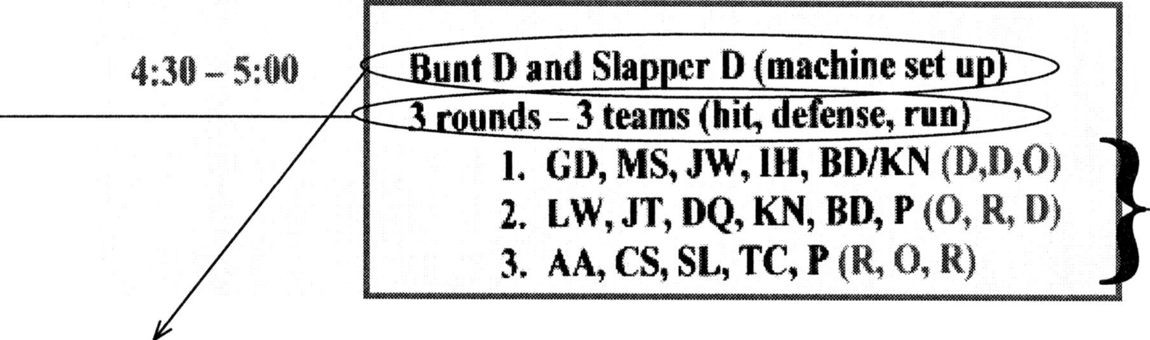
4:30 – 5:00
Bunt D and Slapper D (machine set up)
3 rounds – 3 teams (hit, defense, run)
1. **GD, MS, JW, IH, BD/KN** (D,D,O)
2. **LW, JT, DQ, KN, BD, P** (O, R, D)
3. **AA, CS, SL, TC, P** (R, O, R)

This whole 30 minute section will be on Bunt Defense and Slapper Defense using a pitching machine.

This will happen in 3 different rounds with your team split into 3 teams; one will hit, the other will play defense and the third group will run bases.

These are the initials (first and last name) of the players that will be in each of the 3 different teams/groups, and the order of their rotation:

1. **Team 1**: GD, MS, JW, IH, BD/KN (Defense, Defense, Offense) These are the infielders so they will go twice on defense instead of having a baserunning group)
2. **Team 2**: LW, JT, DQ, KN, BD, P (Offense, Running, Defense)
3. **Team 3**: AA, CS, SL, TC, P (Run, Offense, Run) These are the outfielders so they will not do the defensive group and will run twice instead.

Here's how this would look on the field:

4:30 – 5:00

Bunt D and Slapper D (machine set up)
3 rounds – 3 teams (hit, defense, run)

1. **GD, MS, JW, IH, BD/KN** (D,D,O)
2. **LW, JT, DQ, KN, BD, P** (O, R, D)
3. **AA, CS, SL, TC, P** (R, O, R)

Each group will stay in each location for 10 minutes as follows:

- *Group 1: Defense (10 minutes), Defense (10 minutes), Offense (10 minutes)*
- *Group 2: Offense (10 minutes), Running (10 minutes), Defense (10 minutes)*
- *Group 3: Running (10 minutes), Offense (10 minutes), Running (10 minutes)*

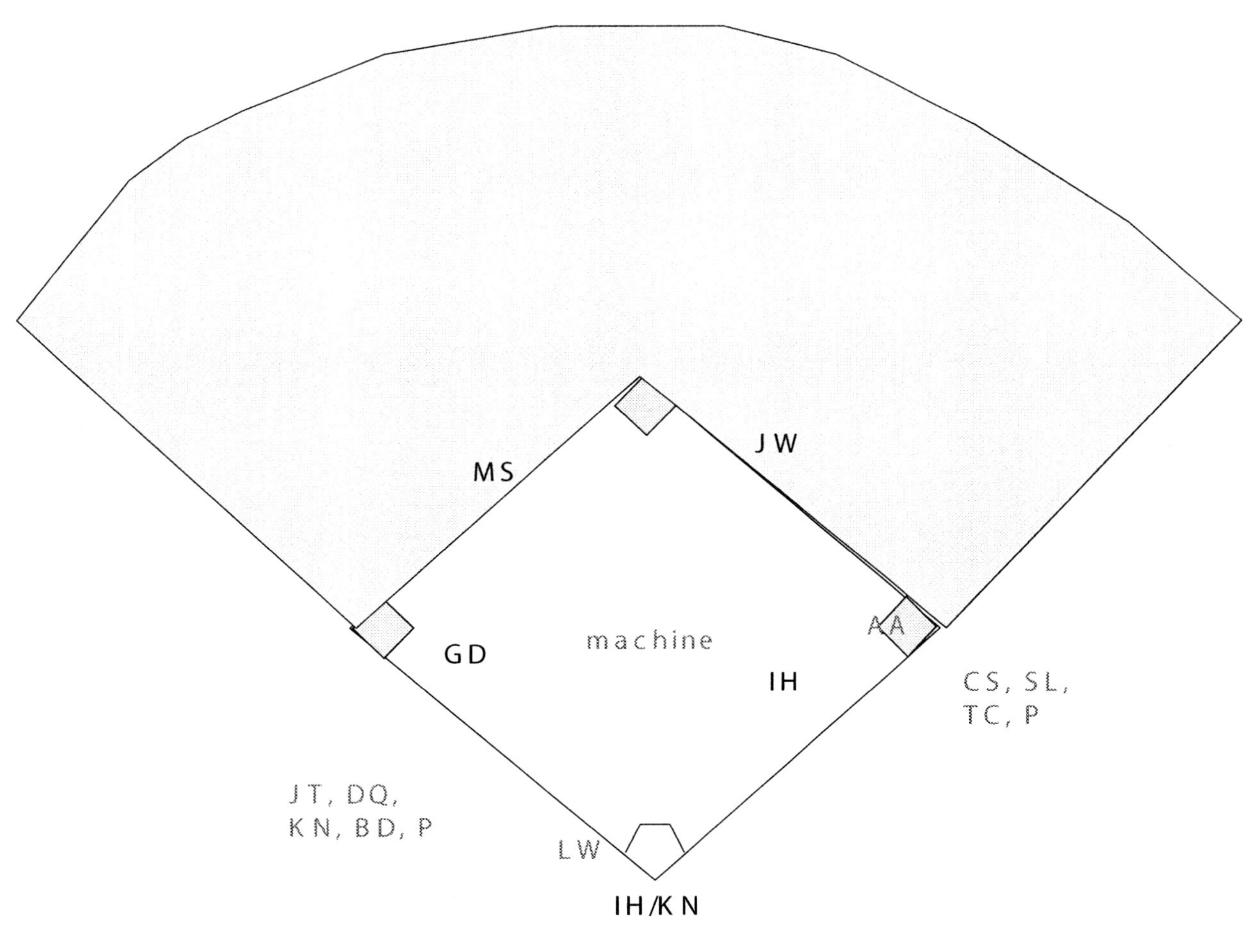

While the last example put everyone on your team in the same location - all playing on the infield either as the defense, the offense or the runners - the following examples will spread your team out to different stations in and around your field. (Keep in mind that if you're practicing indoors that you adjust the space or station locations according to the amount of room that you have).

In this example, there are 7 different stations and each one works on the following:

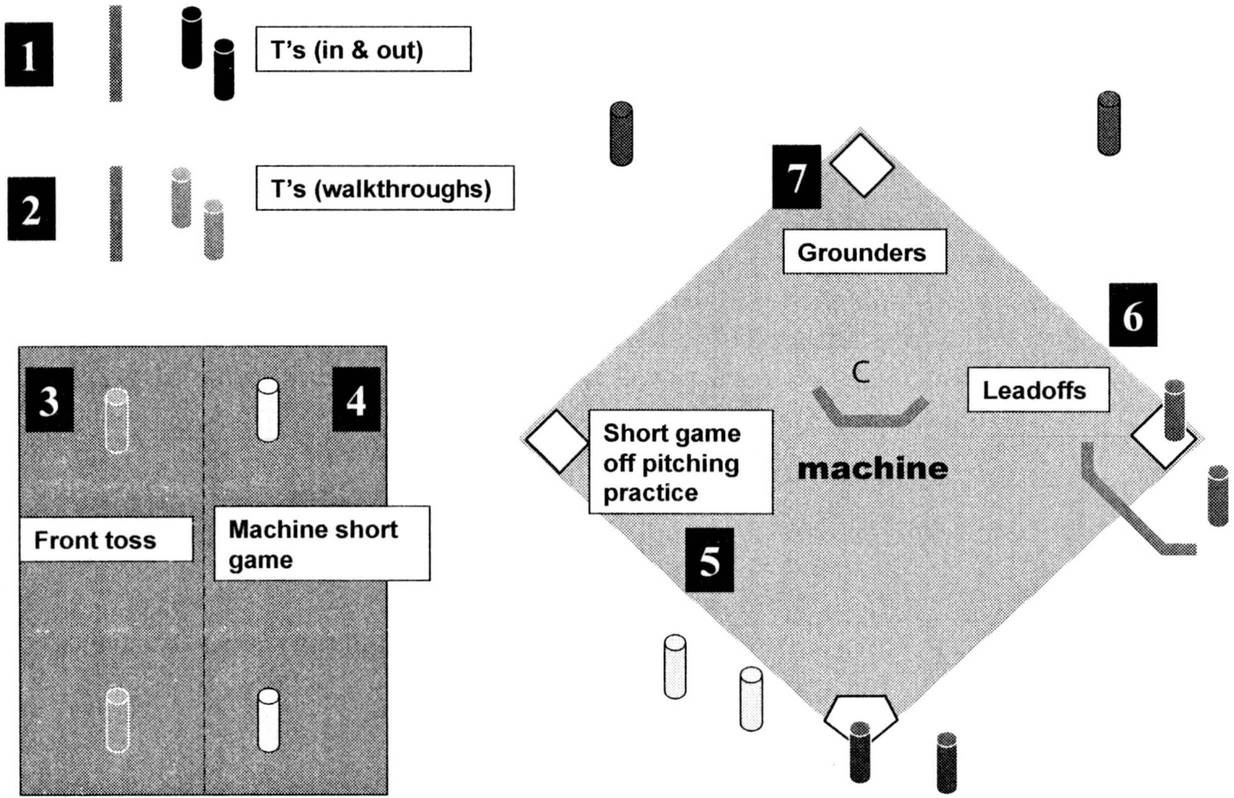

Station 1: Hitters in pairs working on hitting off Batting T's - they're working on hitting an inside and an outside pitch by placing the T either inside or outside.

Station 2: This station is also working on Batting T's - but the hitters are doing a drill called "walkthroughs" where they start a step behind the T and cross over with their back foot then step with their stride foot and the hit the ball...as if they were "walking" into the swing.

Station 3: Hitters are in the batting cage (if you have one) and are working on hitting Front toss - a ball tossed from behind a screen from infront of the hitter from about 4-7 feet away. If you don't have batting cages then use whiffle balls.

Station 4: This station is working on either bunts or slaps off of the pitching machine. If you don't have a machine have someone toss or pitch balls underhand. Slappers will do both bunts and slaps while non-slappers will work on their bunting.

Station 5: This station will involve two things at once - your pitchers will be pitching to their catchers here as their pitching practice for this day. So rotate pitchers and catchers every so often. The other thing happening here is that your hitters will now practice their short game - either bunts or slaps - off of live pitching.

Station 6: Station 6 will help the players work on the timing of their leadoffs. They will be protected from slapped or bunted balls from station 5 by a protective screen that is positioned about 5 feet in front of 1st base and over far enough to cover them while they are actually on 1st base. The baserunners will work on leaving as the ball leaves the hand of the pitchers practicing at station 5.

Station 7: Station 7 will work on groundballs (for infielders) and flyballs (for outfielders). This station will also have a protective screen placed slightly behind the pitching rubber and in-line with 2nd base. A coach **C** will be hitting either the grounders or the flys to the fielders who position themselves on either side f 2nd base. The fielders will not throw the ball back into the coach after each play, but rather roll the ball to 2nd base. When the coach is out of balls then both fielders will hustle over and fill up the bucket and continue.

Remember that this is only a portion of your practice so you won't stay at these 7 stations for your entire practice time. With 5 minutes per station it would take 35 minutes to go through all 7 stations. That would give each player (with 2 per station) 2 1/2 minutes per station. Depending on the number of players you have (this example shows 2 players per station plus your pitchers and catchers so that would be about 17 - 18 players on a team in this format) this segment of practice could take anywhere from 35 minutes to over an hour.

If you need more time per station or are trying to figure out how to give your players more station time without spending too much time overall at this part of practice, then cut down the total number of stations.

Another way to hold a similar type session is to create 4 hitting stations somewhere off to the side of your field,and use your field for a defensive station. That setup would look something like this:

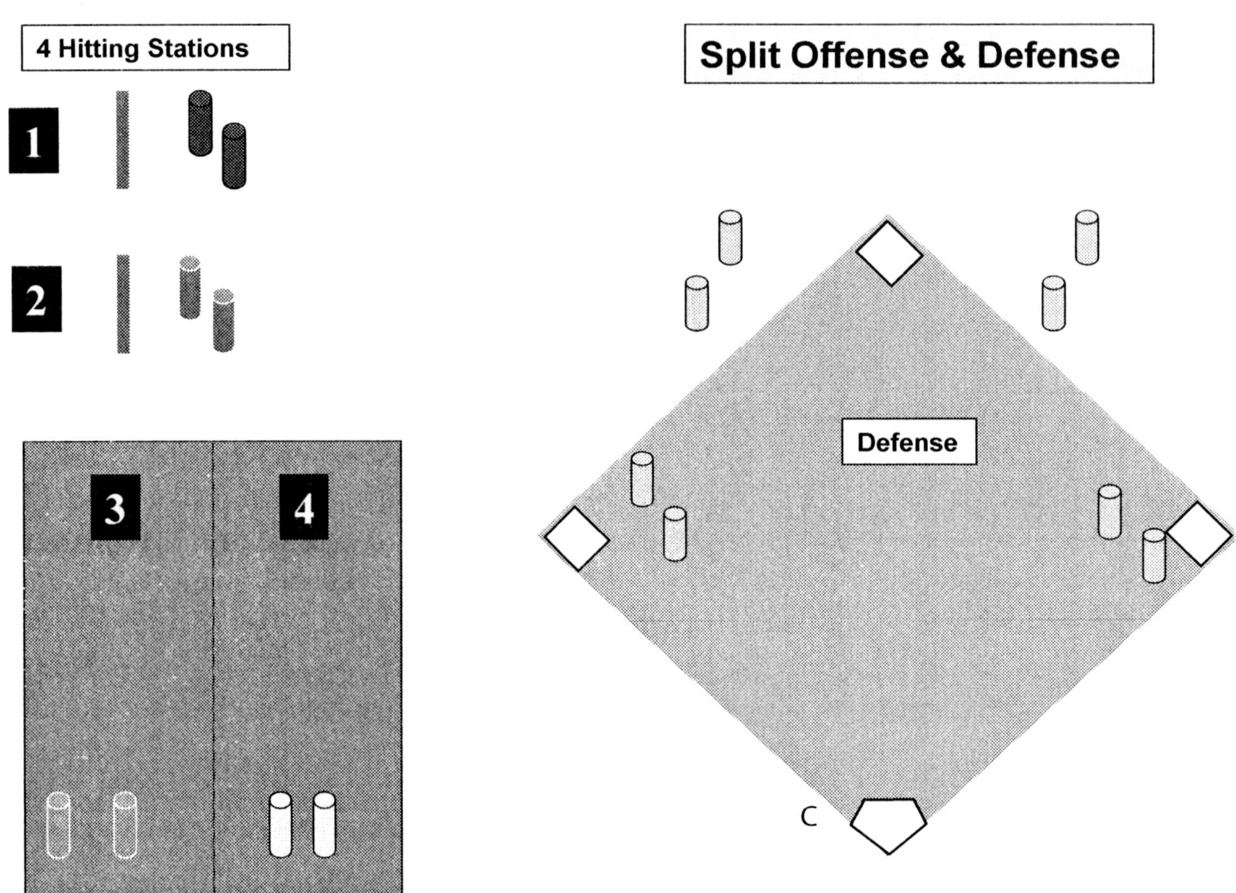

Stations 1, 2, 3 and 4: Are all 4 different hitting stations each working on some aspect of the swing. While this diagram shows Stations 3 and 4 in batting cages they don't have to be. These two stations could be held someplace else if you don't have two batting cages (as most people do not).

Defense: The field will then be used to work on different elements of your team defense. As different players rotate in you could work on either outfield, infield, right side (outfield and infield), left side (outfield and infield) or middle (middle infield and centerfield in outfield) defense. The **C** is the coach who hits flyballs, grounders, bunts and slaps to the defense based on the situation being worked on.

The amount of time you have for each station as well as for the entire segment will depend on the number of players you have, the length of time you want spent at each station and how much total time you want to spend on these things during this practice.

This is almost the exact same format as the previous page, except this setup has 2 different hitting stations instead of 4. So the team can be broken up into groups of four and assigned as follows:

- *Group 1: Station 1, Station 2, Defense, Defense*
- *Group 2: Station 2, Defense, Defense, Station 1*
- *Group 3: Defense, Defense, Station 1, Station 2*
- *Group 4: Defense, Station 1, Station 2, Defense*

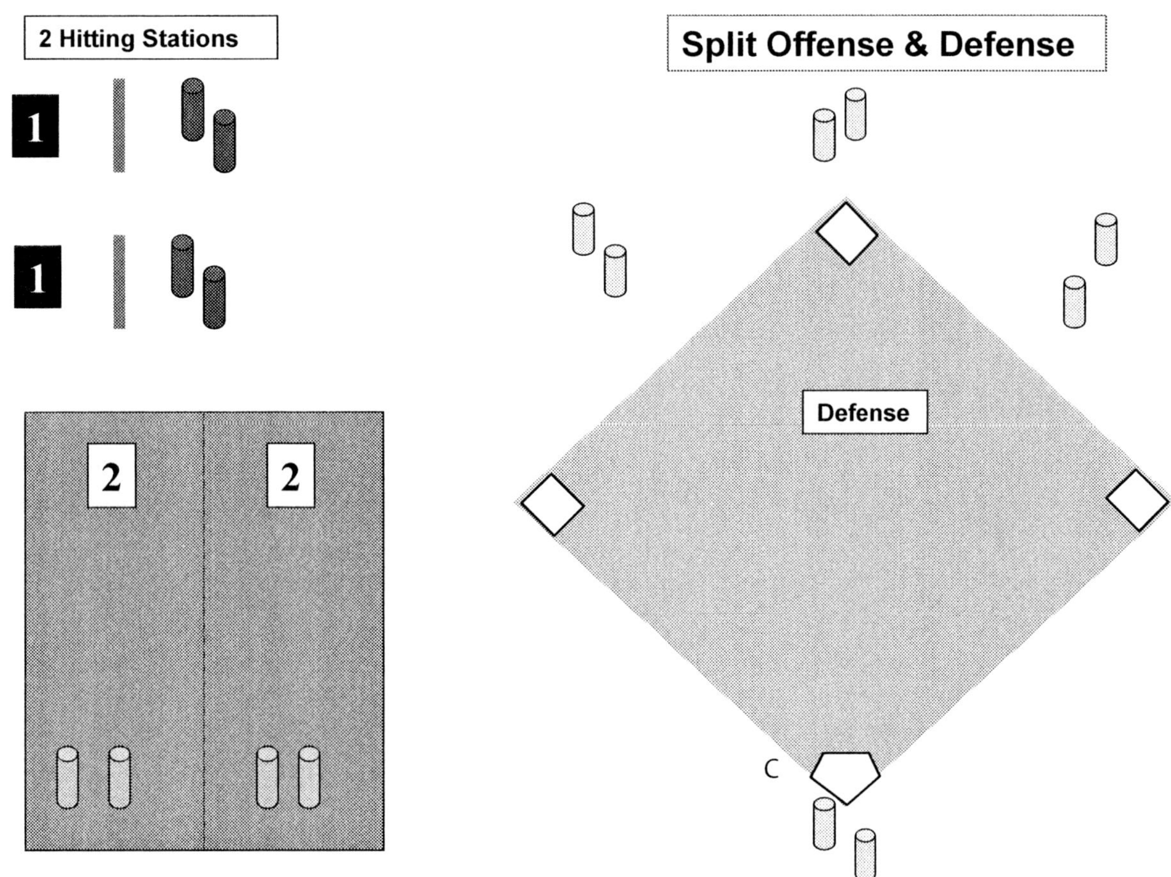

Stations 1 and 2: Are 2 different hitting stations each working on some aspect of the swing. While this diagram shows Station 2 in batting cages it doesn't have to be. These two stations could be held someplace else if you don't have two batting cages (as most people do not).

Defense: The field will then be used to work on different elements of your team defense. As different players rotate in you could work on either outfield, infield, right side (outfield and infield), left side (outfield and infield) or middle (middle infield and centerfield in outfield) defense. The **C** is the coach who hits flyballs, grounders, bunts and slaps to the defense based on the situation being worked on.

Small Teams is another way of working with the concept of Whole Team Situations to give your players practice time and experience actually playing games instead of just drilling on different skills or skill parts.

The idea of small teams is to divide your team up into 2 or 3 teams (I'll show you examples how to do both) and have them play actual games against each other - without needing to have 18 players for 2 teams of 9 each.

Let's take the following example and see how the concept of small teams works:

Small Teams

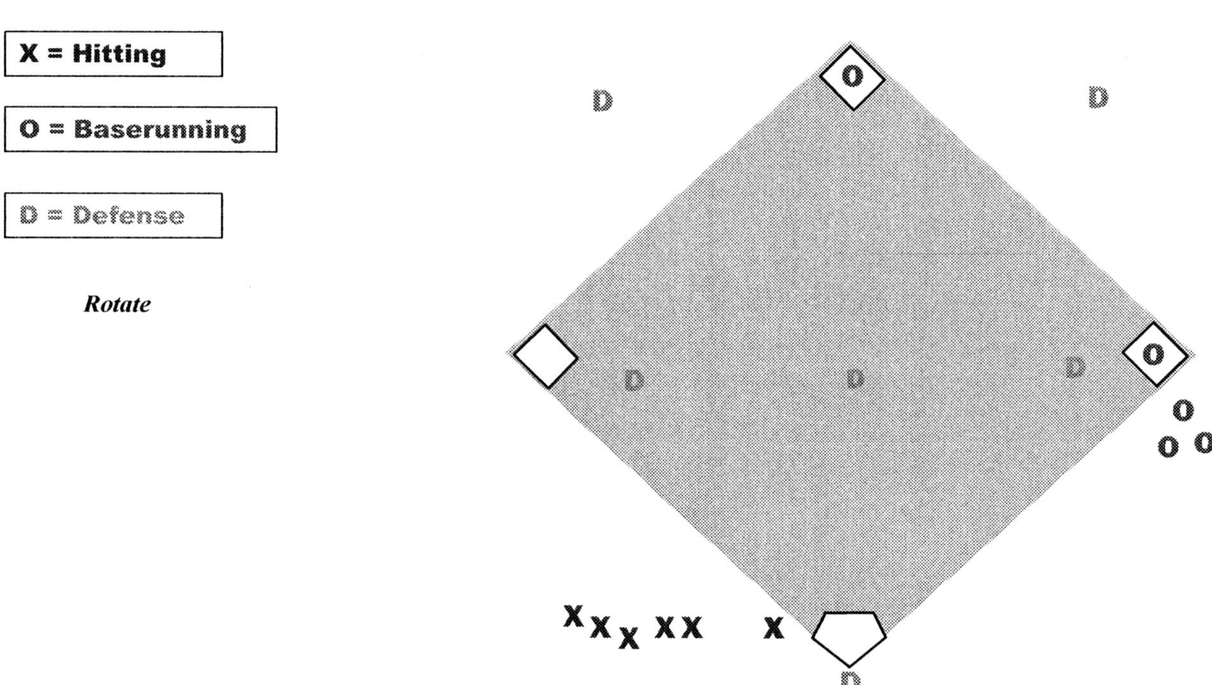

In this small teams example the entire team is split up into 3 smaller teams; one is on Defense (the D's), one is Hitting (the H's), and one is Running Bases (the O's). As you can see by the number of D's on defense there aren't enough players to play every position. While this 3 team setup won't let you practice game-like team defense it will help your players learn to work together and hustle to make sure they have someone fielding the ball and covering the bases so they can get runners out and earn their way up.

Each team would rotate through all 3 locations (Hitting, Baserunning and Defense) and would stay at each one for a set amount of time. To help make this more competitive you could create points for each team based on performance, so things like hard hits or good bunts are points for the Hitting team, getting to the next base or good decisions on-base are points for the Baserunners and outs or great plays would be points for the Defense. Each team would count their points at each of the 3 stations and the team with the highest point total would win for that day.

Small Teams

2 Teams on Defense
(O's & D's)

1 Team on Offense
(X's)

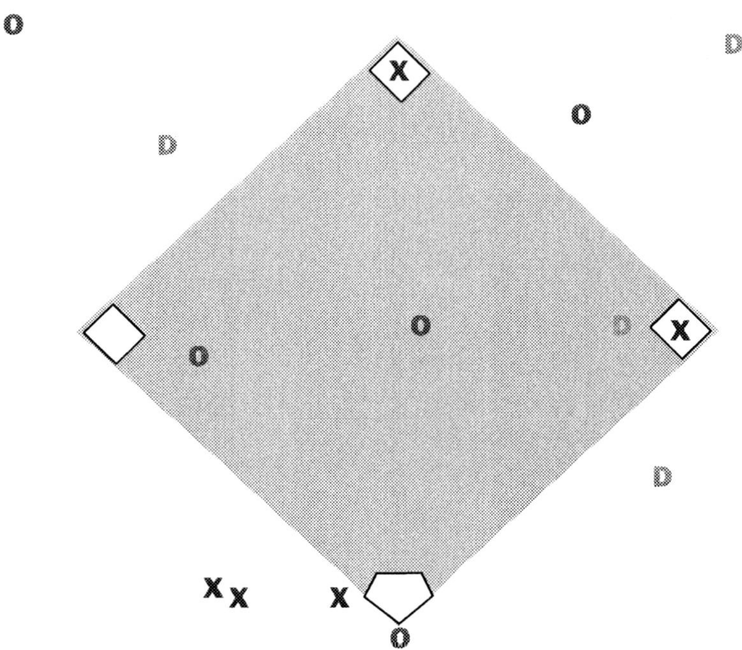

This small teams example still has your entire team broken up into 3 teams, but 2 of those 3 are combined to play defense (in this case the O's and the D's) while the 3rd team (the X's) are on offense. This setup does allow you to practice your team defense since there are now enough players at each position.

You just need to make sure you've done your homework first and you know when the O's are up, what positions the D's and X's are going to be playing so they aren't just making it up themselves or worse yet, you aren't making it up at the last minute. Same goes true when the D's are up and the X's and O's are on defense.

This is a great time to give your backup players game experience or to give players experience playing a second and even 3rd position.

Again, keep score so this is competitive and as game-like as possible.

Defensive Only Practices

These 3 sample practices will be just that - Defensive Only - to help you with those times throughout a season when your offense is doing well and you simply need to spend an entire practice working on your defense.

Defensive Only - Practice 9 Diagram

1 **2:00 – 2:30 Infielders work on defense while outfielders and catchers in the cage hitting**

Hitting In Cages (OF):

Patti 2

Dawn

Lutsi

Scia

T

T

M STREAK

Ground Balls (IF): (10 minutes each pair)

Nina/Randi

Kendall/Crani

Kim/JJ

Work on:

- *Groundball Crossfire*
- *Slow rollers, Bunts and Footwork*

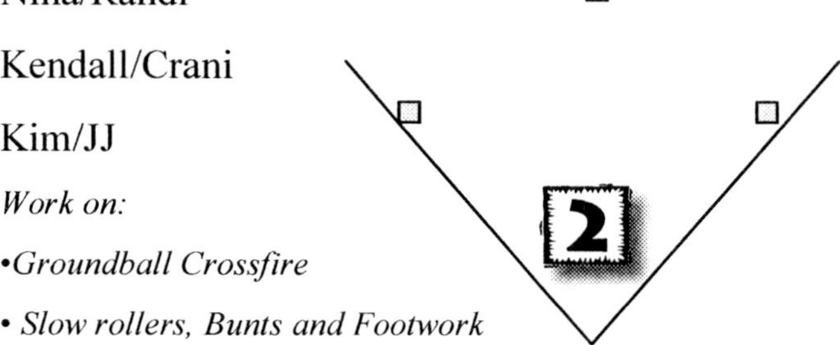

3 *(During last IF group (Kim/JJ) the outfield needs to start warming up their arms)*

4 **2:30 – 3:00**

Outfield: Makes throw to bases with runners, hitters hitting off side-toss. (the pitchers need to warm-up their arms for Bunt Defense)

5 **3:05 - 3:45**

Bunt / Slap Defense – with live pitching and runners.

Work on:

- *Pickoff / steals*
- *Signals from the coach*

6 **3:55 – 4:20** **CONDITIOINING** – Frisbee Football

7 **4:20 – 5:00**

Pitchers work following Frisbee Football:

Des – wants to throw in bullpen

Kaci – wants to throw in bullpen

Klav – wants to throw in bullpen

8 ***WE NEED 3 PLAYERS TO STAY AFTER CONDITIONING TO CATCH THE PITCHERS.***

Defensive Only - Practice 9 Explanation

1 In this 30 minute segment the focus will be on the infielders getting in 30 minutes of defensive work while the outfielders and catchers (who don't also play an infield position) get some extra work hitting in the batting cages (if you have them. If not, then just set up some hitting stations).

2 These 4 outfielders will go down to the batting cages and get in some extra hitting work. This practice shows 2 batting cages, one with a machine (M) and in the other with a Hitting Streak (STREAK). The players feed themselves and make sure they wear helmets. Also in this area are 2 batting T's (T) the players can use as well.

Meanwhile the infielders are put into pairs and 2 coaches work with each pair for 10 minutes. Work on their footwork on bunts (for balance) and their glove work on fielding bunts and slow rollers. The other 2 groups (not being worked on with the coaches) can hit grounders to each other and worked on glove work on groundballs. While this doesn't seem like a lot of time – 30 minutes for the whole infield and 10 minutes per group – it's a great practice and will each player more than enough time of concentrated individual defensive work.

3 During the last infield group of Kim and JJ (names of 2 infielders), the outfielders who had been hitting need to start warming up their arms by playing catch.

4 Outfield – This 30 minute segment is devoted to the outfielders getting work on fielding grounders and flyballs and throwing to bases. Be careful not to have your outfielders throw too much. In order to do this you can have them field one without a throw (just tossing the ball off to the side), and then field one with a throw. The infielders are the hitters for this and also the baserunners and they hit off of side toss from a coach. Meanwhile, the pitchers and catchers are off to the side warming up to pitch for bunt defense.

5 Bunt/Slap Defense – with live pitching and runners - The next 30 minutes are spent going over bunt defense with our infield and getting our pitchers and catchers game ready rotating in quickly. The Outfielders are the ones hitting off of live pitching and alternating at running bases. It works best if you have one hitter stay up for 5 at-bats and the other outfielders as baserunners on the bases. Each at-bat change the bases and the situations for the outfielders. The hitters can either bunt, hit away or slap based on the signals either you or your assistant give them. This is a great time for you to practice your signals.

6 Instead of having them jog and do sprints at the beginning of practice, put conditioning at the end and have them play Frisbee Football for 25 minutes. It's a GREAT game improve conditioning, teamwork and throwing and catching skills.

7 8 In order for the pitchers to complete their workout following conditioning 3 players need to stay after practice and catch for them. Use regular players to catch for your pitchers as often as possible because it not only allows your catcher's to hit during batting practice when their legs were still strong, but also improves your other player's hitting skills by seeing pitches up close behind home plate. (of course they all wear catching gear).

Defensive Only - Practice 10 Diagram

This practice is an actual example of one of the practices I held with a professional team I coached in the Women's Professional Softball League. I've listed it as I originally drew it out to help show you the different ways coaches make out their practice plans. I always drew mine out like this since I'm pretty visual - it helped me know where everyone was going, when they were going there and what equipment we'd need.

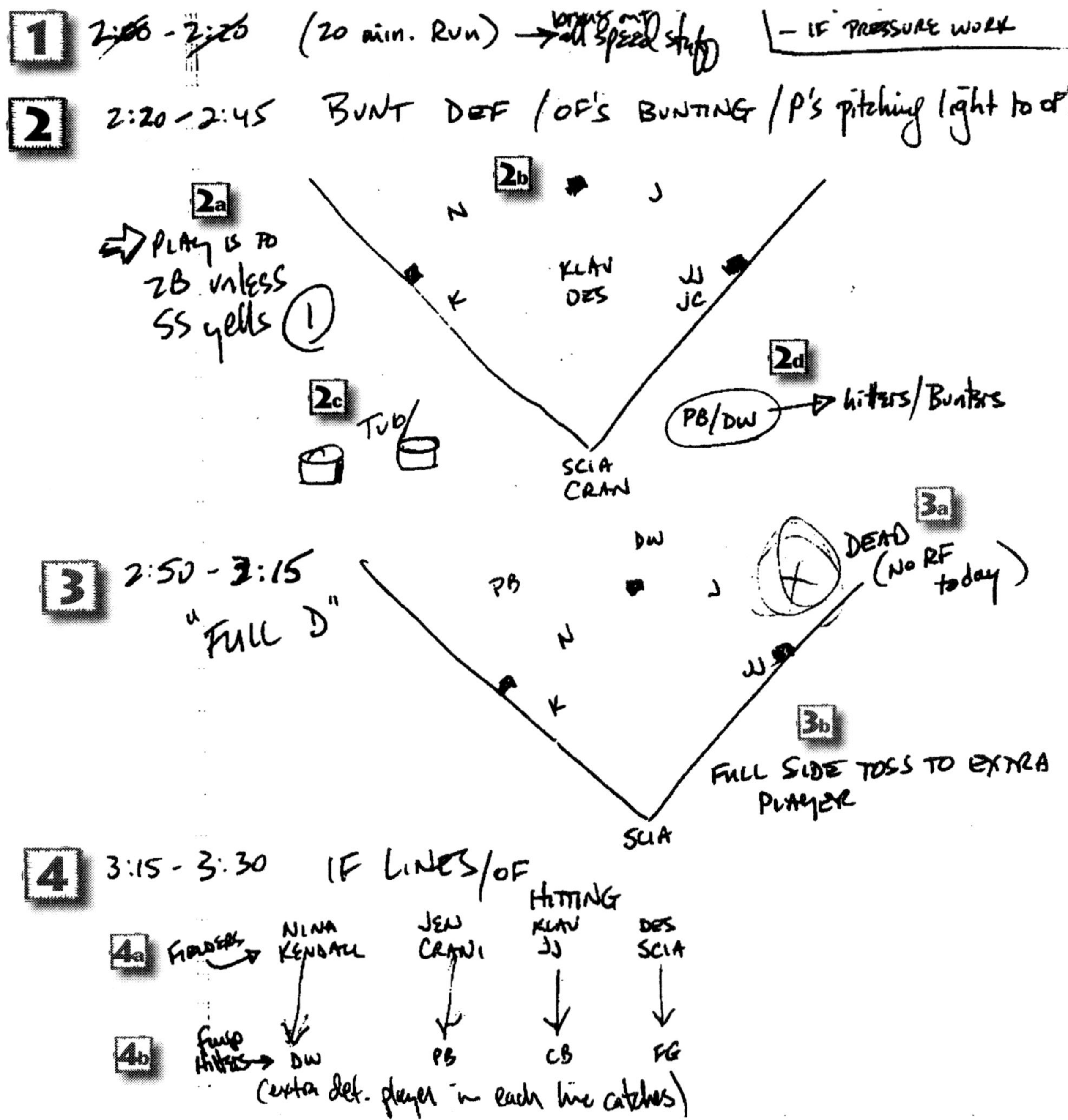

Defensive Only - Practice 10 Explanation

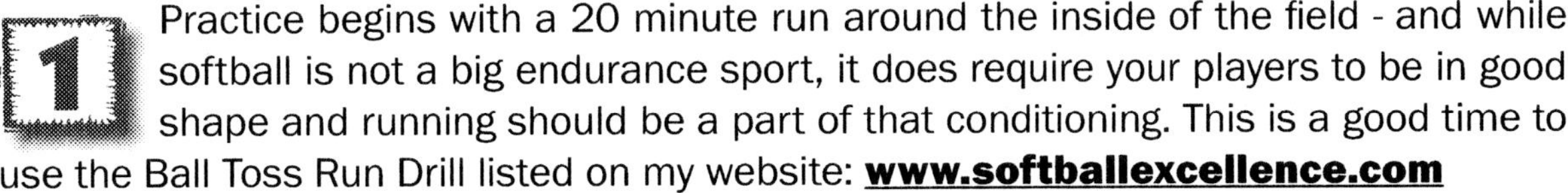

1 Practice begins with a 20 minute run around the inside of the field - and while softball is not a big endurance sport, it does require your players to be in good shape and running should be a part of that conditioning. This is a good time to use the Ball Toss Run Drill listed on my website: **www.softballexcellence.com**

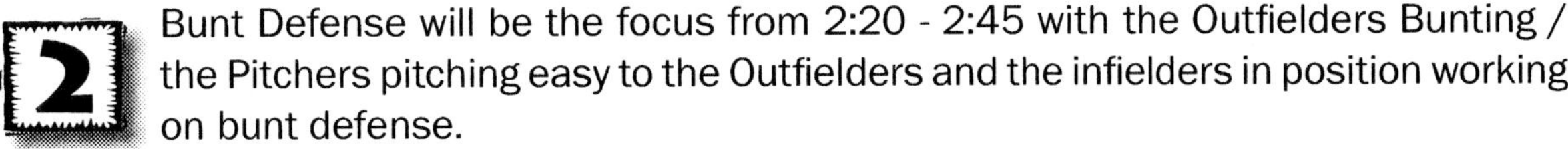

2 Bunt Defense will be the focus from 2:20 - 2:45 with the Outfielders Bunting / the Pitchers pitching easy to the Outfielders and the infielders in position working on bunt defense.

2a This is a reminder that every play is to 2nd base unless the Shortstop yells “ONE”. The Shortstop covers 2nd on the bunt so that’s why she’s the one to yell “ONE” if the throw IS NOT going to 2nd base.

2b I’ve listed by initial what players will start at what infield position. This is a good idea if you have more than one player for each position - it just saves time over you having to figure it out on the spot. Klav and Des are the 2 pitchers that will rotate in gently throwing to the bunters and Scia and Cran are the 2 catchers that will rotate catching and being a part of the bunt defense.

2c 2 big plastic tubs full of balls so we don’t waste time chasing balls during practice.

2d PB and DW are the 2 outfielders (all we had at practice that day) that will alternate between hitting or bunting each time up in order to keep the defense honest

3 From 2:50 – 3:15 working on the “FULL DEFENSE” with all defensive players

3a Since we only had 9 players on this day – including pitchers – we made Rightfield dead, and made the defensive play off of live hits by the extra player (we had an extra 1st baseman that would rotate into defense).

3b We aren’t using a pitcher in this so we have a coach side tossing the ball to our extra player to hit – so the defense can play off of an actual hit ball.

4 We finish practice with the Infielders and Pitchers forming 4 lines (fielders) and the Outfielders and catchers hit groundballs to each line for the 10-in-a-row Drill. The extra fielder in each line catches for the hitter and then rotates with her hitting partner. Each defensive player must field (stop) 10 balls with accurate throws in a row before moving to the next line. Each player must complete each line before finished.

4a The line of fielders (infielders and pitchers) - 4 lines of fielders with only the player in the front of each line working on getting their 10 in a Row. Make the pitchers go through this drill too in order to make good fielding pitchers.

4b The line of fungo hitters and catchers (outfielders and catchers). The switch off hitting grounders to the infielders/pitchers and catching their thrown balls.

Defensive Only - Practice 11 Diagram

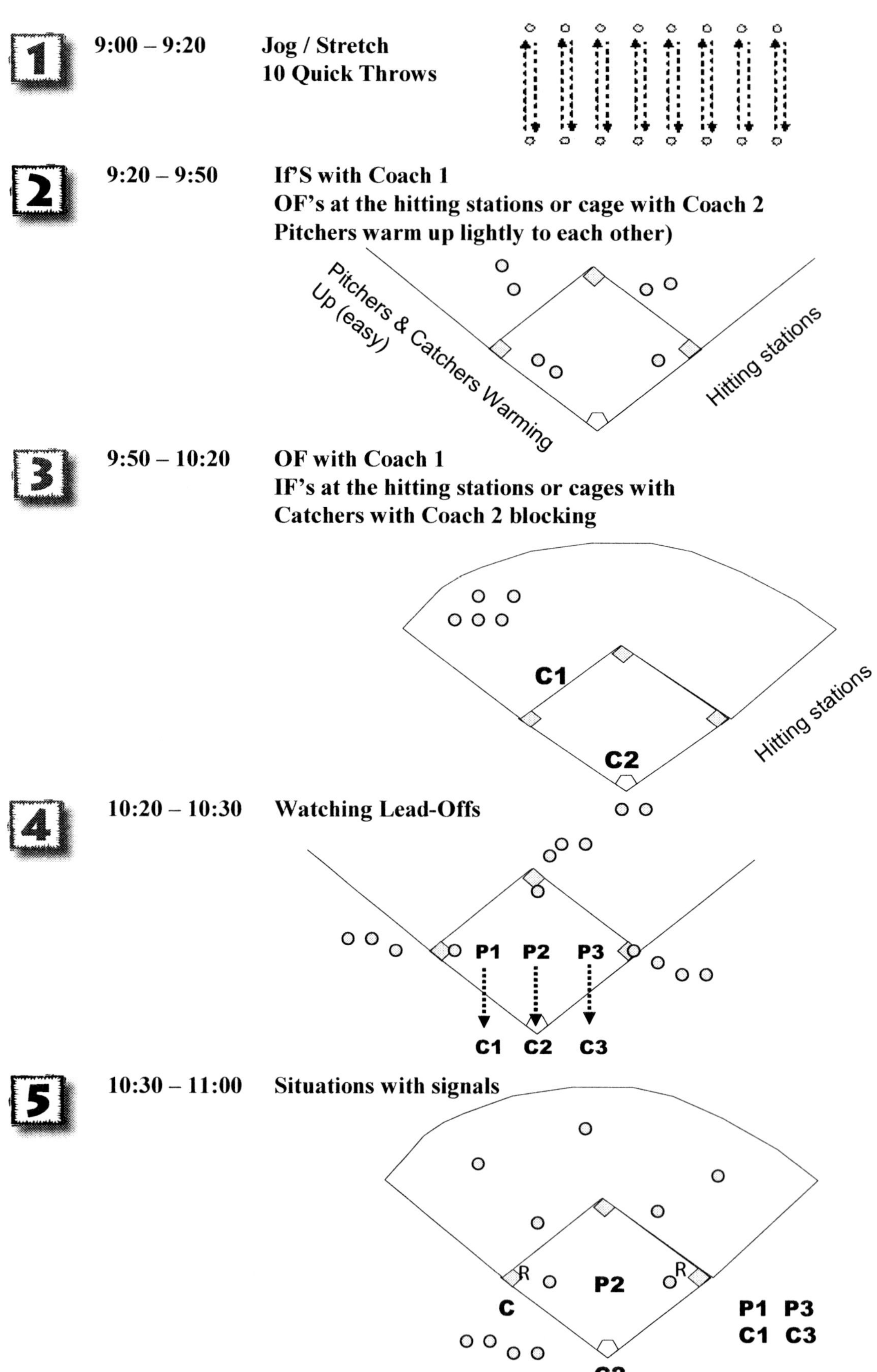

Defensive Only - Practice 11 Explanation

1 **Jog / Stretch** - The first 20 minutes of practice will involve a 15 minute team run followed by 10 Quick Throws – this drill divides the entire team up into pairs, usually the same pairs they're in when they warmup. Each pair has their gloves and a ball. When you say "go" everyone simply has to throw the ball back and forth to their partner 10 times as fast as possible. The first pair to 10 wins. (you can either count "1" each time a partner touches the ball or once down and back is counted as "1".) Just let everyone know before you start the drill how you're going to count before you start.

2 **IF's with Coach 1** - From 9:20 - 9:50, this 30 minute session the main focus will be on infield work. One coach will spend this time with the infielders either focusing on individual fundamentals, infield team defense or a combination of both (depending on the type of work your infielders need at the time of this practice).

The Outfielder's are down the line working on their hitting skills with Coach 2 in either different hitting stations or batting cages if you have them.

Your Pitchers & Catchers are off to side warming up lightly to each other.

3 **Outfielders with Coach 1** - The next defensive session goes from 9:50 to 10:20 and will focus on the outfielders and the catchers. Coach 1 (C1) is with the outfielders working on individual outfield skills like diving, working on balls against the outfield and sideline fences, balls in the sun, going back on balls, or any type of outfield skills. While this is going on Coach 2 (C2) is working with the catchers at home plate on their individual skills like blocking, setting up, throws to 2nd, throws on balls to the backstop or anything else the catchers need work on. The infielders are now in the hitting stations or cages just as the outfielders were in the previous session.

4 **Watch Lead-offs** – Put all of our pitchers on the mound at the same time – stretching them out in a straight line between 1st and 3rd (only one gets the real rubber and the other 2 throw without rubbers) – and have them pitch lightly/easily to your catchers. (If you have more than 3 pitchers then you won't have room for more than 4 at a time so switch them out every-so-often if you have more than 4 pitchers. Also - if you don't have one catcher per pitcher then have your position players work in to catch the pitchers when they aren't working on their leadoffs. They should all wear masks to protect themselves but catching the pitchers will help make them better hitters.

Meanwhile the rest of your players are spread out at 1st, 2nd, and 3rd base (with helmets) and are practicing timing their lead offs and the balance of their landings. They should all try and leave the base AS the ball leaves the pitchers hand (pick one of the 3 pitchers to watch - not all 3).

5 **Situations with signals** - Place your full defense on the field with the extra players hitting off of the pitchers. The pitchers and catchers will work in pairs with only one pair at-a-time pitching they'll still pitch easy but work on their inside and outside targets so they don't get creamed by the hitters. Put runners at either 1st or 2nd or 3rd or mix it up and gave signals to hitters and runners from the 3rd base coaching box. The focus of this drill is TEAM DEFENSE and not offense. After a practice of individual defensive work you are now tying it together in team defensive practice.

Offensive Only Practices

These next 4 sample practices will be Offensive Only practices to help you with those times throughout a season when your defense is fine but your offense is horrible (or else headed that way). Please keep in mind that these Offensive Practice samples are meant to be used occasionally and not every single practice you have.

Offensive Only - Practice 12 Diagram

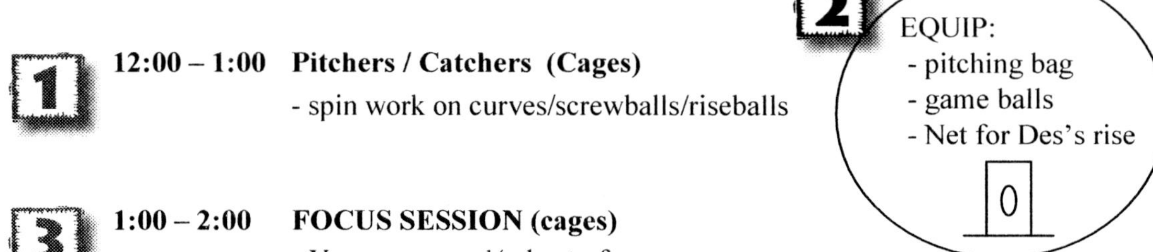

1 **12:00 – 1:00** **Pitchers / Catchers (Cages)**
- spin work on curves/screwballs/riseballs

3 **1:00 – 2:00** **FOCUS SESSION (cages)**
- Your name on ½ sheet of paper
- pick out a piece of paper – put what's awesome about that person

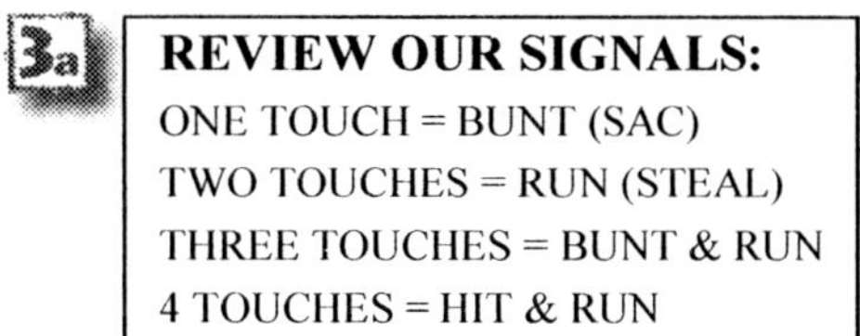
3a **REVIEW OUR SIGNALS:**
ONE TOUCH = BUNT (SAC)
TWO TOUCHES = RUN (STEAL)
THREE TOUCHES = BUNT & RUN
4 TOUCHES = HIT & RUN

3b Talk about runner with GREEN LIGHTS = PB, JB, DW
3-0 Counts / Swinging at pitches / Mistakes / Approach in the Box
- HIT THE BALL vs worrying about me

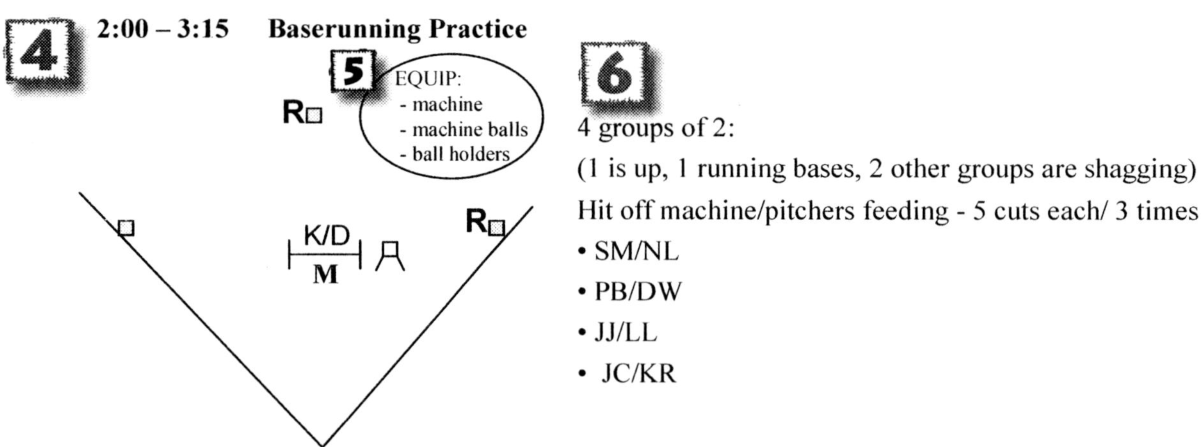

4 **2:00 – 3:15** **Baserunning Practice**

6 4 groups of 2:
(1 is up, 1 running bases, 2 other groups are shagging)
Hit off machine/pitchers feeding - 5 cuts each/ 3 times
- SM/NL
- PB/DW
- JJ/LL
- JC/KR

7 **BASERUNNING RULES**:
- FIND THE BALL!
- If in Air – only tag if you can advance
- All foul balls – TAG
- All fly balls at 3rd base - TAG

Offensive Only - Practice 12 Explanation

1 **Pitchers / Catchers (cages)** - from 12:00 to 1:00 the pitchers will work with the catchers in the batting cage area (or whatever area you have for pitching). They'll work on the spins for the curveballs, riseballs, and screwballs followed by an alternating pitch workout using these 3 pitches. NOTE - your pitchers can practice any of their pitches during this time and not just these 3 pitches.

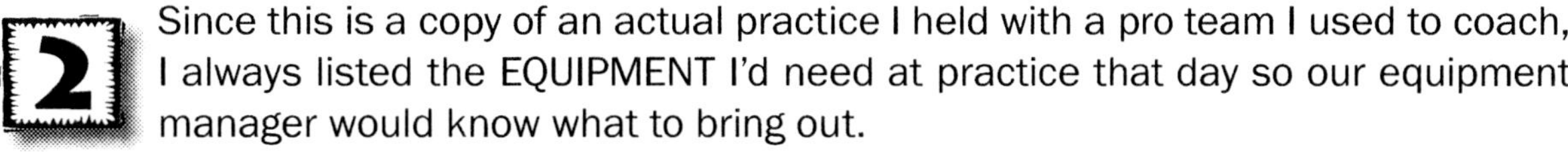

2 Since this is a copy of an actual practice I held with a pro team I used to coach, I always listed the EQUIPMENT I'd need at practice that day so our equipment manager would know what to bring out.

3 We held weekly team building or confidence building sessions that I started calling our "Focus Sessions". During this 60 minute segment from 1:00 - 2:00 we held a Focus Session for 20 minutes, we reviewed our Signals for 20 minutes and we discussed various offensive issues for 20 minutes. This Focus Session (which we held that day in our batting cages) involved every person getting a blank sheet of paper and putting their name on it. Then folding up that paper and putting it into a bucket. Everyone then reached in and grabbed a sheet (other than their own) and simply wrote down 1 - 2 things that they felt were awesome about the person whose name appeared at the top of the sheet they grabbed. They could be anything from "you hit the ball like a rocket" to "you give me confidence the way you cheer"/. Then, fold the paper back up and pick out another person and repeat - do this for 3 people (other than you) and the session is complete. As a coach - you keep these in a bucket and bring out until there is a pretty long list for each person - ten you can share each person's sheet with them whenever they need a confidence boost.

3a We spent the next 20 minutes reviewing our signals and then pointing to different players and telling them to stand up and give the signal for a certain play, or, to have a certain player give a signal and pick another player to say what the signals was.

3b The last 20 minutes we talked with the team about the players that had green lights in regards to stealing bases whenever they wanted to and what that would mean offensively for us. Also what we wanted from them on 3-0 counts, on making mistakes at the plate and in general how we wanted them to focus on hitting the ball hard and NOT on worrying about my reaction to their swing or at-bat.

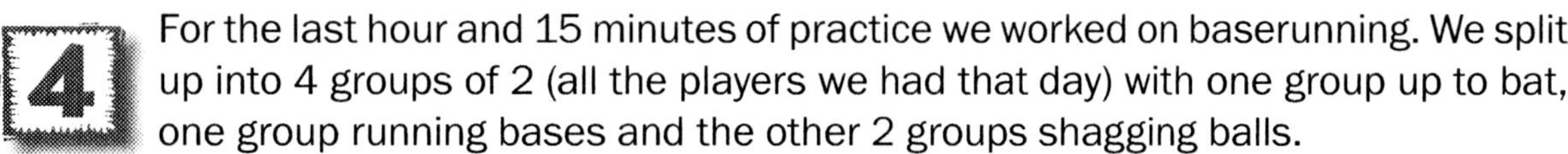

4 For the last hour and 15 minutes of practice we worked on baserunning. We split up into 4 groups of 2 (all the players we had that day) with one group up to bat, one group running bases and the other 2 groups shagging balls.

5 This is a list of the equipment needed for the baserunning session.

6 Here is the list of the 4 groups of 2 players per group. The field layout shows the R's as the group of 2 running the bases, while another group of 2 bats and the remaining 2 groups shag balls on the field. The K/D represent 2 of our pitchers that were standing behind a net and feeding the machine. Players take 5 cuts each off the machine and go through it 3 times before rotating.

7 Since this session of practice was focusing on baserunning, I made sure I had our baserunning rules written down so our runners could work on them with each ball hit!

Offensive Only - Practice 13 Diagram

This practice is designed to provide 10 players, split up in groups of 2 with 60 minutes of intense hitting practice. While this practice only shows 10 players hitting, you can then repeat the same schedule with up to 10 more players during the next hour - while you also hold defensive practice on the field. OR - if you don't have enough people or facilities to do defensive practice while you're also doing this Offensive Practice, then split your team into groups of 3 instead of groups of 2.

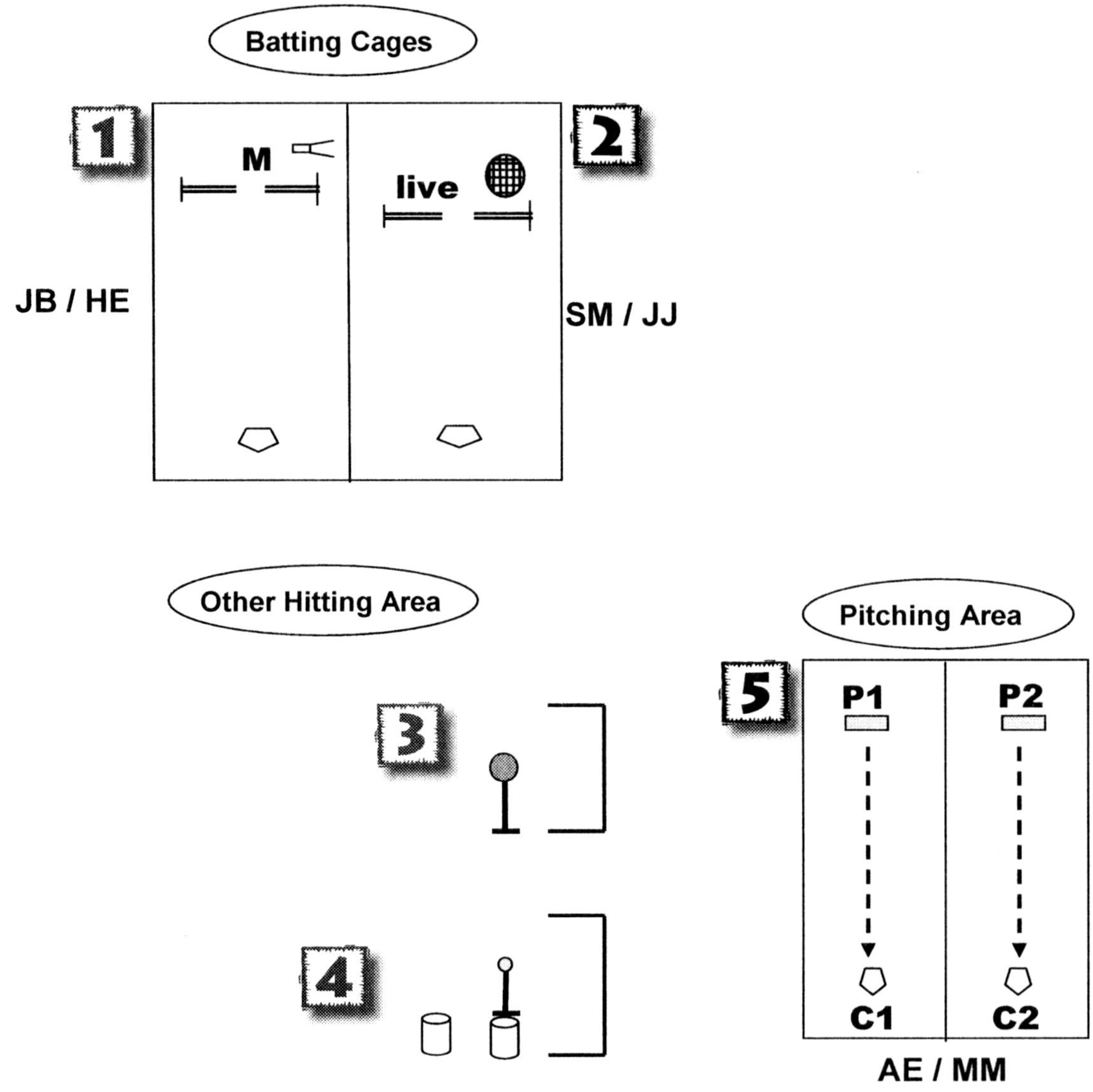

Batting Cages

1 M

2 live

JB / HE

SM / JJ

Other Hitting Area

Pitching Area

3

4

5 P1 P2

C1 C2

AE / MM

6

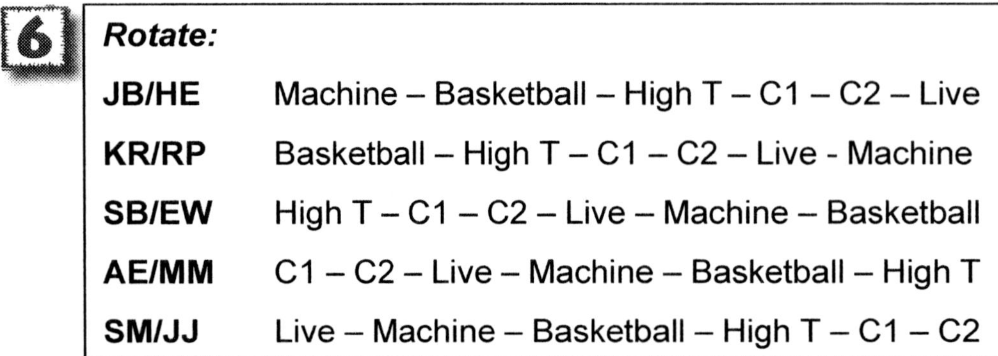

Rotate:

JB/HE	Machine – Basketball – High T – C1 – C2 – Live
KR/RP	Basketball – High T – C1 – C2 – Live - Machine
SB/EW	High T – C1 – C2 – Live – Machine – Basketball
AE/MM	C1 – C2 – Live – Machine – Basketball – High T
SM/JJ	Live – Machine – Basketball – High T – C1 – C2

Offensive Only - Practice 13 Explanation

BATTING – HITTING PAIRS (Rotate after 20 minutes) – This practice is designed to provide your players with 60 minutes of hitting work via 6 different hitting stations. Your team will be split up into pairs and each pair assigned one of 6 stations. 10 minutes per station per pair or 5 minutes per player per station, and rotate after 10 minutes.

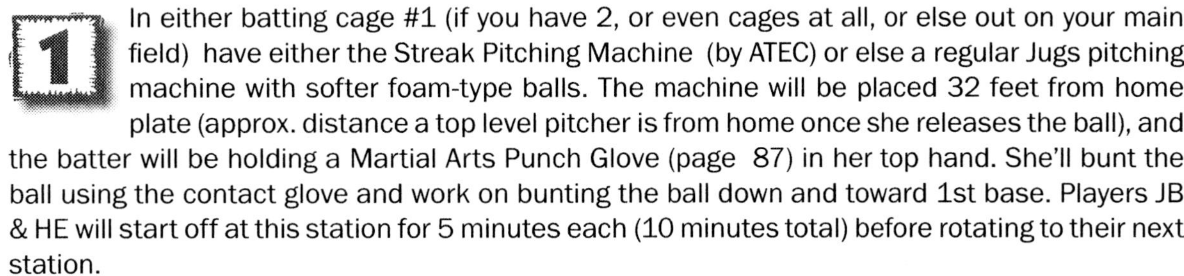

1 In either batting cage #1 (if you have 2, or even cages at all, or else out on your main field) have either the Streak Pitching Machine (by ATEC) or else a regular Jugs pitching machine with softer foam-type balls. The machine will be placed 32 feet from home plate (approx. distance a top level pitcher is from home once she releases the ball), and the batter will be holding a Martial Arts Punch Glove (page 87) in her top hand. She'll bunt the ball using the contact glove and work on bunting the ball down and toward 1st base. Players JB & HE will start off at this station for 5 minutes each (10 minutes total) before rotating to their next station.

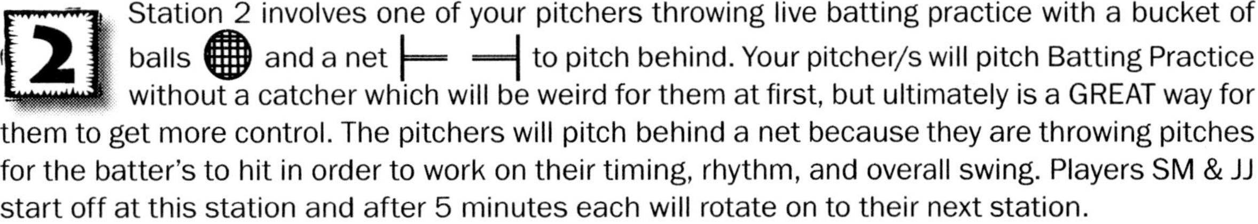

2 Station 2 involves one of your pitchers throwing live batting practice with a bucket of balls and a net to pitch behind. Your pitcher/s will pitch Batting Practice without a catcher which will be weird for them at first, but ultimately is a GREAT way for them to get more control. The pitchers will pitch behind a net because they are throwing pitches for the batter's to hit in order to work on their timing, rhythm, and overall swing. Players SM & JJ start off at this station and after 5 minutes each will rotate on to their next station.

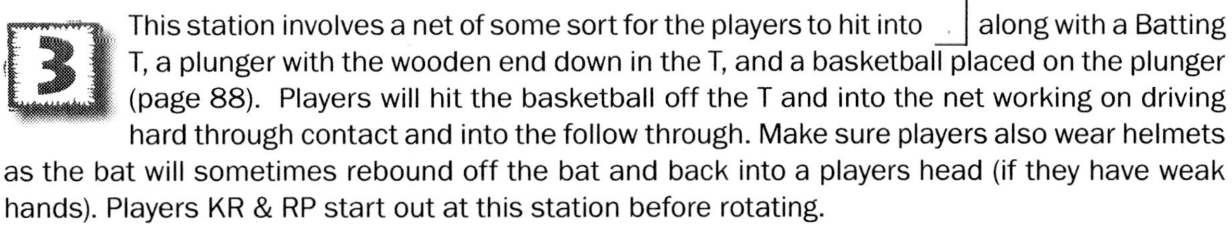

3 This station involves a net of some sort for the players to hit into along with a Batting T, a plunger with the wooden end down in the T, and a basketball placed on the plunger (page 88). Players will hit the basketball off the T and into the net working on driving hard through contact and into the follow through. Make sure players also wear helmets as the bat will sometimes rebound off the bat and back into a players head (if they have weak hands). Players KR & RP start out at this station before rotating.

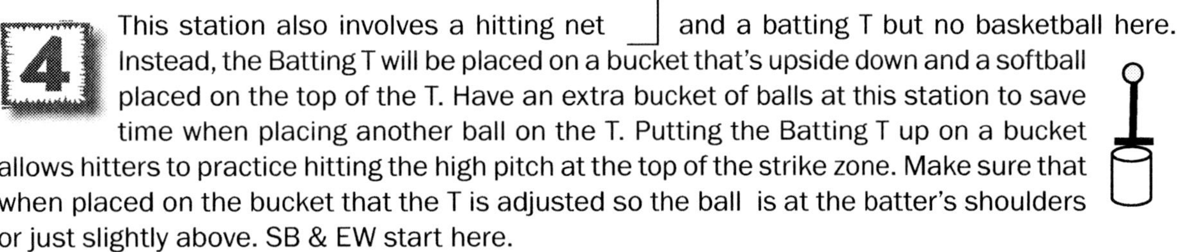

4 This station also involves a hitting net and a batting T but no basketball here. Instead, the Batting T will be placed on a bucket that's upside down and a softball placed on the top of the T. Have an extra bucket of balls at this station to save time when placing another ball on the T. Putting the Batting T up on a bucket allows hitters to practice hitting the high pitch at the top of the strike zone. Make sure that when placed on the bucket that the T is adjusted so the ball is at the batter's shoulders or just slightly above. SB & EW start here.

5 This station is actually 2 identical stations - each one involves a pitcher (P1 or P2) pitching their actual practice workout to catchers that are really the hitters in catching gear (C1 and C2). This might seem weird or even unsafe at first, but trust me, it's not only safe (since they're both wearing all the catching gear) but it's also a fantastic way to improve your hitters by giving them the opportunity to see pitch after pitch come in and really concentrate on catching it. AE and MM start off catching in these two stations. Catchers will switch after 5 minutes and catch the other pitcher to get more experience seeing another pitcher. The pitchers are getting their actual practice workout in while the real catchers are able to go through hitting practice with fresh legs.

6 This is the rotation list so you can always help your players figure out where they're supposed to go next, as you KNOW that someone's going to ask you!

Remember - 10 minutes per group per station or 5 minutes per player per station and then rotate. Total of 60 minutes for all 6 stations.

Offensive Only - Practice 14 Diagram

3:30 – 4:30 **Hitting Stations / Pitchers & Catchers in Bullpen (10 minutes per station)**

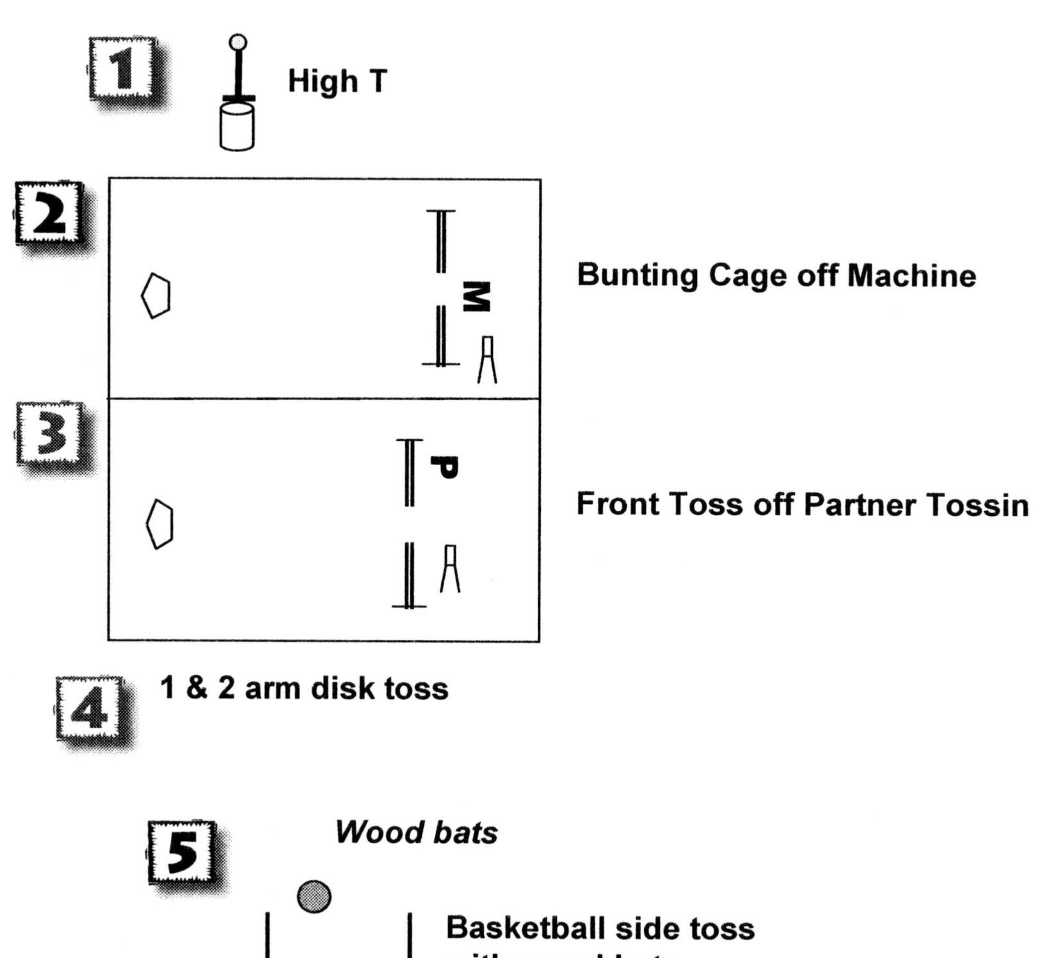

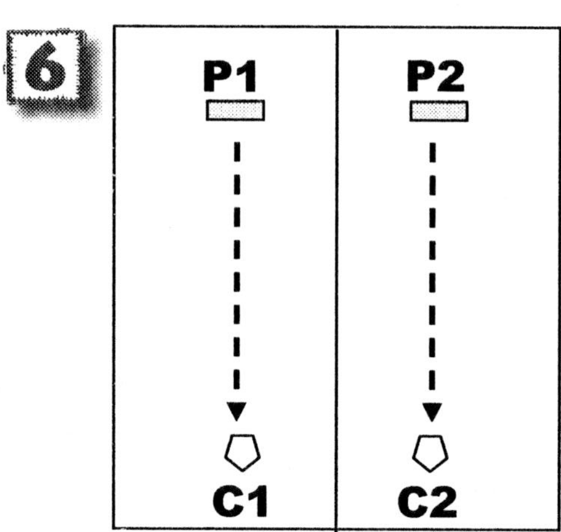

Offensive Only - Practice 14 Explanation

This is a practice that is very similar to the previous practice example - #13. This Offensive Practice also lasts 60 minutes and is based on station work of differing types. Your team will be divided into pairs or groups of 4 if you have a lot of players with each group staying 10 minutes at each station.

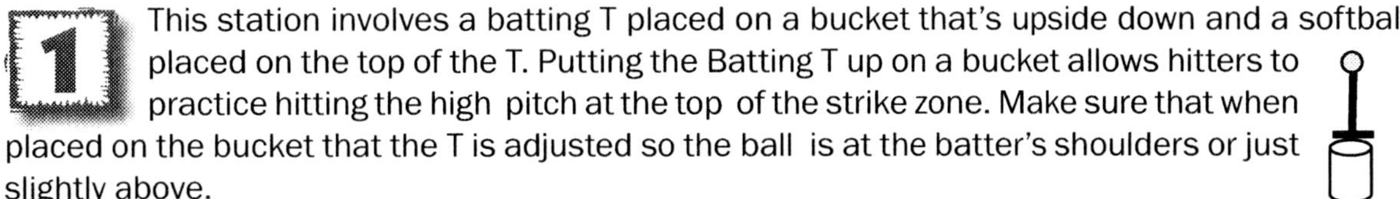

1 This station involves a batting T placed on a bucket that's upside down and a softball placed on the top of the T. Putting the Batting T up on a bucket allows hitters to practice hitting the high pitch at the top of the strike zone. Make sure that when placed on the bucket that the T is adjusted so the ball is at the batter's shoulders or just slightly above.

2 Station 2 involves a pitching machine (M) and a ballbasket (optional) to hold a lot of balls and make it easier for the person feeding the machine. The feeder will make sure the batter is ready each time before feeding the machine, and the batter will have a helmet on and a bat and is working on bunting balls - alternating them as follows: left, middle, right, middle, left and repeating. The machine and person feeding the machine are behind a protective screen.

3 Station 3 involves a player (P) and a ballbasket (optional) to hold a lot of balls and make it easier for the person tossing. The tosser will front toss to her partner who is working on hitting away. The tosser will be about 20 feet in front of the hitter and will be tossing from behind a protective screen and waiting each time for the hitter to get ready. The hitter is working on hitting the ball HARD to left, middle, right, middle, left, etc...

4 At this station the partners will work with the hitting disks on the "One Arm" and "Two Arm Disk Toss Drills". These drills are listed on my site: **www.softballexcellence.com** and are great for helping players learn the correct hand path to the ball for the greatest amount of power and field coverage. This station is set up beside one of the batting cages or else facing a fence as the disks can travel pretty far and just need to go out about 8-10 feet.

5 This station involves a basketball (more than one if you have them), a screen to hit into, a wood bat light enough for your players to swing (you can get one at your sporting goods store) and a helmet for each player. The batter will have her helmet on and will get a basketball side tossed to her from her partner and hit the basketball as hard as possible into the net. Using wood bats helps the players work on using their body and hands for the power source instead of relying on the technology of the bat. And the basketball requires the players to hit to - and through - the contact zone with a lot of power. Again, have them wear their helmets in case their bat rebounds off the basketball and back into their head.

6 This station is actually 2 identical stations - each one involves a pitcher (P1 or P2) pitching their actual practice workout to catchers that are really the hitters in catching gear (C1 and C2). This might seem weird or even unsafe at first, but trust me, it's not only safe (since they're both wearing all the catching gear) but it's also a fantastic way to improve your hitters by giving them the opportunity to see pitch after pitch come in and really concentrate on catching it. AE and MM start off catching in these two stations. Catchers will switch after 5 minutes and catch the other pitcher to get more experience seeing another pitcher. The pitchers are getting their actual practice workout in while the real catchers are able to go through hitting practice with fresh legs.

Offensive Only - Practice 15 Diagram

1 **OBJECTIVES:**
- Get them to swing
- Batting practice off live
- Pitchers work on all pitches with catchers

2 6:00 – 6:25 Conditioning

3 6:25 – 7:00 P/C warmup and IF/OF do 10-in-a-row

4 7:00 – 8:30 Live BP with P/C's

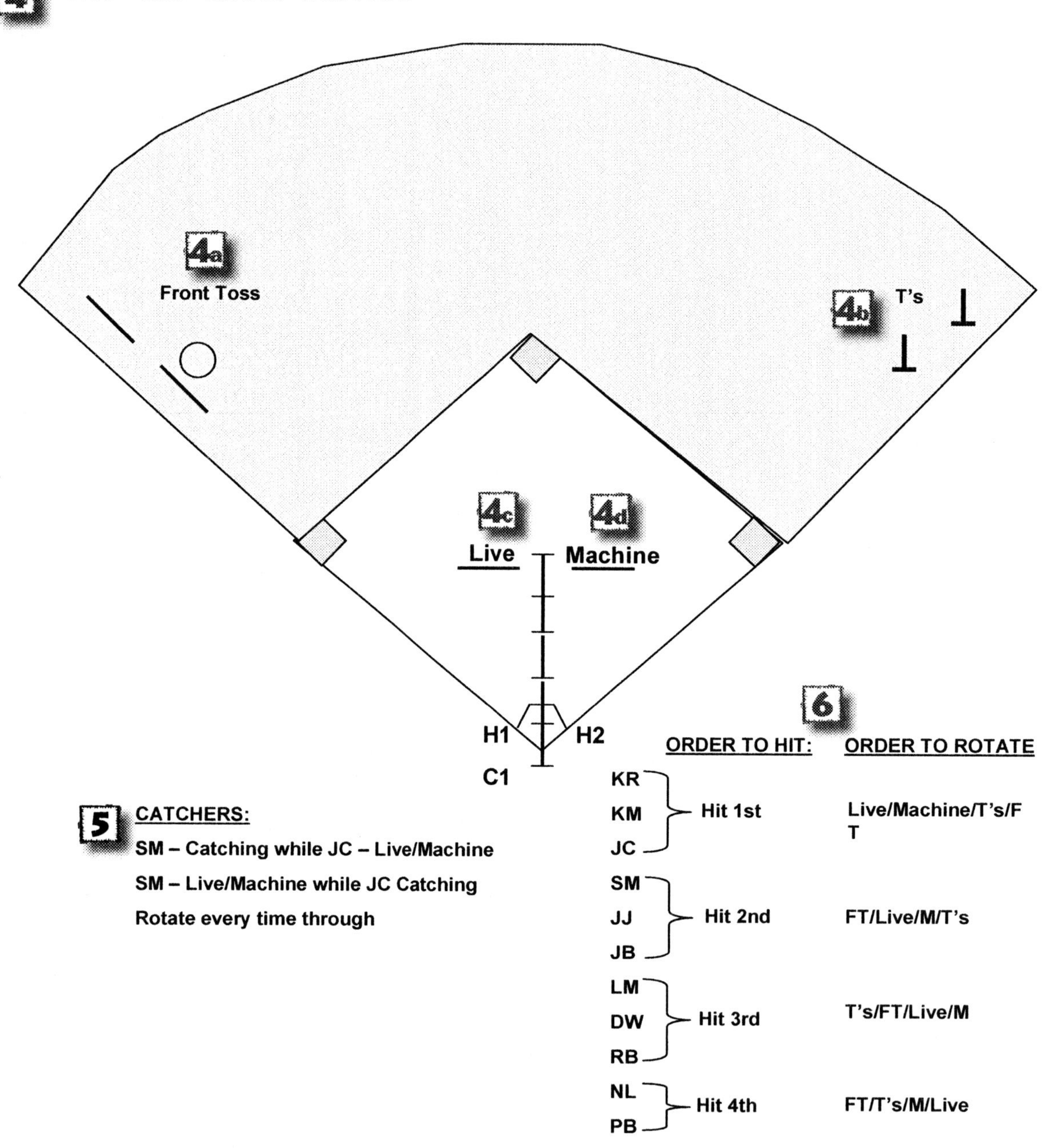

Offensive Only - Practice 15 Explanation

These were the things we were trying to work on for this practice so I listed them at the top to remind both myself and my players. As you can see, they are pretty simple objectives, nothing fancy. And yet this practice was for a professional team. You can never practice the basics enough!

From 6:00 to 6:25 we worked on conditioning. If you're going to use this practice for your team then 25 minutes worth of conditioning and/or speed work that I have listed either elsewhere in this book or else on my website at: **www.softballexcellence.com**.

From 6:25 to 7:00 the Pitchers and Catchers warmup (P/C warmup) while the Infield and Outfielders (IF/OF) do the 10-in-a-Row Drill (explained on page 77).

This is the meat of this practice - Live Batting Practice (BP) using our own Pitchers and Catchers (P/C's), but doing so in a way that not only helps the hitters but helps the pitchers and catchers as well. I know that many coaches don't ever let their pitchers pitch batting practice - I'm not one of those coaches. I think that pitchers can benefit a ton from practicing against hitters instead of just facing them in games, and if you can structure your practice to have your pitchers throwing against your hitters it not only makes them both better, but makes practice go faster as well. This Batting Practice involves a few different stations allowing players a lot of opportunity to work on their swings.

This is a Front Toss station with the tosser standing behind a protective nets, with a bucket of balls, and front toss the ball to the hitters. The tosser needs to be about 5-6 feet infront of the hitter who in this case is hitting the tossed balls out into the outfield.

This station involves 2 Batting T's located way done the right field fence line (or lese someplace out of the way of the balls being hit). The hitters work on hitting off one T set for an outside pitch and the other T set on a bucket for hitting a high pitch.

Now we move to the infield (which is where we set up this particular type of batting practice) but you could do this with Live out on the field and the Machine portion in a batting cage. Anyway, we split the actual pitching rubber down the middle with protective nets (6 total with 4 nets placed end-to-end to split the field in half and then one net in front of the live pitchers and one in front of the machine) and placed another protective net in front of where our pitchers would pitch batting practice. We also used a catcher since our pitchers were using this as pitching practice, and we used a throw-down home plate as well.

On the LIVE side of the protective nets our pitchers would rotate throwing at-bats to 3-4 hitters (only one pitcher at-a-time would actually be out on the field pitching, the others would be over near or even in the dugout). You can see an H1 in the live hitting side of the field - this indicates that one of the 2 hitting partners is hitting in the live side, while her partner (H2) is in hitting in the Machine side. They'll then switch after 5 pitches and do so for a total of 20 pitches (NOT 20 swings), and then rotate as a pair on to another station.

This side of the protective screens is where the machine pitching takes place. The machine is set on a speed that allows the hitters to get some good swings in while making contact and feeling confident in their ability to hit. Either a coach or else one of the pitchers not currently throwing live can feed the pitching machine.

This was how our catcher's would rotate between either catching the live hitting session or else hitting in both the live and machine sessions.

To help me keep track of how everyone rotated I divided the team up into their 3 person groups (with one exceptions which only had 2 players) and then listed what order they hit in and how they each rotated to every station.

Combined Practices

The last 5 sample practices are practices that Cover both offense and defense.

Combined Practices - Practice 16 Diagram

1 9:00 – 9:15 **WARM UP** (jog/stretch/jump rope/swings/sprints/throwing)

2 9:15 – 9:30 **FUNGO WARMUP** **OF's and C's hit groundballs to IF's and P's.**

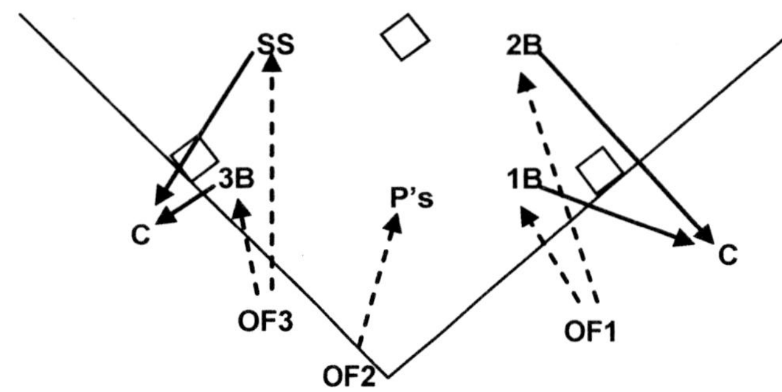

3 9:30 – 9:45 **BUNT DEFENSE** **OF's / P's - Run** **OF's / IF's – Hit / Bunt**

NL RB

KR / KM JC / JJ

JC / SM

4 9:45 – 10:15 **RUNDOWNS / 1st & 3rd's**
(P's and C's warmup for live batting next)

5 10:15 – 11:00 **BATTING PRACTICE**

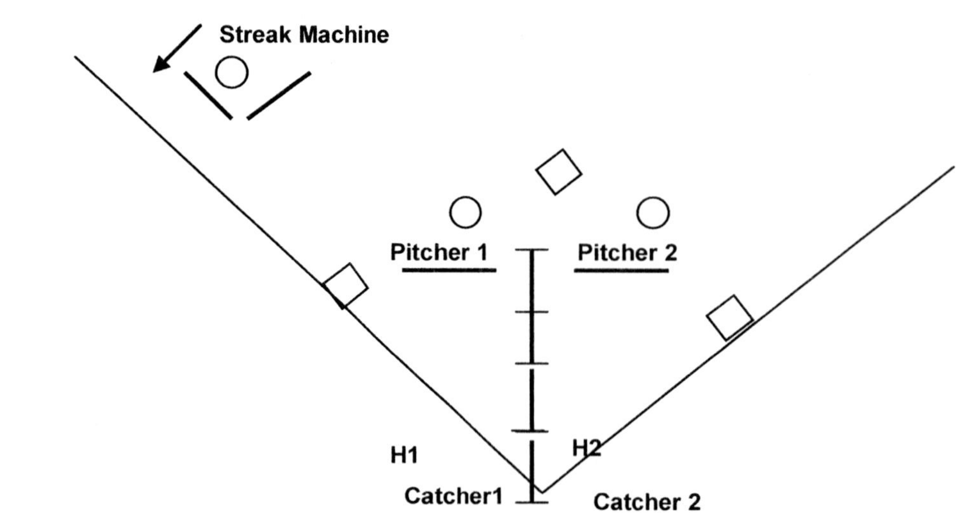

Combined Practices - Practice 16 Explanation

Practice starts with 15 minutes of warmups that involve a jog, some sprints or jump rope, followed by some dry swings with bats and then throwing.

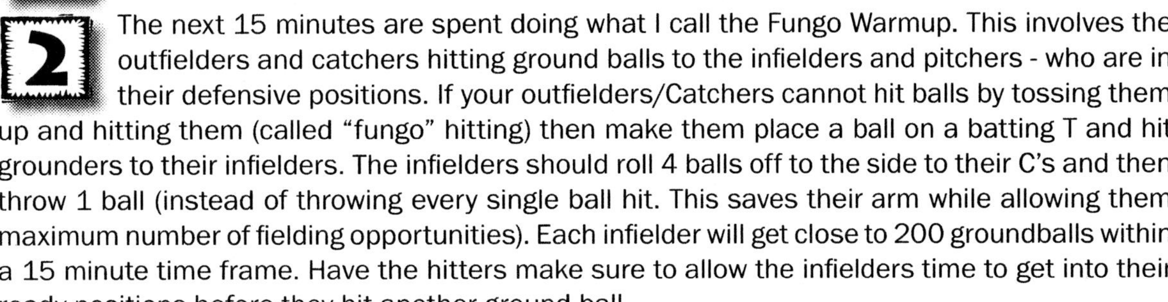

The next 15 minutes are spent doing what I call the Fungo Warmup. This involves the outfielders and catchers hitting ground balls to the infielders and pitchers - who are in their defensive positions. If your outfielders/Catchers cannot hit balls by tossing them up and hitting them (called "fungo" hitting) then make them place a ball on a batting T and hit grounders to their infielders. The infielders should roll 4 balls off to the side to their C's and then throw 1 ball (instead of throwing every single ball hit. This saves their arm while allowing them maximum number of fielding opportunities). Each infielder will get close to 200 groundballs within a 15 minute time frame. Have the hitters make sure to allow the infielders time to get into their ready positions before they hit another ground ball.

In looking at the diagram of the Fungo Warmup, it goes like this: Outfielder 3 alternates hitting groundballs to the 3rd baseman and Shortstop who each roll and throw balls back to their catcher located over near 3rd base. Outfielder 2 hits grounders to the pitchers who are all lined up at the pitchers mound. One pitcher at-a-time fields the groundball and rolls it off back toward homeplate. Outfielder 1 alternates grounders between the 1st and 2nd basemen who roll and throw their balls to their catcher located off the field near 1st base. NOTE: Each hitter should have a bucket of at least 20 balls near them so that less time is spent collecting balls and more time spent hitting and fielding balls.

3 15 minutes of Bunt Defense follows the Fungo Warmup with the infielders in their positions on the field (including catchers) and using the outfielders and pitchers (with helmets on) to bunt or slap, and run. A Pitcher can be in position on defense and simply toss a ball for the batter to bunt or else you can have your pitchers throwing hard and use this as an actual bunting practice. Make sure you also have a runner on 1st (with a helmet) to work on making plays at 2nd as well as to 1st.

The next 30 minutes can be spent with the infielders and outfielders practicing rundowns and then working on 1st and 3rds. Some of the players will have helmets on and will serve as runners for both rundowns and 1st and 3rds. While this is going on the Pitcher's and Catchers are off to the side warming up for throwing live batting practice to follow.

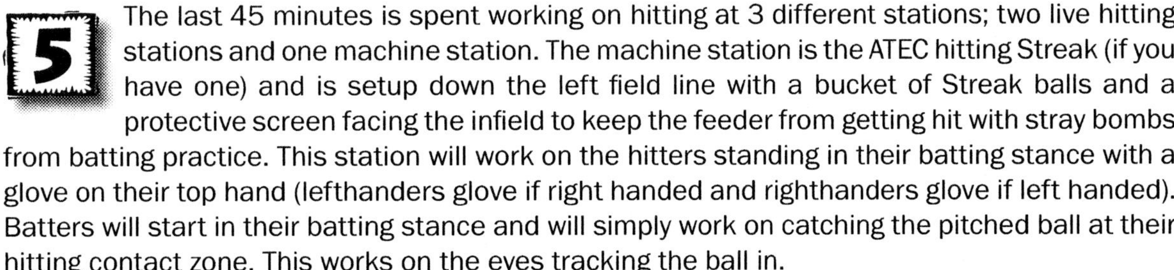

The last 45 minutes is spent working on hitting at 3 different stations; two live hitting stations and one machine station. The machine station is the ATEC hitting Streak (if you have one) and is setup down the left field line with a bucket of Streak balls and a protective screen facing the infield to keep the feeder from getting hit with stray bombs from batting practice. This station will work on the hitters standing in their batting stance with a glove on their top hand (lefthanders glove if right handed and righthanders glove if left handed). Batters will start in their batting stance and will simply work on catching the pitched ball at their hitting contact zone. This works on the eyes tracking the ball in.

The other 2 stations involve splitting the plate in half with protective screens and bringing them out to the pitching mound. This allows you to hold two hitting practices at once on your field (or else use a batting cage if you have one and your infield) - make sure to also put protective screens infront of both pitchers. Each pitcher has a catcher and is working on something very specific: Pitcher 1 is working on an Up pitch and a Down pitch (their choice for each) and pitcher 2 is working on a fast pitch (their choice) and a changeup. Hitters get 5 pitches per station twice through and then rotate.

Combined Practices - Practice 17 Diagram

1 9:30 - 9:50 **Conditioning**

2 9:50 – 10:30 **Bunt Defense and Slap Defense**

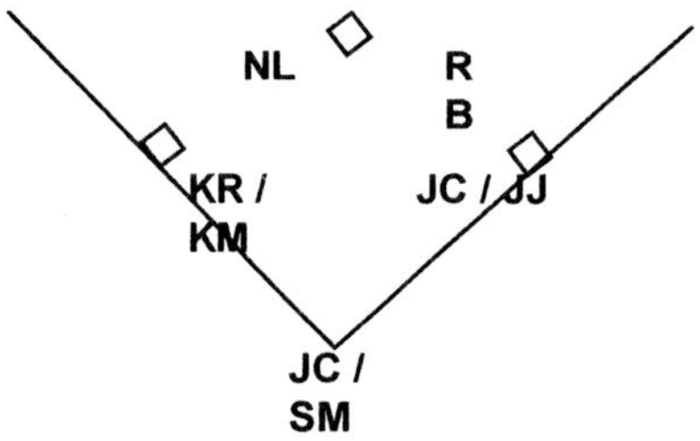

NL
R
B
KR /
KM
JC / JJ
JC /
SM

3 10:30 – 10:50 **Rundown Word and 1st & 3rd's**

4 10:50 – 11:05 **Crossfire (IF/OF Grounders/flys)**

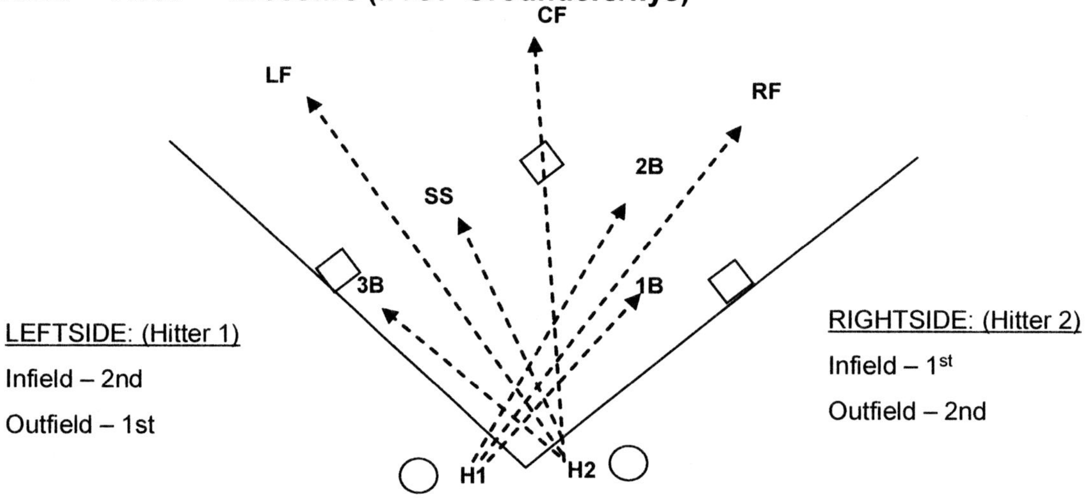

CF
LF
RF
SS
2B
3B
1B
H1
H2
LEFTSIDE: (Hitter 1)
Infield – 2nd
Outfield – 1st
RIGHTSIDE: (Hitter 2)
Infield – 1st
Outfield – 2nd

5 11:05 – 12:05 **Batting Practice**

Karate Gloves
Bunting off
Streak Machine
Machine
Hitting
M
S
2 players front toss to 2 hitters
H1
H2

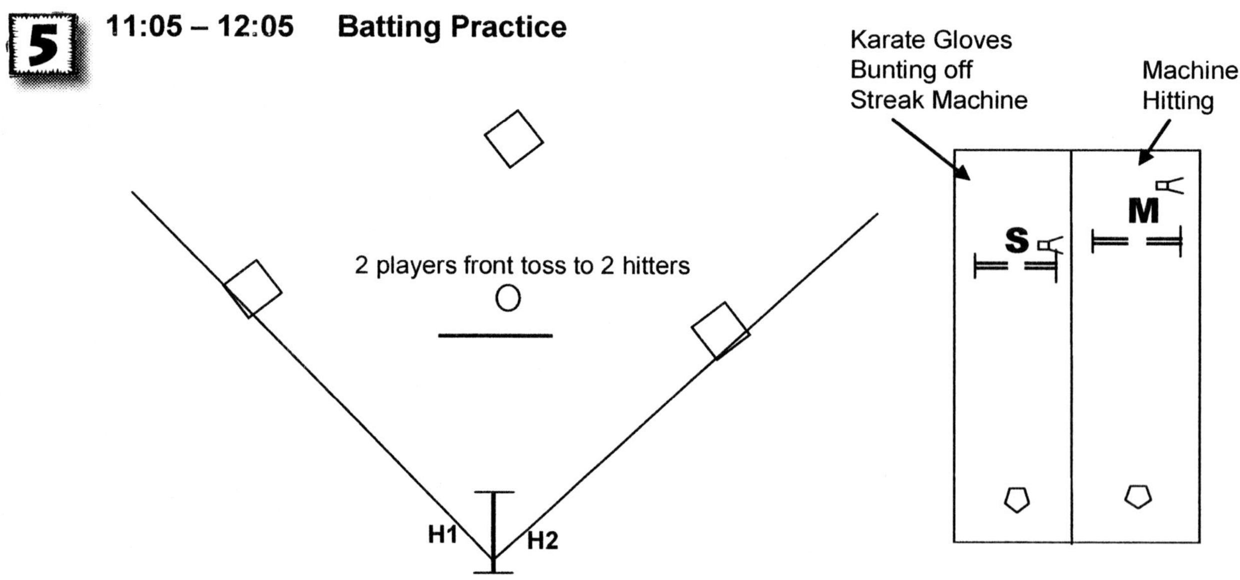

Combined Practices - Practice 17 Explanation

Practice starts with 20 minutes of conditioning - your choice.

The next 40 minutes are spent on Bunt Defense and Slap Defense either 20 minutes on each defense or else 40 minutes total with the hitters either bunting or slapping. Make sure this defense is practiced first without hitters and runners and then add both hitters and baserunners.

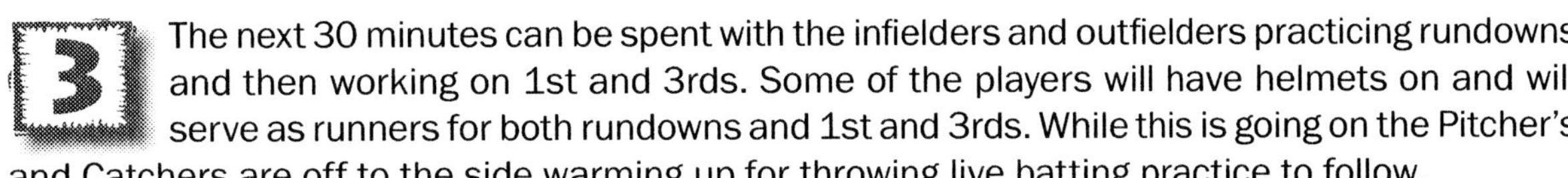

The next 30 minutes can be spent with the infielders and outfielders practicing rundowns and then working on 1st and 3rds. Some of the players will have helmets on and will serve as runners for both rundowns and 1st and 3rds. While this is going on the Pitcher's and Catchers are off to the side warming up for throwing live batting practice to follow.

The 15 minutes from 10:50 to 11:05 involves doing a defensive drill called crossfire. This is a great way to help your players gets tons of groundball and flyball fieding opportunities within a pretty short amount of time. Put your players out in their defensive positions with any alternates off to the side of the field so they don't get hit. They can fill in whenever their posision is being hit to and then move off the infield after that.

There are 2 hitters for this drill - Hitter 1 hits to the right side of the field (2B, 1B and RF) and Hitter 2 hits to the left side of the field (3B, SS, LF and CF). Each hitter has a tub full of balls, a bat and someone to toss them balls if possible. When Hitter 1 is hitting groundballs to the right side infielders - 1B and 2B (no throws, just roll the balls off to the side of the field) Hitter 2 is hitting flyballs to the left side outfielders - LF and CF. Hitters alternate between their 2 fielders and continue hitting to only these players for about 25 balls. After 25 balls are hit, stop and collect all balls back ino the tubs, and then Hitter 1 hits fly balls to the right side outfielder - RF, while Hitter 2 hits groundballs to the left side infielders - 3B, SS. The players not having balls hit to them can just relax until it's their turn again. Do this 2-3 times through or as many times as you can in 15 minutes.

Not having your players throw the balls after they field them allows them to get in so much more defensive practice without adding all that stress to their arm by making that number of throws. This is great to at the start of the year when their arms are still getting strong as well as toward the end of the year when their arms are wearing out.

The last hour will be spent on Batting Practice in 2 different stations; the cages and front toss on the field. If you don't have cages you can do these same things in one of your outfield corners and off to the side of your field.

The cages will involve two different stations - one is a machine with a protective screen to allow your players the chance to get some good, solid cuts in. And the other station is the Streak machine (if you have it) or a pitcher throwing to hitters that, instead of using bats are using the karate gloves on their top hand to work on their bunting. (page 87).

The front toss area involves two hitters seperated by a protective screen and two tossers in front of them behind a protective screen. The tossers are working on inside and outside tosses.

Half your team starts in the cage area (half of them at one station and half at the other) while the other half starts at the front toss stations (half at one and half at the other). Each group stays at each station for 15 minutes and then rotates to the next station. Everyone should have multiple reps within the 15 minutes.

Combined Practices - Practice 18 Diagram

1 9:00 – 9:45 **CONDITIONING** (Cones/Bats/Medicine Balls/Therabands)

2 9:45 – 10:15 **10-IN-A-ROW AT POSITIONS** **OF's and C's hit groundballs**

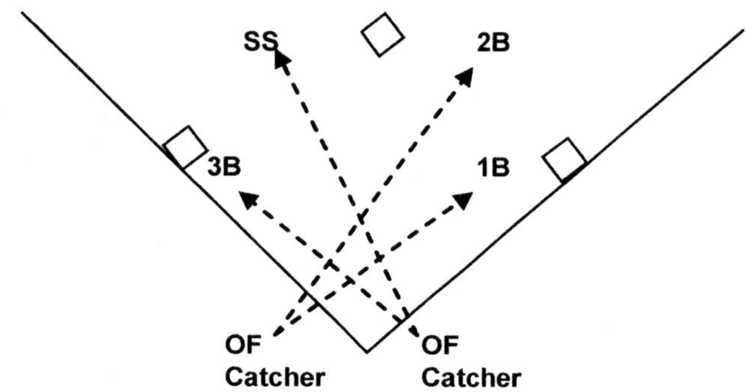

3 10:15 – 10:40 **INFIELD WITH ASST.** **P'S & C's Warm up (one pitch + fastball)**

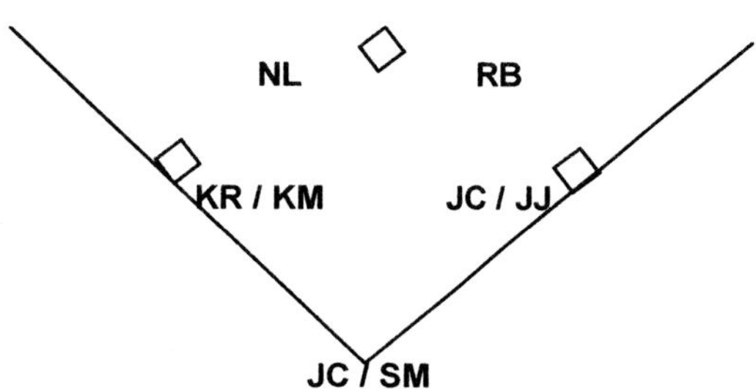

4 10:45 – 11:30 **BATTING PRACTICE**

GOAL – To DRIVE one of 1st 2 pitches!!

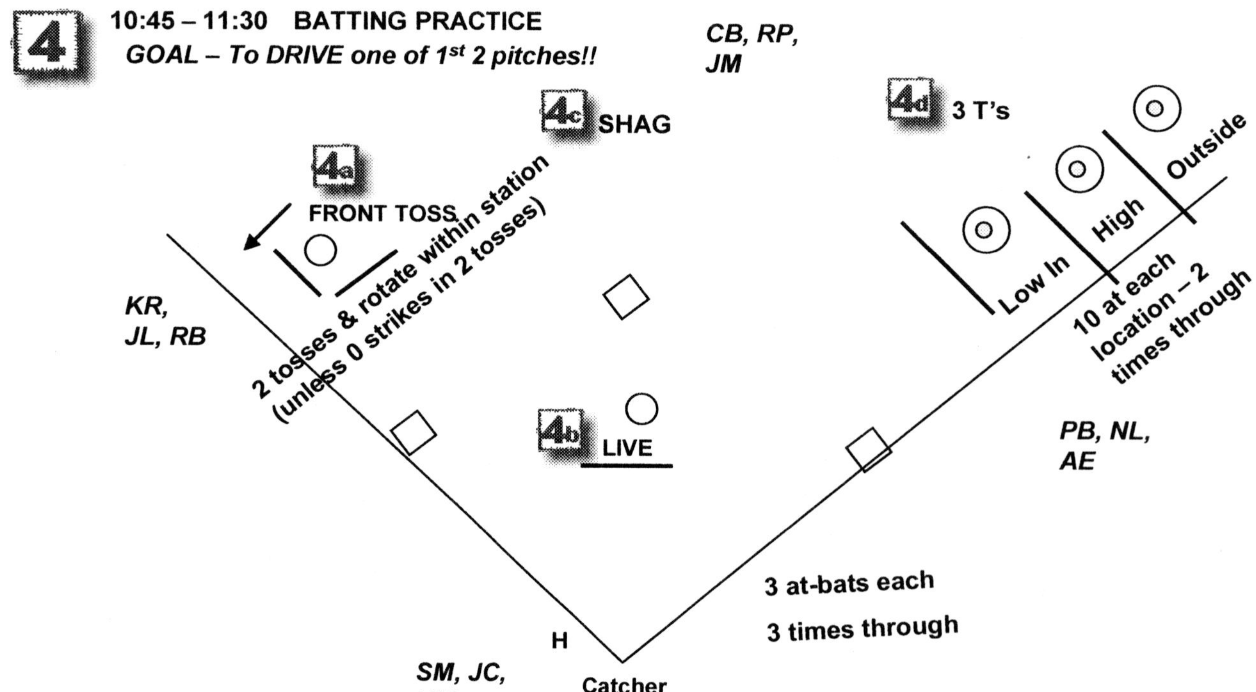

Combined Practices - Practice 18 Explanation

This conditioning session lasts for 45 minutes and focuses on strenght and conditioning. Use the cones for speed and agility training, do wipers with the bats for hand and arm strenght training, the medicine balls for stomach strenghtening and the therabands for strenghtening the small muscles within the shoulder complex.

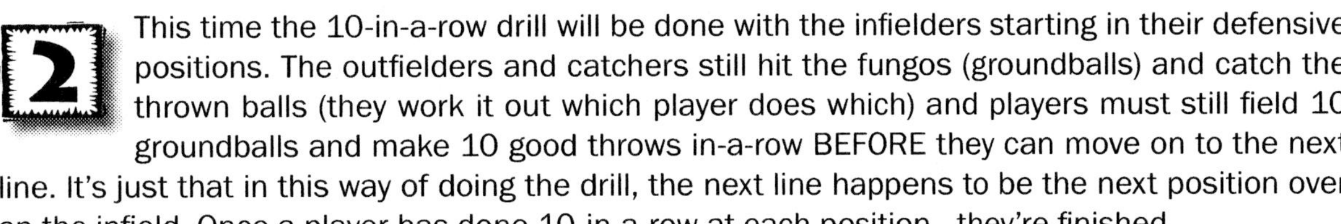

2 This time the 10-in-a-row drill will be done with the infielders starting in their defensive positions. The outfielders and catchers still hit the fungos (groundballs) and catch the thrown balls (they work it out which player does which) and players must still field 10 groundballs and make 10 good throws in-a-row BEFORE they can move on to the next line. It's just that in this way of doing the drill, the next line happens to be the next position over on the infield. Once a player has done 10-in-a-row at each position - they're finished.

3 The next 25 minutes involve the infielders working with the assistant coach (or else the head coach - whoever handles the infield) while the pitchers and catchers warm up. The infielders will work on whatever defensive things they need work on both individually and as a group. The pitchers will warm up one of their pitches - their choice - and the fastball). The outfielders take turns stepping in as batters (with their helmets and bats - BUT NOT SWINGING) as the pitchers warm up.

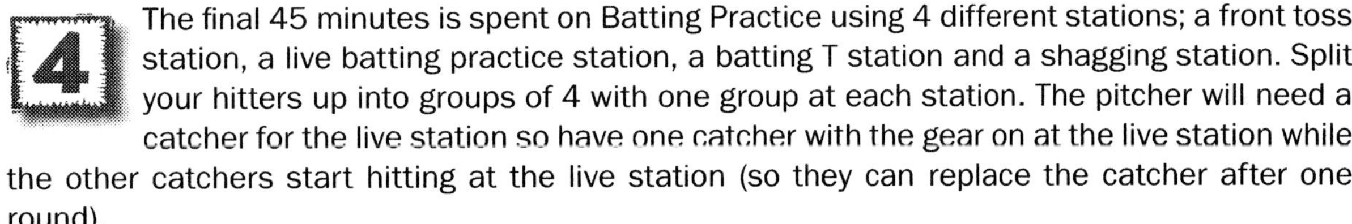

4 The final 45 minutes is spent on Batting Practice using 4 different stations; a front toss station, a live batting practice station, a batting T station and a shagging station. Split your hitters up into groups of 4 with one group at each station. The pitcher will need a catcher for the live station so have one catcher with the gear on at the live station while the other catchers start hitting at the live station (so they can replace the catcher after one round).

4a Front toss - make sure you have a protectice screen in front of the tosser along with a screen (or a player with a glove on) protecting them from the side from any balls hit their way from the live hitting station. This station will focus on getting the players to DRIVE (hit hard) one of the 1st 2 pitches they see so here they'll only get 2 tosses and then rotate within their group. (If not strikes within the 1st 2 tosses they get another toss). Working on being agressive at the plate.

4b The live station will involve a pitcher actually pitching a workout to a catcher in her catching gear. The pitchers will work on their critical counts (0-0, 1-1, 2-2) using the pitch they warmed up and their fastball). The batters work on driving hittable pitches. Each hitter will have 3 at-bats and go through 3 times. The first time through it's a 0-0 count, the 2nd time it's a 1-1 count and the 3rd time through it's a 2- 2 count.

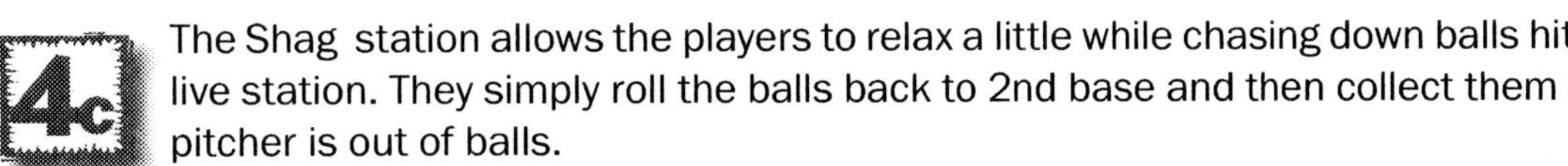

4c The Shag station allows the players to relax a little while chasing down balls hit from the live station. They simply roll the balls back to 2nd base and then collect them when the pitcher is out of balls.

4d The 3 T station lets the hitters work on hitting pitches in 3 different locations; Low and Inside, High and Outside. The T's are set up in relation to a home plate so that the hitter can easily tell the location of each pitch. Hitters will hit sponge balls into the fence if no hitting nets are available. Hitters will hit 10 at each of the 3 T's and go through twice before rotating.

The circled intials represent the players that will start at each station

Combined Practices - Practice 19 Diagram

1 5:00 – 5:30 WARM UP & CONDITIONING (jog/stretch/jump rope/swings/sprints)

2 5:30 – 5:45 THROWING WARMUP
- Infielders throw to each other to warm up
- Pitcher's throw easy to outfielders to warm up partially

3 5:45 – 6:15 BUNT / SLAP DEFENSE
- Pitcher's alternate throwing to batters EASY as they continue warming up
- Outfielders run at 1st and hit (either bunting or running slap) based on defense
- Infielders work on their bunt and slap defense, coverage and communication

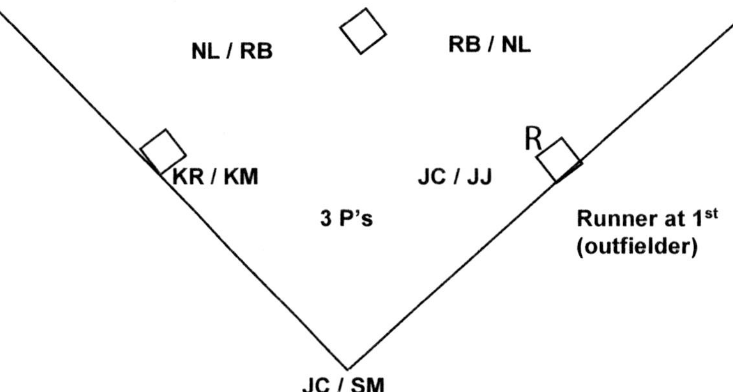

4 6:15 – 7:00 BATTING PRACTICE

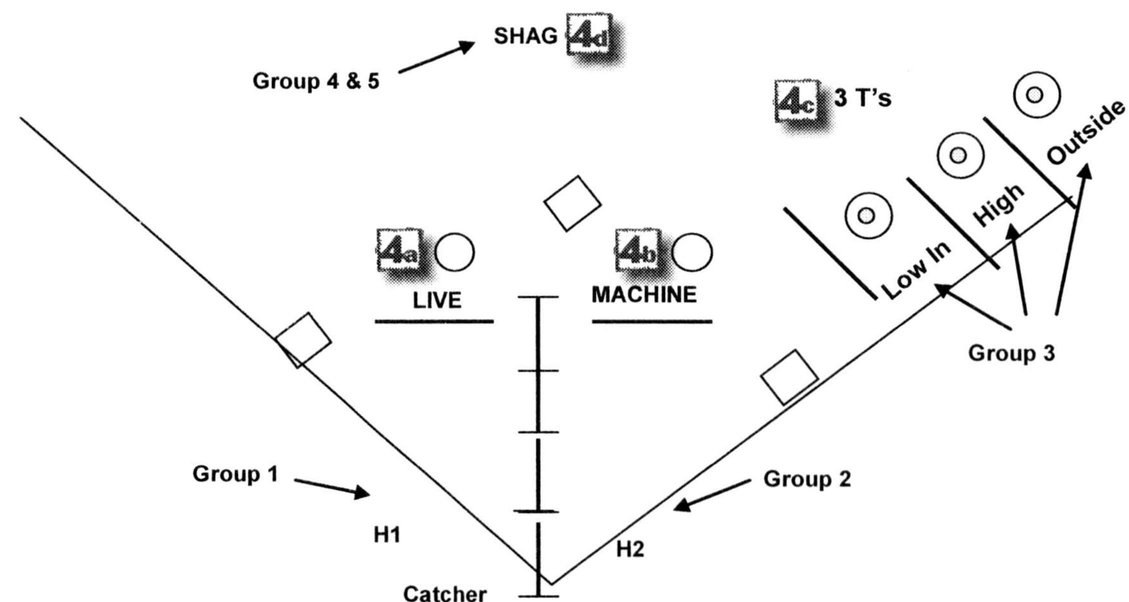

Combined Practices - Practice 19 Explanation

Practice starts off with a 30 minute warmup and conditioning session. Players can jog, stretch and then jump rope, do some dry swings with bats and then get some sprints in.

The Throwing Warmup lasts 15 minutes and is happening in two groups; one group is the infielders and catchers who are all throwing to each other to warmup, and the other group is the pitchers and outfielders who are also playing catch - except the pitchers are throwing underhand to get warm while the outfielders are obviously throwing overhand. The pitcher's don't have to completely warm to begin the next session as it will allow them to continue warming up.

The Slap / Bunt Defense session involves the entire team working in some role. The infielders will be in their defensive positions (both starting and backup positions and can switch out throughout this session), the outfielders are the hitters and runners during this session, the catchers will have their gear on and will be catching during this session and also playing live defense and the pitchers will pitch easy during this session (to batters) and continue to warmup.

The outfielders who are serving as the hitters will NOT hit the ball hard on full out swing - but instead will practice reading the defense and bunting or slapping based on where the defense is positioned. The pitchers will throw easy since the hitters are not hitting away, and both the pitchers and catchers will play on defense as well. The outfielders will make sure to always have a runner at 1st (with a helmet on) so the defense is playing for the out at 2nd or 1st.

Switch out infielders as needed to give them all opportunities to practice at both their primary and backup positions. To make this competitive keep score of OUTS made at 2nd by the defense versus RUNNERS SAFE at 2nd by the offense.

The last 45 minutes will be spent on Batting Practice in 4 different stations; Live hitting, Hitting off the Machine, Hitting off 3 different Batting T's and Shagging.

The live station will involve a pitcher actually pitching a workout to a catcher in her catching gear. The pitcher will work on the critical counts (0-0, 1-1, 2-2) and the batters work on driving hittable pitches. Each hitter will have 3 at-bats and go through 3 times. The first time through it's a 0-0 count, the 2nd time it's a 1-1 count and the 3rd time through it's a 2-2 count.

The machine station involves a pitching machine, a feeder with a large bucket of balls behind a protective screen. This station is to allow your players the chance to get some good, solid cuts in, to work on their timing and to build up their confidence. Make sure the feeder shows the ball to the hitter before feeding the ball (to allow the batter to time the pitch).

The 3 T station lets the hitters work on hitting pitches in 3 different locations; Low and Inside, High and Outside. The T's are set up in relation to a home plate so that the hitter can easily tell the location of each pitch. Hitters will hit sponge balls into the fence if no hitting nets are available. Hitters will hit 10 at each of the 3 T's and go through twice before rotating.

The Shag station allows the players to relax a little while chasing down balls hit from both the live and machine stations. They simply roll the balls back to 2nd base and then collect them when the both stations are out of balls. 2 groups will be at this station at once.

Combined Practices - Practice 20 Diagram

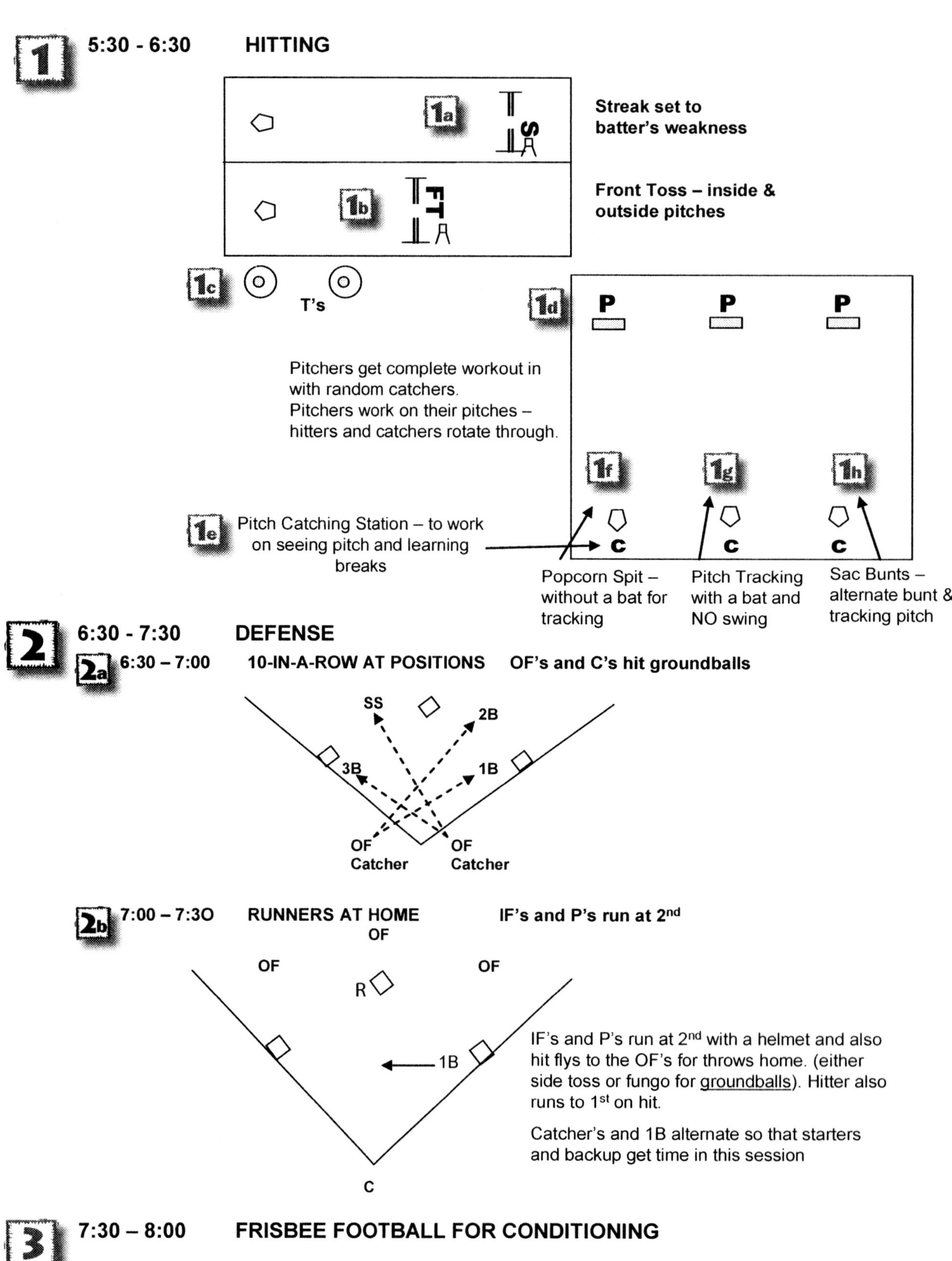

3 7:30 – 8:00 FRISBEE FOOTBALL FOR CONDITIONING

Combined Practices - Practice 20 Explanation

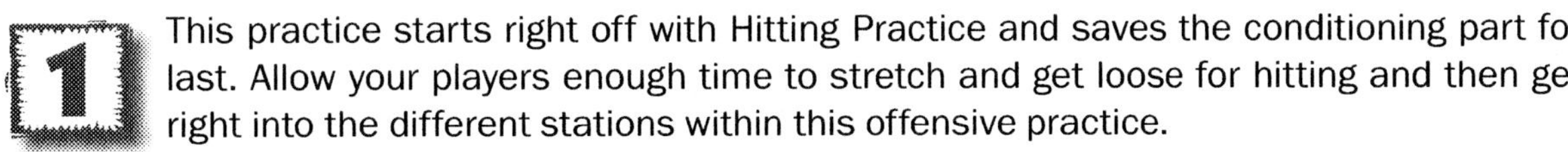

1 This practice starts right off with Hitting Practice and saves the conditioning part for last. Allow your players enough time to stretch and get loose for hitting and then get right into the different stations within this offensive practice.

1a This station can either be held in a batting cage if you have one or else out on your field. It involves the ATEC Streak Machine (if you have one and if not, then the regular pitching machine) set to throw to the batter's weakness (worst location). Make sure whoever is feeding the machine is protected by a screen.

1b The next station involves front toss from behind a protective screen and closer to the hitter than the Streak Machine station. The tosser works on tossing inside and outside tosses and always waits for the hitter to get ready before tossing again. Also toss from behind a protective screen.

1c The T's station involves at least 2 batting T's set up for outside pitches and for a high pitch (put the T on a bucket so ball is at shoulder level for hitter). Hit into nets.

1d Part of this hitting session involves the pitchers in their normal pitching workout. The pitchers (in this case 3 of them) will go to their normal practice locations and will begin working on their practice for that day.

1e Instead of using regular catchers to catch the pitchers, the catchers will be one of the hitting stations. So regular position-players will catch the pitchers in their pitching routine. Make sure the catchers all wear protective gear even though none of the hitters are actually hitting the ball - it's for safety. Having your position players catch your pitchers really helps them learn to see how pitches move and to watch the pitches much closer.

1f This hitting station involves the batter stepping into the box without a bat and with a kernel of unpopped popcorn in her mouth. The Popcorn Spit drill involves the hitter spitting the popcorn kernel at the ball at the point of contact. So the hitter will act like she's swinging at the ball but without a bat. This really shows her where her head is pointing when she's trying to hit the ball (based on where she spits the kernal of popcorn)!

1g This station involves the hitter simply tracking the ball into the catcher's glove (no bat, no swing).

1h The final hitting station involves the batter alternating between a sac bunt and simply tracking the ball into the catcher's glove. Make sure the catcher has gear on at this station.

2 Defense is next so let your infielders and pitcher's warm up their throwing arms for a bit.

2a The infielders and pitchers will do the 10-in--row drill in their positions.The outfielders and catchers hit the fungos (groundballs) and catch the thrown balls and players must still field 10 groundballs and make 10 good throws in-a-row BEFORE they can move on to the next line. It's just that in this way of doing the drill, the next line happens to be the next position over on the infield. Once a player has done 10-in-a-row at each position - she's finished.

2b The outfielders are next so they warmup their arms while the pitchers and infielders warmup their legs. Outfielders in their positions and the IF's and P's take turns hitting ground balls to the outfielders and running home from 2nd. The OF's work on throwing home through te 1B as the cutoff.

3 Practice ends with 30 minutes of conditioning by playing a game of Frisbee Football.

CHANGES FOR PRE, IN, & OFF-SEASON

Now that you've got the idea about how to hold better practices and have seen 20 actual practice examples you still might face the challenge of what to do with your players and team throughout the year. In other words, how should practices differ for the three main seasons in a year: pre-season, in-season and off-season?

That's a great question that really needs some time spent on it to help you see the main goal for each of these parts of the year. The concepts I'm going to talk about in this chapter apply whether you're coaching a college team that you have under your direction all year long or a summerball team that you see mainly during the summer but then only briefly the rest of the year.

PRE-SEASON

The Pre-Season is whatever you consider the part of your season leading up to time when your games start. This might be only a week or two if you're coaching high school ball or summerball where you can't work with your players until they complete HS ball, all the way up to 6-8 weeks for some college programs. Whatever your Pre-Season time frame is, the key is to take complete advantage of whatever time you do have instead of complaining about the amount of time you need.

Skills & Conditioning

The main focus for your Pre-Season should be developing your players Skills and improving their Conditioning. This applies whether you're practicing once a week or everyday. When you sit down to create your Pre-Season practices make sure that you're allowing time for defensive and offensive "Everydays" for all of your players and that conditioning is built into each practice.

This part of your season is where you build up the skills and fundamentals that will carry your players through their games and that will determine what type of strategy you can or can't implement throughout the season.

If your team can't bunt the Pre-Season is where you fix that. If your pitchers can't get ahead of the hitters then this is where you help them fix that. Outfielders that can't throw accurately need to spend time in the Pre-Season correcting that problem as do infielders that struggle with charging a ball or going to their backhand.

You have an advantage if you coached your team last season as you'll already know what skills need to be improved on and by which players. But coaches, I want to caution you that YOU shouldn't be the only one that knows what each player needs to improve on and why - the player needs to know too! Take some time either at the end of the regular season or at the beginning of the Pre-Season to sit down with each player and let them know the things they are strong on and those skills they need to work hard on to improve. And, that you're going to help them improve on those things but they're going to have to put in the effort.

Let players know where they stand with their skills and how they can expect to benefit as a result of improving their weaknesses. For instance, will they see more playing time, or get a chance to start? If you can help your players understand why all that extra work will help them in the long run, instead of simply being another one of your diabolical plots to torture them, then they'll be far more motivated to work hard and improve - which helps you and the whole team in the long run.

While the Pre-Season focus is on individual skill building and conditioning, you will still need to spend some time on team offense and defense as these will be needed in your first few games. I just want to caution you not to spend your entire Pre-Season focusing on team skills or else you'll never have the players to successfully execute your grand schemes.

IN-SEASON

This is what we all live for - Softball Season! The time of year when all we seem to do is play and practice, and usually too much of the first and not enough of the later. In-Season practice is usually many things - tough, scarce, inconsistent, negative (based on the type of season you're having), short-handed (injuries and/or vacations depending on level of commitment and team), etc...Our job as coaches is to keep the focus of In-Season practice in mind, and that focus is:

Repair & Prepare

That's right! Repair from your last game and Prepare for your next one. Once the season starts you're probably spending most of your weekends playing tournaments plus a game or two during the week. That doesn't leave much time for practice. You're probably only squeaking out one practice a week so you've got to be smart about how you use it and make the most of it.

Repair Work - The first part of your practice can be devoted to fixing things that happened in your last game. Instead of holding those horrible post-game bitch sessions that don't do anyone on your team any good and only serve to somehow help you feel better, skip them. After a game - win or lose - let your team know that we'll talk about this game at our next practice or game (based on your schedule) and then remind them of their next team activity, time and location.

When you meet next as a team then simply ask your team, "How do you think we played last game?". Trust me, your team will be much harder on themselves then you ever could be, but when you handle it in this way it's much more constructive since you can then immediately do something to change it (either play better if you're next meeting is another game, or else work to fix it if your next meeting is practice).

The Repair portion of your practice can be spent on individual as well as team fixes, and skill as well as confidence fixes. Get over being a critical, judgmental ogre as a coach and get tuned into the Repairs that your players and team desperately need to make before your next game. It's your job as a coach to help them fix their problems and put them in a position to succeed and this Repair part of your In-Season practice is a perfect time to do just that. Anyone can simply point out the problems, but what they're supposed to do to fix them must come from you!

Prepare Work - The second part (it might not be half since this means the two parts are even) of your In-Season practices will involve Preparing your team for their next opponent. Now some of you are in a better position than others to know who your next-game opponents will be, great. Either way, try to find out as much as you can about who you're playing next and then spend time preparing to face them. If you don't know anything at all about your next opponent try looking them up on the internet and checking out their schedule. Chances are you'll know someone who has played them before so call that coach and find out as much as you can. You should know things like: Are they fast? Does their pitching dominate or is it hittable? Are they aggressive? Who are their best hitters? Do they hit more or bunt more? Do they have any lefty slappers?

Once you know any or all of these answers you can spend the rest of your practice time working on the team defense you're most likely to play against them, working on how your pitchers should pitch them, what your hitters should expect to see from their hitters and how aggressive your runners will need to be on the bases.

Practicing like this during your season will put your team in a much better position to have a successful season and prevent those slumps that teams tend to go through but that can be shortened or prevented. Remember coaches - Repair and then Prepare!

OFF-SEASON

When your players leave following the end of your season, those that are returning to your team should each know exactly what skills they need to improve on over the Off-Season and HOW they should go about working on them. The more specific of a workout you can give your players the greater chance they'll actually follow them.

Learn, Experiment, Improve

I suggest that you make their workouts fairly simple to do or else they might not ever do them. For instance, you might have your infielders work on 20 forehands, 20 backhands and 20 front-throughs (groundballs caught directly infront of them with a forward motion of the hands and glove) everyday. You might ask your outfielders to do 25 high tosses to themselves everyday, and ask your pitchers to throw at least 40 fastballs and 40 changeups to someone or a wall everyday.

Now, if everyday is WAY too much to ask, then send your players home with a chart that must be initialed by the player and the parent saying that they did their skill work at least 5 of the 7 days a week. Then, have each player email their sheets to you each month so you can tell whose falling behind and might need a little call, email or other form of motivation.

The Off-Season is the perfect time for players to learn new skills (like pitches for pitchers), experiment with things (like slapping for hitters) and to generally improve on how they did last year (like all of your players).

Stay as in touch with your players during the Off-Season as your rules allow and you'll be amazed at the results once the Pre-Season roles around!

Bright Idea:

One thing to remember when practicing is to allow your team the chance to wear their uniforms at least once in practice before their 1st game. This is especially helpful for those new players who will be awed by the uniform - it's better to get that all out in practice than in your 1st game.

Also - if you can ask some umpires to come out to one of your practices it will not only help your pitchers and hitters but will also build some good relations with the umps. They need practice too and offering them a chance for some practice along with getting your players used to having Balls and Strikes, Outs and Safes called - helps everyone!

Best of Luck with your season and work to out-practice your opponents!

Here's to your team's success and to holding better practices!

Notes

Notes

About the Author

Cindy has over 20 years of softball experience as a player, coach, administrator, instructor and television analyst. As a player Cindy pitched and played firstbase on the college and professional levels before going into college coaching. She served as an assistant coach at Arizona State University and a head coach at both New Mexico State and Wichita State. Following her college coaching career Cindy served as National Director for Junior Olympic Softball for the Amateur Softball Association and then Director of National Teams and Coaching Development for USA Softball. Cindy coached for 5 seasons in the Women's Professional Softball League before working for the International Softball Federation as Director of Development. Cindy is a member of the National Fastpitch Coaches Association Hall of Fame and has conducted close to 500 clinics worldwide. THE ULTIMATE SOFTBALL PRACTICE GUIDE: A Revolutionary Approach to Organizing & Planning Your Practices is Cindy's 8th book and Softball Excellence - via softballexcellence.com - is Cindy's latest efforts to share her teachings and experience with the softball world.